# AN ELEMENT OF LUCK

# AN ELEMENT OF LUCK

## OF LUCK

*To South Arabia and Beyond*

## MICHAEL CROUCH

The Radcliffe Press
London     New York

To Lynette, who has shared so much,
with love

Published in 1993 by
The Radcliffe Press
45 Bloomsbury Square
London WC1A 2HY

175 Fifth Avenue
New York
NY 10010

In the United States of America
and Canada distributed by
St Martin's Press
175 Fifth Avenue
New York
NY 10010

Copyright © 1993 by Michael Crouch

A full CIP record for this book is available from the British Library
A full CIP record is available from the Library of Congress

ISBN 1–85043–739–4

Copy-edited and laser-set by Selro Publishing Services, Oxford
Printed and bound in Great Britain by WBC Ltd, Bridgend, Mid Glamorgan

# Contents

# Acronyms and Abbreviations

I have tended to revert to the letters by which an institution or office was known and this may occasionally prove confusing for some. Here, for easy reference, are the most commonly used:

| | |
|---|---|
| ADC | Aide de camp |
| AAND | Assistant Adviser Northern Deserts |
| BA | The British Agent (Western Aden Protectorate) |
| BBC | The British Broadcasting Corporation |
| BP | British Petroleum |
| CO | Commanding Officer |
| C in C | The Commander-in-Chief (Middle East Command) |
| DGs | Desert Guards |
| EAP | The Eastern Aden Protectorate |
| FG | The Federal Guard |
| FLOSY | The Front for the Liberation of South Yemen |
| FOO | Forward Observation Officer |
| FRA | The Federal Regular Army |
| HBL | The Hadhrami Bedouin Legion |
| HMG | Her Majesty's Government (in Britain) |
| HQMEC | Headquarters Middle East Command |
| JAA | Junior Assistant Adviser |
| MARA | The Military Assistant to the Resident Adviser |
| MECAS | The Middle East Centre for Arabic Studies |
| NLF | The National Liberation Front |
| PCL | Petroleum Concessions Limited |
| PO | Political Officer |
| POL | petrol oil and lubricants |
| PSP | The People's Socialist Party |

| | |
|---|---|
| RA | The Resident Adviser & British Agent (E A P) |
| RAF | The Royal Air Force |
| RHA | The Royal Horse Artillery |
| SAL | The South Arabian League |
| SAS | The Special Air Service Regiment |
| UNO | The United Nations Organization |
| u/s | unserviceable |
| VIP | Very Important People |
| WAP | The Western Aden Protectorate (later to become the Federation of South Arabia) |

# General Foreword
# to the Series

A. H. M. KIRK-GREENE

Lecturer in the Modern History of Africa, University of Oxford, and
formerly of the Colonial Administrative Service, Nigeria

A whole generation has passed, nearer two in the case of the Asian
sub-continent, since Britain's colonial territories in South-East Asia,
Africa and the Caribbean achieved independence. In the Pacific the
transfer of power came about a decade later. There was little interest in
recording the official or the personal experience of empire either in the
inter-war years — viewed by some, often among those personally
involved, as the apogee of the British empire — or in the immediate
aftermath of empire. And in this latter period attitudes were largely
critical, largely condemnatory and even positively hostile. This is not
surprising: such a reaction is usual at the end of a remarkable period of
history.

   With the passing of time and with longer historical perspective it
was possible to see events in a better and more objective light and the
trend was gradually reversed. In due course there came about a more
sympathetic interest in the colonial period, both in Britain and in the
countries of the former empire, among those who were intrigued to
know how colonial government operated — in local, everyday practice,
as well as at the policy level of the Colonial Office and Government
House. Furthermore, those who had themselves been an integral part of

the process wanted to record the experience before, in the nature of things, it was too late. Here was a potentially rich vein of knowledge and personal experience for specialist academic historians as well as the general reader.

Leaving aside the extensive academic analysis of the end of empire, the revival of interest in the colonial period in this country may be said to have been stimulated by creative literature. In the late 1960s there were novels, films and radio and TV programmes, now and again tinged with a touch of nineteenth-century romance and with just a whiff of nostalgia to soften the sharp realism of the colonial encounter. The focus was primarily on India and the post-1947 imagery of the 'Raj': there were outstanding novels by Paul Scott — surely destined to be one of the greatest twentieth-century novelists — J. G. Farrell and John Masters; epic films like *A Passage to India* and *Gandhi*, the charming and moving vignette of *Staying On*, and, for Africa, *Out of Africa* and *Mister Johnson*.

In the second half of the 1970s there emerged a highly successful genre of collective 'colonial' memoirs in the *Tales of ...* format: Charles Allen's splendid trilogy *Plain Tales from the Raj* (1975), *Tales from the Dark Continent* (1979) and *Tales from the South China Seas* (1983), followed by others like *Tales of Paradise: Memories of the British in the South Pacific* (1986) and *Tales of Empire: the British in the Middle East* (1989), all good history and good reading.

Throughout the period from India's independence until that of the last crown colony there had, of course, been those splendid works which combined both academic history and creative literature: for example, Philip Woodruff's *Men who Ruled India: The Founders* (1953) and *The Guardians* (1954); and Jan Morris's *Heaven's Command*, *Pax Britannica* and *Farewell the Trumpets* (1973–8).

Finally, as the 1970s gave way to the 1980s, those voices which had remained largely silent since the end of empire now wanted to be heard. The one-time colonial officials, be they district officers, agriculturalists, veterinary, medical or forestry officers, policemen or magistrates, and just as often their wives, began to write about their experiences. They wrote with relish and enthusiasm, with a touch of adventure and few personal regrets. There was a common feeling of a practical and useful task well done, although some thought that more could have been achieved had independence come about more slowly.

## General Foreword to the Series

These memoirs often began as little more than a private record for the family, children and grandchildren, some of who had never seen a colonial governor in full fig, shaken hand with an emir or paramount chief, discussed plans with a peasant or local politician, or known at first hand the difference between an *askari* and an *alkali*, an *amah* and an *ayah*. By 1990, the colonial memoir had begun to establish itself as a literary genre in its own right.

The initiative of the Radcliffe Press in harnessing and promoting this talent, primarily autobiographical but also biographical, promises to be a positive addition to both the historical and the literary scenes. Here is a voice from the last Colonial Service generation, relating from personal experience the lives and careers involved in the exercise of latter-day empire. They were part of what was arguably the most influential and far-reaching international event of the second half of the twentieth century, namely the end of empire and the consequent emergence of the independent nations of the Third World. It could also perhaps be argued that this is part of an even greater process — decolonization 'writ large', a sea-change in world affairs affecting greater and lesser powers into the late twentieth century.

It may well be that by 2066, the centenary of the closing down of the Colonial Office, great-great-grandchildren will find the most telling image of Britain's third and final empire in these authentic memoirs and biographical studies, rather than in the weightier imperial archives at the Public Record Office at Kew or in Rhodes House Library, Oxford.

# Foreword

Michael Crouch in *An Element of Luck* has written an absorbing account of his time as a political officer in South Arabia. He also tells of his family background which had much to do with him choosing a career in Her Majesty's Overseas Service, and of his family's time in Western Australia once that career had come to an end with the British withdrawal from Aden.

The events in South Arabia he writes about seem far removed from those of today. Apart from being of great interest to those who served there and all those interested in obtaining the authentic feeling for the last years of the British presence, it will be invaluable to students and researchers. A political officer was given great responsibility, a little guidance and trusted to get on with it. His life was never boring, sometimes frustrating and often extremely dangerous. I was fortunate to serve in Aden and the Western and Eastern Protectorates as a young Army officer with both the Welsh Guards and the SAS, and came to know many of Michael Crouch's colleagues. He has written about the eccentrics, the awkward and those of independent character who existed in the service and I suspect through diffidence, not so much as he might have about the very many patient, hardworking and imaginative men who were dedicated to those they felt they were responsible for. I, myself, saw how Michael Crouch himself, Ralph Daly, Jim Ellis, Godfrey Meynell, Bill Heber Percy and John Shipman were selfless in their commitment to South Arabia and its future.

The British withdrawal was a painful process and as with other nations and colonies, disentanglement left many scars. The perception of what was right was often very different in Westminster and Whitehall to what it was in Aden. Tragedy befell many and hundreds were killed when the British departed, and it is understandable that

## Foreword

Michael Crouch, with his experience as a political officer, writes so vehemently about this period over 25 years after the event.

*An Element of Luck* brings back many memories for all of us who knew South Arabia, and Michael Crouch has produced an excellent record of what he experienced and felt during the last 10 years of the British presence there.

General Sir Charles Guthrie KCB LVO OBE ADC Gen
Commander-in-Chief British Army of the Rhine

# Acknowledgements

This has been a six person effort: my drafts were painstakingly reviewed, first in England by my sister Sabrina, then by my wife Lynette in Australia who would consider some recollection of the Aden days and say, 'But it wasn't like that at all! Do you remember ...?' I would then try to get it right. I am so grateful to them for their tolerance and good memory. It was an interesting exercise for us: we do not seem to have had the time or inclination to discuss our past life. The catharsis has been refreshing.

The draft was then passed to daughter Catherine who read each chapter through, with a wholly objective if at times unflattering response. 'Dad — what on earth does that mean?' My thanks to her for all her efforts. Charles from Melbourne added his most useful responses to some of the criticisms raised from the first reading — he knows how I have appreciated this.

Finally, I am indebted to Dr Lester Crook for his time and trouble during my visit to England, when we went through the project together, and for his subsequent constructive comment on the end result.

To all those old friends and colleagues who were part of the mutual support on which we relied in those tiresome if fascinating times, I want to make it clear that the opinions in this book — made clearer by the benefit of hindsight — are mine alone. They are neither intended to boost nor destroy my fellows' reputations; they are included just because they seem important to the context. If I have unintentionally offended anyone, I apologize. If I have omitted something which really should have been included, please put it down to the tyranny of distance — and to the selective recollections of antipodean middle age.

Michael Crouch

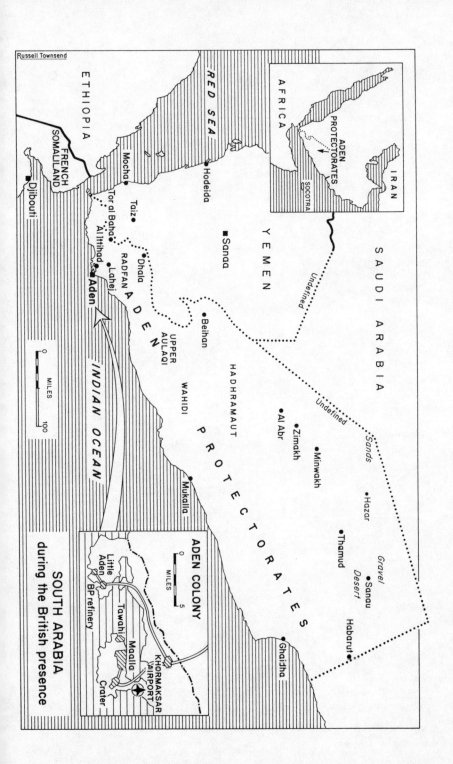

Russell Townsend

SOUTH ARABIA
during the British presence

ETHIOPIA

FRENCH SOMALILAND

Djibouti

RED SEA

AFRICA

ADEN PROTECTORATES

SOCOTRA

IRAN

Mocha

Hodeida

Taiz

Tor al Baha

Al Ittihad

Aden

Dhala

Lahej

RADFAN

YEMEN

Sanaa

SAUDI ARABIA

Undefined

UPPER AULAQI

Beihan

WAHIDI

HADHRAMAUT

Al Abr

Zimakh

Minwakh

Undefined

Sands

Hazar

Gravel

Desert

Sanau

Thamud

Habarut

INDIAN OCEAN

PROTECTORATES

Mukalla

Ghaidha

ADEN COLONY

Little Aden

BP refinery

Tawahi

Maalla

Crater

KHORMAKSAR AIRPORT

0 MILES 5

0 MILES 100

# Introduction
## The Fruits of Existing Seeds

'Agitations are the fruits of existing seeds'
— General Gordon

THE metal cylinder with its fluted tail tinkles on the floor. It is the casing of an anti-tank bazooka missile, keeping open our bedroom door. Its sinister shape is at odds with the peaceful setting of our Western Australian home. Perhaps though it is a desirable reminder to us, in our privileged Antipodean tranquillity, of the nasty little wars breaking out across the troubled world of the 1990s. It is also a memento of a distant interlude, one incident in a colourful period from my past. It was several decades ago, during my first career, as a political officer in HM Overseas Service from the late 1950s through to the British withdrawal from South Arabia, almost a decade later. Seemingly I am destined to be the last of a family that has thrived on serving the Crown, in a particular way of life that used to offer adventure and advancement to young men, eager to make their lives and risk their reputations, all over the world.

It had all started four generations before mine, on my mother's side. Her paternal grandfather was born into a family called Chesney. My great-great-great-grandfather had emigrated to America and returned to County Antrim after the American War of Independence (he was a Loyalist). His eldest son, General Francis Rawdon Chesney explored the Euphrates River and was named 'Father of the Suez Canal' by de Lesseps with whom, as the British representative, he worked on the construction. A nephew of General Chesney, Lieutenant-Colonel Charles Cornwallis Chesney RE, was a renowned military critic of the

1

time. A professor at Sandhurst Military Academy, he wrote books on strategy and is still remembered for the 'Waterloo Lectures' there. But it was Colonel Chesney's brothers who cemented the family tradition of serving the monarch overseas; General Sir George Tonkyas Chesney, another engineer, served through the Indian Mutiny and became the Military Member of the Viceroy's Council in India. He later became a member of Parliament and wrote a number of books of which his best known was *The Battle of Dorking*, a fictionalized account of a contemporary invasion of England. One of his other brothers was Major Algernon Moir Chesney, that paternal grandfather of my mother's and my direct link with those enterprising military engineers.

Algernon Moir Chesney had also served through the Indian Mutiny; he had been in the Madras Army and after he retired he went out to Australia to some cousins (possibly named 'Mayne') where he ran sheep on their property. He had quarrelled with all his family and been separated from his first wife who became insane (as did their son who, on being invalided from the Indian Army, threw himself overboard into the Red Sea). Algernon Moir Chesney altered his name by simply changing it without legal authority, and returned to England where he worked as a private tutor, an 'Army and General Coach'. A brilliant classicist and linguist, he remarried, again with a careless disregard for legal niceties (no check as to whether his first wife was still alive). His third son, Arthur Mayne, followed the family tradition of service in India.

Arthur had fallen in love with my grandmother's portrait in his friend's rooms at Cambridge; he had been a 'Senior Wrangler' there (he was an accomplished mathematician who, as an old man, fascinated me with his mental arithmetic) and passed second in his year, into the prestigious Indian Civil Service. After a first tour in India of the usual seven years he had panned enough gold from the small stream that ran through his district to fashion a wedding ring; he persuaded my grandmother to marry him and to accompany him to India, where they started to raise their five children in the years leading up to the First World War.

My maternal grandmother was descended on the one side from (to quote her) 'the Barnetts: a worthy line of typically English middle class' engineers (who built many of the roads and railway bridges of

Imperial India), solicitors and doctors, interspersed with an Admiral, a famous horseman and (by marriage) Captain Webb, the first man to swim the English Channel. Her mother's family was predominantly Huguenot French, called 'Bonnycastle' (originally 'de Belcastel'), of whom the most noteworthy was one John Bonnycastle, Professor of Mathematics at Woolwich, and Astronomer Royal. There were Bonnycastle engineers too, who, together with a fair sprinkling of bohemian eccentrics, combined with all the other empire builders and soldiers to make up the proud, generous, impatient and sometimes explosive genetic mixture that was my mother's contribution to my character.

My father's antecedents were different: descended from a respectable but dull (by contrast with my mother's family) line of gardening chapel goers, it was his great uncle George Crouch who first showed any urge to leave the mother country; he emigrated to the Victorian goldfields in 1852, ostensibly apprenticed to a draper in Melbourne. Finding no gold, he was involved in helping to run a liquor still for thirsty miners, and later prospered as one of the founder fathers of the goldmining city of Ballarat. He had claimed to his Victorian colleagues that he was directly descended from a baronet; the claim was later indignantly refuted by Lyon King of Arms, so the sturdy gardening ancestry has had to be reluctantly accepted. That line of Australian Crouches since died out: it was left to my father to venture next overseas. After war service at Gallipoli and in East Africa, he took his medical skills to the savage splendour of the Ethiopian Court, and later to the Sudan.

Accompanying my forebears abroad, where it was allowed, were those indomitable women who made homes under often primitive conditions, and reared the children, sharing the hardships, including the dangers, of lives threatened by disease, unfriendly locals, and the tyranny of isolation from one's kind. Lynette, my wife and partner of 30 years, knows all about it. Her family background is also one of colourful soldiering in India, pioneering in Africa and in Australia. The Saxony merino sheep is one legacy of her family's ancestral initiatives; still prized for its fine wool it was introduced to van Dieman's Land (Tasmania) in the 1830s and later to the Australian mainland.

Reflecting on the challenges of past hardships is a form of pleasant escapism in itself, not confined to elderly men in London clubs; it is perhaps a kind of nostalgia for a world where those in positions of isolated authority could make decisions, remote from today's instant electronic back-up and instruction. It was also distant from the contemporary flood of often trite material on disastrous global events that leaves one feeling isolated from where it is all happening. The 'information culture' has permeated all aspects of modern existence since the early 1980s, when it was just starting to irritate my elderly mother. Ten years on the information flow is even more relentless. How today's pace of events would have appeared to someone of my mother's generation it is possible to surmise: she had lived through the political and social upheavals of two world wars; perhaps she would not be too surprised (or concerned, even) by immediate exposure via TV to our contemporary scenario of worldwide recession and militaristic bickering. She did worry, though, about those parts of the world where she had lived.

From my mother's fiercely idiosyncratic perspective and personal knowledge of the countries concerned, it was the collapse of the rule of law throughout the Sudan that really affected her, towards the end of her life. In the 1950s she had seen the Sudan ready to run itself, with a local judiciary, a medical service, educational structures and a transport system that were the pride of expatriates and the envy of less well-served neighbours. In a mere decade or less, all this was to collapse into the anarchical chaos that typified that million square miles of bloodshed and slavery, a century or so, earlier.

She had seen me off to Aden, the centre of British influence in South Arabia, at the same time as the Sudan was going it alone; and her expectations of the future of that part of the world were nothing like those for the Sudan. Even then she had seen South Arabia as a potential blot on the British reputation for leaving something worthwhile behind, though she liked the thought of her son following in the traditions of his forebears — South Arabia's mixture of medieval colour, its squalid tribal feuding and intrigue, and its unsettled past suggested to her, even then, that the British influence was ephemeral. She was a wise old thing.

She and I knew Aden itself as being the biggest bunkering port in the world, outside New York. As a family we had been among thousands of tourists in transit who had shopped for duty-free goods in Crater, often after dark when there was some respite from the fierce summer heat and humidity. There had been a distinct degree of goodwill and a deal of mutual acceptance of the British presence, then: there was prosperity to be shared.

It was not to last, of course: the decline in British influence, and accompanying values, was hastened by changed political philosophies and priorities, in a world that saw a colonial paternalism, together with a cynical exploitation of the masses, inherent in every British initiative. It was sad that there was enough of this same cynicism, among many of my British colleagues in South Arabia, to mask the genuine efforts of a small handful of British advisers outside Aden, and the administrators in Aden itself, to help the locals to help themselves. The latter of course meant nothing to the ideologists in Europe and the United Nations Organization (UNO) politicians in New York. So it was that the eventual Aden debacle depressed me more than it did my mother who had seen it all happen before. I was part of the latest pattern of enforced change, with the challenge to be forced out of me.

The story that follows is of an interwoven pattern of upbringing and of personal experience, of a life shaped by my family's imperial service, and coloured by a period in South Arabia that still impinges on my thoughts, some 30 years on.

An old friend and colleague penned a light-hearted piece of doggerel, which reinforces the memory of an unusual way to earn a living. He borrowed an elegiac format to capture the bitter-sweetness of an Arabian world then fast disintegrating into chaos.

> A curfew marks the end of one more day,
> The bragging bedou from their haunches rise,
> A silence falls on those who have to stay,
> Save for the daily hymns of hate from Taiz.
> Now fades the glimmering heat haze from our view,
> The Union Jack descends its downwards track.
> Far off explodes a hand grenade or two
> And still is heard the sharp bazooka's crack.

It concludes:

> The Flag is down, another flag is raised,
> Gone is the symbol of the heir to Rome.

### An Element of Luck

The Bedou stop and stare, amazed,
And, empty-handed, wander slowly home.

(With grateful acknowledgment to Peter Hinchcliffe)

I could not have summed it up better, myself — just the right note of realism, tinged with regret.

# 1

# Embryo Imperialist

IT is said by a certain member of my family when exasperated that I am 'just like that grandfather.' Unlikely, I feel, given his brilliance at mathematics; besides, I am sure he lacked my ebullience although a family story had it that my mild mannered grandfather once impaled a waiter's hand with his fork, to the plate. This piece of unlikely folklore was to impress on me that I should not, as did that unfortunate waiter, hurry at mealtimes. I could hardly reconcile such a coldblooded act with the gentle, elderly man who had stayed with us in Kenya, but having learnt something of his determination and obstinacy, even ruthlessness, as a younger man, it could have been true. I could even imagine the ensuing dialogue (the waiter's imprecations being part): 'My dear fellow. Was that your hand? I thought it to be my steak. Pray, wrap your hand, you must not bleed on the table,' and so it might have gone.

Arthur Mayne had had a strong sense of compassion for not only the more impoverished members of his family (whom he supported financially for years) but for the under-classes in general. As an up-and-coming member of the Indian Civil Service his career suffered; he combined Fabian principles (which prevented him from accepting a knighthood on two occasions) with acute hypochondria. The latter impelled him to opt out of social gatherings, much to the dismay of my grandmother who rather liked to attend the Viceroy's Reception at Simla. But even as her glittering formal dress was laid out on her bed, it was, 'Emily, my dear, I feel my fatigue poisons coming on. I must retire,' which he did, to his wife's chagrin. If it was not the 'fatigue

7

poisons' it was another imagined malady, 'the worm', consuming his inner being.

This usually amiable but trying eccentricity having brought his Indian career to a halt before the First World War, he had transported his children back to the United Kingdom over a period of some years; they toured the Far East, the United States, Canada and New Zealand, the children spending time at various schools along the way and picking up an appreciation of the wide world in their formative years. My grandfather continued to be an inveterate traveller who even in late middle age could persuade his wife to accompany him in a small motor vehicle — with those contemporary wire wheels — to above the Arctic Circle, and (on another memorable journey) through the Balkan States.

Once established in the Channel Isles, Arthur had knitted socks for the troops and then volunteered to drive an ambulance in Northern Italy. His immense skills of organization brought him to the attention of the International Red Cross; he was to take charge of the repatriation of Allied prisoners of war from Germany, which he accomplished with distinction. It was really his wife's misfortune that the anticipated second offer of a knighthood never materialized; Arthur Mayne had been urging the returning prisoners of war to vote for the Labour Party.

And so in retrospect I feel gratified at being compared to my grandfather. Eccentricity aside (and perhaps I confess to some) there was much in Arthur Mayne to admire. Essentially he combined principle with pragmatism. The fact that social events brought on the male equivalent of a mild fit of the vapours counted for little, when measured against the whole man.

His middle daughter, my mother, had no such social inhibitions. She was given to vocal expressions of approval in public, accompanied by what she saw as the appropriate moves. It was just prior to my receiving a degree from the hands of the chancellor of Cambridge University, in 1962. My mother, in company with my bride of one month, had been sitting in the Senate House, surrounded by the paraphernalia that my mother insisted was necessary to her wellbeing — rugs, spare shoes, opera glasses, baskets, and the like. Just as the stately procession was entering the Senate House, she exclaimed in clear tones that there was a much better location from which to view the ceremony, on the other side of the chamber. Seizing Lynette's hand and strewing her essentials as she rose, she darted like a ferret, under the feet of the

8

approaching dignitaries. Not for the last time Lynette had prayed for the earth to open.

My father was a fair-haired, blue-eyed sportsman who had graduated from the London Hospital after a star-studded progression through the Merchant Taylors' School and Cambridge. He was just in time for the Gallipoli campaign where, lying slightly wounded on the beach at Suvla Bay, he had shared a cigarette with an ANZAC who, it turned out, also bore the second name of 'Armstrong' and family name of 'Crouch'. They never met again (this was Lieutenant-Colonel Richard Armstrong Crouch, the illustrious descendant of that enterprising George Crouch, my father's great uncle, who had emigrated in the 1850s to seek a fortune on the Ballarat goldfields, in Victoria, Australia).

My father had ended the war in Africa with a Military Cross and a determination to return to Africa. His first appointment was as Court Physician to the Empress of Ethiopia: 'All raw meat, silver dollars and "shifta" [bandits] hanging from trees,' was the summation. He then joined the Sudan Medical Service: ten years on a paddle steamer, the 'Lady Baker', converted to a slowly mobile hospital in the steaming swamps of the Southern Sudan, which was a major means of clearing up that revolting tropical ulcer disease, yaws.

My father had met my mother via Sudan connections; he had been an old friend of her first husband. She had married well: John Beavan was wealthy and well connected, a District Commissioner in the elite Sudan Political Service. He had beaten a swarm of her admirers, to carry her off from her London existence, that of a dancing teacher and a typical 'flapper' of the 1920s. They lived initially at Renk, in the Southern Sudan where she was one of the first European women allowed to share a husband's lonely life in those remote parts. The happy union lasted for just 18 months. He contracted blackwater fever. She nursed him fiercely on the paddle steamer carrying him to hospital in Khartoum. He died within sight of the town.

My father, then still a bachelor in his early forties, had done his best to assuage her grief. After a time they married. He was to die before he was 60, and my mother was widowed for the second time; she was not yet into middle age and she had two children to bring up, alone.

My parents had displayed a tremendous zest for life that ensured they were not to be tied down in the humdrum life of a nine-to-five job back in Britain. My father in particular saw the need to break away from some of his kinsfolk who, by contrast with his years of doctoring under the most appalling conditions, were preoccupied with a comfortable existence and a narrow-minded ignorance of the world, outside their complaisant daily lives. My parents therefore tended to surround themselves with relaxed colleagues on leave from distant climes. Their company also included my father's younger brother, Dick. He too had felt the need to break out from those family confines but, in so doing, he earned the reputation of being the traditional 'black sheep'. He was chronically short of cash; on one occasion he had pawned a set of silver tankards won by my father in polo tournaments. They were engraved with my father's initials 'H.A.C.' Dick persuaded the pawnbroker that the set was part of the mess silver of the Honourable Artillery Company — and worth a lot.

I believe that those family traits that are inheritable have been the principal determinant of my personal life patter, rather than the hotch-potch of outside influences and the behaviour of others. Indeed, the sheer variety of conflicting impulses — the romantic versus the practical, for example — has often resulted in a deal of mental conflict, as in, 'Where to, now?' Leaving aside the demands and needs of family, surely the most pressing influence on the decisions made by the breadwinner, the conformist middle class in me sits at times uneasily with the urge for an individualistic (some might say, irresponsible) lifestyle. My mixture of Franco/Anglian roots, I am sure, has contributed to some tortured rationalizing on my part; my parents' families have contributed Huguenot French and Ulster genes, with an overlay of good old English.

So, from my mother's side I suspect I have inherited whatever flair I have displayed with an, at times slapdash, interest in taking on new challenges. This might account for the eight or nine changes in career since university, each of them of overwhelming absorption at that time. As for my father's family influences, if that is what they are, I can only perceive, perhaps, the positive element of determining to achieve, often in some isolation from other support systems. What I seemed to have inherited from both parents was a determination to live and work 'in the sun'. My adopted home, Australia, is perhaps destined to provide too much of the stuff, but there is no doubt that the physical environment has won out over the strong cultural pull I still have towards things British — a leaning at times in conflict with the apparent values of Australia. Here, for over 25 years, Lynette and I have lived happily; we have raised a family together, in the security of a well ordered society, isolated from world turmoil. Over 55 years ago it would have seemed just as secure to me — but then I was only three.

Earliest memories are twofold: the first is of crawling on a grassy bank, near a cliff's edge. This was at Bude, in Cornwall. The second, still vivid, memory is of my swinging on a farm gate which was not on its hinges. It fell, pinning me in a bed of stinging nettles. This last flashback was from near the Rectory of Charlwood, in Surrey: Canon Grainger Thompson was my father's best friend at Cambridge; they had studied medicine together. A rugby accident had resulted in injury to his arm which was later amputated. A one-armed doctor was out of the question but a cleric so handicapped could still serve the Lord. So he did. He also played a very good game of golf, his drives being short but accurate. During these games he would compose his sermons and my father, on leave from the Sudan, would contribute inspiration.

Just before the outbreak of war in 1939 my father was already back in Khartoum. He was Assistant Director of the Sudan Medical Service, now in uniform as a lieutenant colonel in the Royal Army Medical Corps and in a couple of years to take charge of all medical arrangements at the Battle of Keren (which kept the Italians in Ethiopia from invading the Sudan). My mother was in England: she was anxious to evacuate my infant sister Sabrina and me, away from Europe. We were shipped, with other Sudan families, to Port Sudan. Among those others was an Australian mother and her small son, Hugo, who borrowed a tray from a steward and approached each mother, with an angelic smile and a request to borrow just one toy. His tray full, he walked to the side and, in full view of them all, tipped the contents into the sea. He ran to the protection of his mother who assured the infuriated women that he was a 'sensitive child' — not untypical of other such sensitive Australians I was to meet in later life.

Port Sudan was to have different memories for me years later, but at that stage it was the excitement of boarding the gleaming Sudan Railways coaches for the very slow but comfortable journey (the sleepers were laid on sand) to Khartoum.

My parents' house was right next to the zoo which was no ordinary British zoo of the time, with dejected animals behind bars. It had

11

enclosures where the animals could actually mingle with the visitors. Those animals likely to harm their admirers were usually suitably confined, but the general effect was of minimal restraint. Among the creatures wandering freely was the fearsome shoebilled-stork; there were ostriches and there was a sign saying in Arabic and English, 'Beware of the ostriches!' This had only been erected after the authorities had discovered a couple of Sudanese fingers lying in the dust, close by the ostriches. (No member of the public had ever come forth to claim them.)

My mother would frequently be asked to nurse various zoo orphans, among which were cheetah kittens. Their parents would have been hunted for their pelts and the babies rescued. Consequently, while other children grew up with dogs, cats or guinea pigs my sister Sabrina and I had cheetah round the house. They were enchanting. They are nothing like leopard in temperament, being essentially timid; they padded round the place, overgrown nursery toys, purring like machine tools: they seemed a mixture of dog and cat in that my parents could take them when they went riding, and they loved to chase a ball. Practically the only time they needed to be tied up was during tennis matches, on my parents' grass court. It was off-putting for players to have a blurred shape hurl itself across the net and seize the ball.

I made friends with Sudanese fishermen who helped me construct a raft of 'ambatch', a balsa-type wood, on which I could float across the Nile to a shallow island from which I caught peculiar fish with long snouts, called 'khoshm al banat' (literally 'noses of the girls'). They made kissing noises. Then there were the sinister slimy catfish with their whiskers and poisonous dorsal spines which demanded careful handling.

Khartoum was laid out, according to legend, by General Kitchener so that machine gunners could control intersections. This was meant to result in a street design of a Union Jack; however, the roundabouts subsequently introduced to cope with vehicles made it hard for the camel handlers who saw no need to go round a traffic island, with their long caravans of camels. Shouting, sweating policemen furiously directed the huge and laden beasts, each padding patiently straight ahead, long eyelashes covering lustrous eyes, great jaws moving rhythmically, chewing a cud.

## Embryo Imperialist

The river front led to the Governor General's palace. Each afternoon, our nannies (usually Palestinian) wheeled or walked us in the deep shade. Along the road the gleaming horses clip-clopped, either single riders, or ponies and traps. Horses were very popular: polo, early morning rides, even a hunt at one stage (until the hounds had to be destroyed because of a rabies scare).

Near the palace stood the statue of General Gordon on a camel. Like most children of the period I used to think the camel was called 'Gordon' and wondered who the rider was.

The Khartoum baths were the other main ingredient in a small boy's pantheon of delight. The design was Roman, it was colonnaded and very deep; I learnt to swim early. Once I even had a lift on the back of a stout man who was passing through Khartoum at the time; my parents were acquainted with the Duke of Gloucester whose elder brother, when Prince of Wales, had toured the Sudan. My father had been his physician in the Southern Sudan.

During the early stages of the war when there was fear that the Italians would occupy the Sudan, from the south, Egypt had seemed a safer bet for women and children. My mother took Sabrina and me to stay with her younger brother and his family, then based in Cairo. Apart from cutting my scalp open at the Gezira Sports Club pool when I fell, and learning something about electricity by putting a finger in an open socket, the other excitement was the approaching war. Egypt looked increasingly under threat.

We were in Alexandria, on the seafront, when the Italian bombers dropped their bombs harmlessly into the harbour: the sirens and searchlights were exciting. Back in Cairo, my mother heard that Rommel's outriders has been sighted near the Pyramids: it was time to head south again. But how? She and her sister-in-law headed for Cairo railway station where they were swept up by pushing, fearful humanity, all trying to get away. A locked train pulled into the platform. Always resourceful, my mother broke a carriage window with a golf club and somehow got her very pregnant sister-in-law and we three small children aboard. After a long wait the train jerked its way out of Cairo. It went as far as Luxor, a few hundred miles up the Nile Valley. There it stopped: what next? A sullen Greek offered a bed for the night; my mother and I walked to the airstrip, deserted except for the incongruous sight of a German Junkers aircraft, presumably forced down and captured. I trailed my fingers over the corrugated sides of the fuselage and the black and white cross. It was baking hot, the summer heat radiating off the sand.

Suddenly, there was a drone and a small Lockheed 'Loadstar' dropped onto the runway. Two South African sergeant pilots looked surprised at the woman and child. They had landed to make some temporary repairs to an engine, before resuming their flight south to Khartoum. It was an ambulance plane, with no seats. Doubtfully they agreed to take on the women and children.

It was my first of many dangerous flights. Not so my mother: she had crash landed at the end of her first time aloft, before the war. Having taken off on this occasion, one of the engines stopped, and we flew all the way to Khartoum on the remaining engine. We had nothing to hold onto except the bare struts of the sides. We were sprawled on the floor, flung violently about by turbulence. Nearly everyone was sick and went on being sick; my mother and I were unaffected.

We landed late in the day at Khartoum and my father learnt for the first time what had happened to his family, from whom he had heard nothing for days. Immersed in a conference he sent one of his junior doctors to meet us, a taciturn Scot, who put Sabrina in the front seat, to revive. 'How's the wee girlee?' he enquired. Sabrina gave him a look of loathing and threw up in his topee.

Khartoum life continued equably from then on. The war stayed away and apart from the procession of service visitors in transit, including Noel Coward and Ralph Richardson with introductions to my parents, it was as if the pre-war life had never ended. I went to school.

My earliest formal education was at a nursery/primary school class, at the 'Clergy House', part of Khartoum Cathedral: bright eyed British children, topped up by the occasional active Greek child, chanted songs, did some reading and writing, and mastered basic arithmetic. I needed extending. My parents, as it happened, decided to retire, about then, to Kenya. They had purchased 25 acres in Limuru, some 20 miles out of Nairobi, where they intended to do some desultory light farming, ride a lot, and concentrate on tennis and golf. It sounded idyllic to their Khartoum friends, but it was a wrench to leave. They had been a popular couple, with a reputation for throwing splendid parties, in between working hard. My Sudan days were over.

# 2

# Paradise More Or Less

THE sendoff from Khartoum station still leaves a trace of nostalgia when I look at the photographs in the album, and think of the hordes of well-wishers, British and Sudanese, who came to see us off, on that baking day in 1944. We travelled in style. The train was made up into a series of self-contained suites; the cook prepared meals, and we had a sitting area as well as sleeping berths. Then it was a transfer into the comfortable existence of a Nile paddle steamer. They were remarkable vessels.

They had very shallow draughts, to negotiate the frequently changing water courses of the White Nile. Great barges were lashed on each side and sometimes to the bows. On these barges travelled the most colourful and polyglot of humanity. Whole families, plus their livestock, mingled in a humming, buzzing ants' nest of daily routine.

We journeyed on the top decks of the steamer, in what, at first sight were wired-in 'meat safes.' This was a precaution against the anopheles mosquito of the Southern Sudan. Our cabins were comfy. Sudanese waiters provided all the amenities, as we steamed at a majestic ten miles an hour, against the slow current. It took three weeks before we were to disembark. Sleeping and waking one was aware of the thud-thud-swish of the huge paddle wheels at the stern. Every so often we might gently nudge a bank. Shouted orders, a reverse of the paddles and we would back off to resume a safer passage.

When we tied up at some rickety jetty there was a flood of humanity on and off the barges. The greetings, the shouts of joy, the reunions made it clear that the Nile steamer was the only regular means of maintaining contact with the outside world. Roads were few and unusable in the wet season. I used to watch the intriguing ritual of a goat being ceremoniously slaughtered for the evening meal. Or, great excitement here, a successful fisherman would haul on board one of the enormous Nile perch, which could weigh hundreds of pounds.

Now we were coming into that forbidding part of the Nile waterway, known as 'the Sudd,' 40,000 square miles of floating papyrus grass, on which whole populations existed, human and animal. The latter were plentiful, from the ubiquitous crocodile on a mud bank, to herds of elephants, sometimes swimming the Nile (they do swim, with their trunk tips just out of the water). It was the locals, though, who caught the eye: unclothed, mostly over six feet in height, covered in ash (to ward off the insect life) and usually standing motionless on one foot, leaning against a long spear. The placid hump-backed cattle grazed, wherever there was a clearing.

The paddle steamer disgorged us at Juba. The rest of the journey into Uganda was mainly by vehicle. You could continue that way, but the best was to take two more water journeys. The first was a 24-hour one, on a converted Channel steamer, the *SS Robert Coryndon*, up the long narrow Lake Albert. The neatest little conventional steamer, all brass and gleaming white superstructure, complete with burly ex-RNR captain, with his four rings and rows of ribbons. Once again, the wild animals stood placidly on the banks, oblivious to our passage.

The ship took us past picturesque little centres, such as Pachwach and Rhino Camp. To the west was Arua, later the home territory of Idi Amin. At Butiaba, on Lake Albert, there was a bus to carry passengers as far as Masindi Port, on shallow Lake Kioga. The (then) prosperity and greenery around Masindi town contrasted with the primeval scenery of much of the southern Sudan.

A slow shuddering journey in another paddle steamer on Lake Kioga brought us to join a cartoon of a train: a tiny engine with huge smoke stack pulled one carriage to join the main Kampala–Nairobi line, at a station called Mbulamuti. The transition to the Nairobi Mail was dramatic.

It was the luxury of a railway that personified the best of British Imperial Africa, in its prime. The dining car with its efficient and smiling Goan stewards, the sleeping compartments with their three window layers — the ordinary shutter through which you could hear sounds of the African night, the glass which cocooned you, and the insect screen. With none in place, I could lean out to see behind me the long line of coaches. To the front, as we went round a bend, there were the two wood-fired engines, great plumes of smoke, the odd smut, and the snake-like convoy of maroon carriages eating up the African miles. It was all very exciting and satisfying to be heading towards the Highlands of Kenya.

At most of the frequent stops, the engines panting as more wood or water was taken on, little 'totos' ran alongside, offering their wares to the passengers leaning out. In Uganda there were great sticks of bananas, ranging from the giant red plantain type to little yellow ones. They always seemed to cost about 50 cents a stick (half an East African shilling) and, hung in the carriage, they ripened overnight.

There were tiny local chicken eggs, the size of ping-pong balls; there were carvings; there were sometimes wretched bundles of fluff, baby mongooses or live birds. We bought a mongoose, once; it developed into the most affectionate of pets, sleeping on my pillow or nestling round my neck.

You could smell the difference between the Sudan and Kenya. You could hear the difference. In Khartoum it was the dry dusty ochre-yellow of an early morning's walk along the Nile, with the 'bulbul' (sparrow) chirping, against a background of rank overlay of camel/goaty smells, a brilliant early light that blurred into the opaque of the morning. In Kenya, by contrast, it was all fresh-turned earth, rich grassy compounds of dew-soaked dark red soil, and smoke, acrid and claustrophobic in its effect and associated with the dark interiors of African huts, burning green wattle logs and a not unpleasant concoction of goat and of African peasant farmer. The noises of Kenya too were so different. Those maddening birds that constantly sing a few notes but never finish, the harsh scream of a hyrax — and the soft laughing African conversations from the collection of Kikuyu huts, their population of grotesquely shaved and bowed women, their dangling ear lobes crammed with metal circles of beads and one-cent pieces.

Limuru was over 7000 feet and the mists and drizzle were relished by those sheltering from Sudan heat. There were fields with luscious fat cattle; there was clear running water; there was a carapace of tea bushes and there were spreads of dark sinister forest. Our house had sweeping views across a steep valley, with just a glimpse of one other roof ('Suburban,' remarked a rancher from the north, to my parents' annoyance). The new home, originally a small stone cottage, had to be extended — two more room, stables and a separate guest area added. There were lawns to be planted, fencing to be put in and a ram to be installed on the little stream 80 feet below the house.

A ram pumps water uphill by a series of valves that are opened and shut by the passage of the water. Provided nothing jams the valve and there is sufficient water in the stream to keep out air, the ram kept the tank filled. Every so often the valve jammed and then it was a tramp down the steep slope, armed with hefty tools; it was usually the remains of a large frog caught as a tadpole, grown up in the pipe and pulverized in the valve.

Limuru life was much like English village life; certainly all the village trappings were there. The little stone church, the golf club, the pony club — hardly the popular overseas image of a Kenya remembered in terms of 'Happy Valley,' with its scandals and its endless parties. My parents had been discussing the wartime murder of Lord Errol. 'Do you know,' said my mother incredulously, 'That night he died, *21* husbands were asked for alibis?' My parents seldom had the time to gossip. Theirs was the hard-working routine of establishing a home and earning their place in the Limuru community of tea planters, farmers and those who worked in Nairobi but who preferred to come home to the hills.

There was a cheerful gang of Limuru children. Felicity and I were the entrepreneurs; we raised funds for the war effort by running elaborate pantomimes, which visiting service men on leave were bidden to watch and then relieved of their petty cash. We took full advantage of the wattle trees, planted for the tanning industry, to plan scenarios of wolves and maidens tied to trunks. We got carried away, stripping the bark off a dozen trees to achieve a ghostly white effect (we were to be severely lectured about ringbarking). There were parts for everyone, including the youngest. Ian was a rabbit, told to squat in a hole until he heard his cue. Unfortunately it was overlooked in the dramatic excitement; long after the audience had been allowed to leave Ian was found, still squatting stoically, all big ears and lumps (he had been bitten by ants).

We all went to the local school which was really for girls only but which was persuaded to take a handful of small boys, it being wartime

18

*Paradise More or Less*

with shortages of space. It was not a success. We loathed being at a girls' school and we hated the girls who despised us. We had to join in dancing classes and wear button-over gym shoes. It was too much and we played up. Places were found for us in proper boys' prep schools. I spent the next three years at Kenton College, just outside Nairobi, where I was well prepared for the Common Entrance to English Public Schools. Kenton was run on traditional British lines and, on the whole, we were looked after well. There was only one activity I did not enjoy much — compulsory boxing. We little boys used to pummel each other furiously, tears of pain streaming down our faces, parents and friends cheering us on. I was Best Loser in my last year, watched proudly by my father, just beginning to show signs of the lung cancer that was to kill him within the year.

I never heard from him again, after that boxing match. He was flown to England by my mother who wrote regularly from London that he was feeling a little better. I was looking forward to their return when I opened a letter from a well-meaning friend. 'You will be very brave, now that your father has died.' A great wave of tears blotted out the dining hall, I was led to the headmaster's study where a letter from my mother lay in front of him. The news had been badly handled.

Marlborough in England had already accepted me but my widowed mother could not bear the thought of losing me. I was sent to the Prince of Wales School in Nairobi, at that time the only school for European boys from the three territories of Kenya, Uganda and Tanganyika. 'European' applied to anyone who was not of African or Asian descent — there were sons of Greek merchants from Dar es Salaam, Italians, Germans and a strong Afrikaans contingent from 'up-country', Eldoret. These were the descendants of those who had trekked right up north from South Africa, often for the very practical reason that they were too dark to be classified as 'white' down south.

The Eldoret contingent was tough, intolerant, sometimes violently anti-black and often as strongly anti-'rooinek' (literally 'red neck', the epithet for those of British descent). There were times in my five years at the Prince of Wales when I suffered agonies. There was institutionalized bullying at the end of each term, with unfortunates like me forced to run gauntlets of knotted towels, being nearly drowned in cold baths and occasionally being forced into one-to-one fights. I learnt to fight back, of course, sometimes to my cost. I once took a swing at a

19

tormenter, he ducked, and my fist hit the concrete wall. I had to sit through a Sunday service with broken knuckles, dripping blood onto my Sunday grey flannels.

Needless to say, like most others I was resilient, but it set me against ever educating my children away from home influence, particularly in single-sex secondary boys' schools. Otherwise, I flourished at the Prince of Wales, which maintained the usual offering of games and activities. I enjoyed rugby, hockey and soccer, tolerated athletics and loathed cricket.

Academically it was an excellent establishment, under the great 'Percy' Fletcher, ex the famous Australian school Geelong Grammar, inspired mathematician and dynamic leader. He was grotesque to look upon; tall with wisps of red hair, a riveting stare, his few decaying yellow teeth clamped round a disgusting pipe, he wore turn-of-the-century rounded collars and always had large sweat stains under the arms. His speech was direct, punctuated by loud sniffs. We were in great awe of him. He had some excellent ideas: among the student body there was no smoking problem because prefects had that privilege, under certain circumstances. I knew of no prefects who actually did more than take a very occasional puff — and you could be sure that no one else did. The prefects guarded their privileges zealously.

Our staff, in general, were excellent, dedicated teachers, well read and each a character in his own right. I was to pass into Cambridge, one of 36 in my year to be accepted for British universities, with about half destined for Oxbridge.

My sight had always been a problem since I had measles in Egypt. I wore glasses permanently and had developed a slight squint which did nothing for my self esteem and was one of the reasons I was bullied so unmercifully. My mother had taken me away from the Prince of Wales for a term, to fly to South Africa where the squint was corrected surgically. It was agonizing: the ether anaesthetic made me vomit, jerking at the stitches in the anchored eyeball. My misery was exacerbated by having to lie, both eyes bandaged, in a hospital ward listening to ongoing commentaries of the cricket Test then being played. After eleven commentaries in three days, five of them in Afrikaans, I developed that distaste for cricket that is still with me. I could never see the ball, anyway; at least with rugby, you could run where others ran.

School was incidental to the serious business of enjoying living in Kenya. Every August the family tired of Limuru mists and headed for the coast. Usually it was by the Mombasa Mail, an overnight train that pulled out of Nairobi just when it was light enough to see the grazing game on the Athi Plains, barely bothering to notice the noisy intrusion. There was the familiar thrill of those hard bunks, longing for the morning which, when it came, presented a tropical Kenya of palms, white sand and damp heat.

Sometimes we drove all the way from Limuru, a pre-dawn start, only a few miles of bitumen and then the tedium of a bumpy, dusty road for 300 miles, occasionally alleviated by meeting an elephant, or even a rhino. Once on the coast and headed towards Malindi, there were the two ferries to be negotiated, one towed by cheerful locals who hauled us across on a long chain, chanting the while and celebrating touching the other bank with an impromptu dance, the leader honking his accompaniment on a large conch. 'Baksheesh' flowed. Past the turn off to the Blue Lagoon, the approach to the mysterious remains of Gedi and the breath-taking exhilaration of first viewing the surf creaming in — just time to change, select a (body) surfboard — and in! The routine was always the same. We lived in basic but comfortable 'bandas' (the local dwelling units) through which the sea breeze blew constantly. We slept under nets and had been taking anti-malarial pills weeks before, in preparation. It was a busy routine, of surfing, of peering into little rock pools for tiny jewels of fish at low tide, of long walks as the sun went down, on a golden beach with the phalanxes of sand crabs moving sideways like well-drilled troops.

Kenya offered other unique opportunities to those who wanted to make their own entertainment. Safaris tended to be well organized expeditions, with lots of back-up. I had a small circle of close friends who looked to do something quite different. One year two of us cycled that dreary road to the coast, a slog of dust and desolation with the occasional twinge of panic when great grey shapes floated across our front, and eyes gleamed from the scrub at the side in the early dawn. Another year we climbed Mt Kilimanjaro, from the Kenya side, with just a few porters to supplement the heavy packs we hauled to the snow line. I was fearfully sick at the summit. One year three of us were dropped near thick bush in the Chyulu Hills, a game reserve. It was only for a week but the isolation, the horrors of being temporarily lost in dripping rain forest with huge ants attacking us as we lay shivering in our sleeping bags, then stumbling out into high grass, to be confronted by an irritable rhino — it was heady stuff.

In my final year at school I had acquired a taste for archaeology, joining a school expedition to excavate Chinese remains on the Kenya coast. Pieces of porcelain were often found on the reefs offshore; the Chinese had traded with the East African coast for hundreds of years. The discipline of careful excavation was hard to take, but I learnt enough to count it as meaningful experience even then, reckoning it would be useful for when next I was to be considered for a similar enterprise. More important though there was a more intrinsic recognition of its worth, perhaps reflecting the spirit of my mother's antecedents — the thrill of being in touch with other civilizations.

It all reinforced a healthy curiosity about life that is not only the essence of a progressive spirit; it is the antidote to the malaise of introspective (and ignorant) self-satisfaction. In the words of my sensible old maternal grandmother, when I was to meet her a year or so later, in Britain, 'Michael, my dear. You must try everything, at least once. Otherwise you will never know what you may have missed.'

# 3

# Towards Man's Estate

URING my last years of school (1951–53) it was apparent to
most Kenyans that changes in the old order of things were
imminent: to those adults, back from the war, many of them
from leading their African askaris in the King's African Rifles, it was
especially clear that Africans were beginning to question their lack of
status, and the future. Not all Africans, of course — the patient Kikuyu
peasants, and those more elderly men who were used to a symbiotic
relationship with the 'bwana' and the 'memsahib', they showed no
thirst for change.

Gradually a new name came to be talked about in the clubs, the
schools, at any gathering where 'law and order' was the theme: Jomo
Kenyatta, the well-educated, politically-astute Kikuyu, he of the fly
whisk and the sonorous tones. Concurrently the papers started to report
on an increasing tide of terror and of murders and intimidations. The
victims were nearly all African. Indeed, that was the pattern throughout the emergency, with relatively few European deaths (albeit under
horrible circumstances) to which the expatriate community reacted
with shock and an increasing concern. Their staff were molested, their
valuable stock mutilated and destroyed. The Kenya Police Reserve
expanded, farm labour was screened, isolated farms were protected and
a pattern of fences, watch towers and patrolling guards became the
norm.

People took to wearing side arms quite openly. The Mau Mau came
to formal notice in 1952: the insurgency only lasted a matter of a few
years and was far smaller overall than the concurrent war in Algeria,
although at its height there were 10,000 soldiers and 21,000 police

23

employed. It was significant in its results: independence for Kenya followed a mere decade later.

I was personally affected as a teenager, in three ways: the most dramatic was one evening lying at home in my bed, reading. I happened to glance at the locked door which led to the outside: I saw the handle quietly being turned. I was terrified: I knew it could only mean Mau Mau. I tiptoed out of bed and whooshed out our Alsatian dog; there was a tremendous woofing in the undergrowth, then — silence. The combined Army/Police patrol found nothing. I too took to carrying a side arm which, apart from time at school (I was in my eighteenth year) and in the army, travelling to and from the UK and my time at university, was habit for the next 13 years.

We had to be careful with longstanding and trusted staff (everyone did) who might be pressured into killing their employers. They had to be locked into or out of the house, and checked on entry, to ensure no 'panga' (machete) was being carried, for instance, under a tray. I was too young officially to join the Reserve, but was invited to support patrols, during the school holidays. The limited game shooting I had done took on extra significance: gingerly I had learnt how to handle a 'light' heavy game rifle, a .375 magnum Holland & Holland, with the proverbial kick like a mule. Later I was to take this weapon to South Arabia; its stopping power was tremendous — and it helped my reputation.

My third direct involvement with the emergency was at school (which had been wired in) where there was a shortage of guards. Senior boys were rostered to patrol during the night: boring it was, but it was fortunate it interfered little with preparation for final exams. I had already been offered a place at Cambridge.

First though there was national service, which entailed an initial six-months' training in what was then Southern Rhodesia, well away from the deteriorating security situation in Kenya, until we were properly trained. We had queued at dawn to board our Dakota aircraft, in crumpled civilian clothing, our army issue dragging over our arms. We returned, smart and confident in our military competence. The British Army had detailed some of their toughest non-commissioned officers to train 100 self-satisfied Kenya youths; they had done an excellent job.

The six months in Rhodesia were not all a whirl of oaths, khaki figures and mind-numbing routine, though: we had some wonderful days off. Someone of my father's generation had remarked that, 'Officers retired to Kenya, other ranks to Rhodesia.' I did not find anything particularly different in the hosts who looked after us, the hospitality and lifestyle seemed the same as at home, although one comment struck me, 'Mau Mau? Can't say I'm surprised. You people up there have problems. You never knew how to treat your Africans. Here it's a different matter entirely. No trouble. Never will be. Better come and settle here, young fellow!'

Back home, in mid-1954, I found Limuru had changed; the emergency was much in evidence, with social gatherings restricted and practically all expatriate males in uniform, in support of the various British regiments stationed throughout the areas affected. I had been released from further military service, with my university place assured. My mother had had enough of her solitary life, running a small farm on her own. Her son was off to Britain. She and Sabrina would come too. We packed up and sailed for the UK, with our possessions crated, and our corgi, but leaving behind our other beloved dog.

My base for the next four years was Hampstead, in north-west London. For the first few years we took over part of the Georgian residence belonging to my glamorous Aunt Henrie, in exclusive Church Row. To me it was a strange existence, to be living in a smart house in an exclusive neighbourhood, but it helped to improve on my first impression I had gained of England from my initial view of Tilbury dockers, securing ropes round bollards, in a thin drizzle. Apart from the surprise of seeing Europeans performing a role I had associated with Africans at Mombasa, it was the shock of observing such small and stunted beings, 'going slow'. We had had to carry our own suitcases off the ship.

The weather was awful (and this was the first and almost the last time English weather upset me). Even allowing for the contrast with the sunny Mediterranean to say nothing of glorious Kenya, it was the wettest summer since whenever ... I noted gloomily that it had been snowing on high ground in Yorkshire, and it was August. I turned my face to the wall and wished I were back in the army, performing meaningful tasks in the sun. This did not last long. It was time for me to 'go up' to Downing College Cambridge, the third generation to study there. This was a bigger event than joining the army; I could dimly recognize it as the first really adult step in doing something purposeful with my life — because it was my choice.

On my first day, by contrast with the dismal summer, it was one of those hazy, sun-shimmery interludes in autumn when my mother shifted me and my few belongings into college. Through the rather drab outer rim of Cambridge and down past the railway station, there, opening like a flower from the grey street outside, was the green quad of Downing College, bounded by the honey-coloured stone of the college buildings.

Downing should have been founded sometime in the latter half of the eighteenth century. It was endowed by Sir George (of Downing Street connections). Being married to the profligate Lady Downing (who did her best to spend her husband's money, before it could be wasted on a mere seat of learning) it was 1800 before enough funds were available for the new college to open its doors. Her portrait hung in Hall, wicked of eye and careless of dress.

I lived for the first year in college, with the last two in lodgings. There was nothing particularly remarkable about my three years' study, but the mid-1950s'.population of undergraduates was an interesting mixture of those who had completed national service (often in Korea, Malaya and Kenya) and those who had come straight from school. The contrast in an individual's maturity of outlook and behaviour could be noticeable; this is surely a case for insisting on a 'gap year' between school and university. In public though the behaviour of members from either group on occasion differed little. It was the period of the Suez conflict and of the start of the Campaign for Nuclear Disarmament: idealism, misplaced or otherwise, was the common skein.

My college had a name for medicine and for law, my discipline for the last two years, after a year reading economics. Downing also boasted the presence of the redoubtable F.R. Leavis, who could be seen striding angrily across the grass, his open neck and overtly aggressive sideburns an apparent expression of contempt for the world's conformity. Behind him would straggle a variety of adoring disciples.

There were clubs, and the appropriate ties, for everything, ranging from political to religious, from sporting to dramatic and social. I seemed to join a lot of them the first year (having specifically avoided the rowing and the Student Christian Movement, having been urged vigorously by their representatives to join, almost as soon as I had settled in). I disengaged from most of them in my second year, but joined the Cambridge Union Society, fondly seeing myself debating with the great. That never happened; it was essentially a rather seedy London-type club in my time. There was a very old man always asleep in a chair, near the entrance. One day he was not there: apparently the committee met and voted to send a wreath to the funeral. The next day he was back.

I did attend several debates which were usually entertaining; one of them featured Gerald Hoffnung, very drunk, with a sousaphone with him. I also managed to see the Footlights each year I was up; Jonathan Miller was in his last year when I was a freshman.

It appeared as if all we did was to enjoy ourselves: not so. I learnt how to devote at least seven hours out of a normal day to study. I had soon realized from the comments on my essays and during the papers I delivered at supervisions that I would never be first-class material. A good 'second' would be my best. I did not achieve even that. I was placed top of the 'thirds' for Part I of the Tripos, with a Part II result of a '2 (2)'. My middling best I found to be markedly superior at the Australian university I was to attend 22 years later.

I did not work at all during vacations (hence my indifferent degree). My first summer I joined the Cambridge University Archaeological Expedition to Libya, through claiming a spurious knowledge of Arabic and in-depth archaeological experience from Kenya. We spent months digging in a massive cave near the Cyrenaican coast, led by a fanatical Cambridge archaeologist who cared little for the welfare of his diggers, but craved professional acclaim. Getting to and from North Africa, Libya itself, still scarred by the North African campaigns, the extensive Roman remains stretching from Tunis to Cyrene, the friendships made with fellow diggers and with members of the British Military Mission to Libya (training the local militia near where we were digging), these were the highlights.

I returned on my own to Libya the following summer, having travelled fifth class across the Mediterranean, in company with French troops returning disconsolately to that terrible Algerian war. I helped in the excavations at Cyrene and collected flints, miles into the bleak deserts, south of the village of Sirte.

While in Tripoli, from the security of a neighbouring balcony, I witnessed a mob trying to destroy the US Information Service Library (those plate-glass windows must have tempted anti-US mobs all over the world): it was part of the tide of anti-Westernism sweeping the Arab world, post Suez, under the leadership of the charismatic Egyptian Gamal Abdul Nasser. He was to dominate the next period of my life.

Less than a decade later I would be sitting with Bedouin friends, round a glowing fire, talking idly about the local happenings. Someone would half apologetically take a small transistor radio out of a skin bag and switch on. The familiar end to the rousing music would thump to a close, and then, in rolling tones, '*Salaam aleikum was rahamtulah al barakatu! Saut al Arab min al Kahr*' (the traditional greetings followed by, 'Voice of the Arabs, from Cairo!'), thereafter the news, followed by a colourful commentary, often as not containing exhortations to the faithful to dispose of the infidels in their midst. Millions of listeners who, even if they knew the 'news' to be fanciful, believed because they wanted to — it was heady, exciting stuff. That morning in Tripoli though, it was just an exciting incident to relate to those back in England.

In Cambridge it had been coming up to my final year and to making plans for the rest of my life, or at least for that part of it beginning to peer over the horizon. After two summers in Libya, there was really no doubt: I was destined in my own mind (and in that of my mother) to take on whatever was available in the way of service overseas. It was a matter of working abroad, in one of the few dependent territories remaining, before I lost the chance to follow my forebears, albeit into a post-colonial world, to become a possible victim of the whims emerging from newly-created democracies and the United States' foreign policy of the late 1950s (I was already cynical, with the arrogance of youth, about its self-proclaimed role).

I did not view the British diplomatic service as being likely to recognize my talents, such as they were; the Foreign Office seemed to require rather clever, multilinguists. Besides, I belonged to no 'Establishment': with a middle-of-the-road degree, a smattering of Arabic, Swahili and French, plus some useful travel backing up my early experiences in the Sudan and Kenya. What was I good for outside Britain, other than a commercial career? And somehow that never appealed at that stage. I applied for Her Majesty's Colonial Service, shortly to become HM Overseas Service.

There was still (just) a Colonial Office, headed by Mr Secretary Lennox-Boyd, and while I did not necessarily want to serve in a 'real' colony, I felt there might be scope for me to do my bit, in the footsteps of my father and grandfather, both photographed respectively, resplendent in their formal uniforms, moustached and confident. I could see them looking down at me.

I was interviewed initially by a district commissioner from the South Pacific, serving a term in London, who asked me what appeared to be quite random questions about nothing in particular. The subsequent board of three was also pleasant, but preoccupied. I had a stiff medical at the hands of the oldest doctor I had ever met (he had served in Africa at the turn of the century). That was it: I was accepted provisionally for training as a cadet.

During this selection process I had opted for where I should like to be sent. It was my mother's influence that had been decisive: 'Go where you get the best pay and conditions, Michael. Government is never generous, but they have to look after you.' There were two postings that met her criteria — Sierra Leone and Aden. The former I had heard had a foul climate, endemic diseases and unintelligible lingua francas, except to the missionaries devoting their lives to translating the Bible into Mende. I had passed through unattractive Aden, when the temperature was at its hottest and it was humid to match. I remembered the trip ashore for the large goats in the street, chewing old newspaper and cardboard boxes. I knew it to be a duty-free port and a minor military base, but there was a hinterland that sounded interesting. The Aden Political Service it was to be. On that basis I studied Muslim law as one of the subjects in my final year (it was so esoteric that I forgot it all — a lot to do with dividing the ownership of a palm tree according to various customs, as I recall).

Cadets for the service had to do a year's preparation at Oxford or Cambridge. Being a Cambridge man it was expected that I would stay up; however, my contemporaries were going down and so I opted for Oxford, where I was accepted for Downing's 'twin', Lincoln. I filled the last summer between Cambridge and Oxford by working in Canada, in a lead smelter, and travelling round North America on the proceeds.

Waiting for me in Hampstead on my return from the United States was a letter welcoming me to the Commonwealth (previously Colonial — the name was changed at the start of my time there) Services Club in Oxford, a residential centre for those undertaking the pre-posting course. I felt the whole tone of the letter had a refreshing informality that combined a no-nonsense approach to me, with a signal that I had really started on my adult life. It was actually rather misleading, in that Oxford, while a period of great fun in my life, contributed little in the way of practical preparation for the career ahead.

We were a polyglot crowd: apart from the recent graduates like me, there were jovial West Indians, a quiet, delightful Somali, a number of overwhelmingly earnest Africans who tended to look askance at the uninhibited behaviour of their British clubmates, and a different group composed of senior officers taking a year off, to undertake a bit of study. The latter were composed of administration and of forestry. We also mixed with a number of the lecturers and others who tried to teach us what they thought we needed.

As it happened, most of the course material was of peripheral use and significance to me; I was to be an Assistant Adviser in the Eastern Aden Protectorate, with no direct responsibilities for the territories to which I was being posted. The course emphasis was strongly on the African territories, and the law that a junior magistrate would be expected to apply. I found myself losing interest in the course as a whole; besides, Oxford was great fun, after the reasonably hard slog of my final year at Cambridge.

The most useful part of the course was my attachment to Dorking and Horley Rural District Council. The services offered were roughly on a par, if not in sophistication at least in scope, with what was attempted in two of the Aden Protectorate sultanates (of which more, later) or so I was to discover. Language should have been important and so it was, but the Oxford professor who tried to teach me was a classicist. I really needed intensive tutoring in colloquial which was not available (I was the only student going to South Arabia). The result was that when I was required to cut short the course right at the end, I sailed for Arabia knowing I had failed all my exams, but having painfully memorized a sentence in classical Arabic that the professor of Arabic assured me would be useful, because it contained a number of different grammatical points. The sentence was (translated), 'The daughters of the judges have flashing eyes.'

I was the last Aden candidate to do the pre-appointment year. The only lesson learnt from that pleasant interlude was how important it is to tailor course material to the actual, rather than to the perceived, needs of the students.

I had been kitted out by my mother, with the help of F.P. Baker & Company of Soho. The Colonial Office provided lists of necessities and useful advice, on what to wear and when. My mother saw to it that I had a complete dinner service (in replaceable earthenware) and all the comforts for trekking, in the best Sudan traditions. I had a formal uniform made, having been solemnly measured for something that made me feel like a cross between the Viceroy of India and a P & O steward. My enormous Wolseley helmet I had hitherto only seen on marine bandsmen. Finally, I purchased the brass buttons, the helmet coat-of-arms and the collar tabs with their one gold strip, for either side of my neck. Gloves were not forgotten. My sword had been my father's; I enjoyed the feeling of family continuity.

I was ready: on 4 July 1958 my mother drove me to Liverpool; my crates of gear had gone ahead. We were rather silent, with none of the light-hearted chat we had enjoyed when first we drove up to Cambridge.

The *SS Salween* was ready to depart for Aden, via Port Sudan, and on to the Far East. She was small and rather shabby, but my four-berth cabin (I was on my own) was palatial. My mother brushed aside the helpful Goan steward and unpacked for me. We embraced briefly and she left me briskly, without looking back. For a moment I had stared fixedly at the porthole, seeing nothing. Then I came to with an effort and opened the letter that had been awaiting me at the ship.

'This brings you our best wishes for a good journey and success in a pleasant and satisfying job ... take plenty of exercise, eat the best food you can get, and broaden your mind whenever you can. Be kind and considerate and polite, and I expect you will get the best out of life.' An old family friend, from the early Sudan days, had made my setting off, all on my own, sound so sensible, so matter-of-fact.

After a while, I folded the letter and went up on deck.

# 4

# Arabian Introduction

JULY 1958: the *Salween* nosed her stubby way towards Suez. There was to be no visit to Port Said, at the north end of the Suez Canal, so the first real stop would be Port Sudan. The North African coast was visible to the right, from Algiers to Cape Bon: the constant stream of shipping all flew their national flags, which was unusual when out at sea. The ostensible reason for the display was provided by the long, low shapes of lurking French destroyers, often within view and prepared to intercept any vessels they thought might be engaged in running arms to the Algerians, engaged in that increasingly desperate war with the French.

On board, any thoughts of bloody strife were absent. I spent my time eating a series of curries, sleeping them off and reading in desultory fashion about Aden and its history. I had obtained before I left an original copy of the Royal Geographical Society's journal, *Volume the Ninth* dated 1839; it contained (on page 125), 'Memoir, to accompany a Chart of the South Coast of Arabia from the Entrance of the Red Sea to Misenat.' There followed the most detailed description of the South Arabian coast — just names to me, at that stage of course, but the maps were beautiful.

Captain Haynes was shortly after to capture what he described as, 'a ruined village of 600 persons.' This was in apparent retaliation for the locals having been unpleasant to the survivors from a ship wrecked there. The 'Pax Britannica' was one thing: however, Aden was to become first a coaling station, on the way to and from India and, some hundred years later, one of the world's biggest bunkering ports; it was

32

administered until just before the Second World War by the government of India and thereafter, until 1967, by London.

One of Aden's uses was as a punishment station for British regiments that had misbehaved in India (which perhaps said something about its climate, long before its recognition by my mother, as a suitable posting for her son). Gradually, the mainly commercially based and multi-cultural population had increased as the shipping flowed, but towards the interior, parts of which seemed to resemble the moon's surface, judging by a photograph in another book I was studying, the Bedouin tribes had remained truculent and xenophobic. It looked like fun. I put Captain Haynes, and the companion volumes on Arabia, away and went to join my fellow voyagers.

Socializing on board was limited. There were only a few passengers: a large lady was off to Rangoon, to try and recover some of her family's property, seized by the government there when her folk fled the arrival of Japanese troops. There was an anonymous sort of person due to join the Aden Public Works Department, and a pleasant girl also off to Aden to stay with a brother 'in oil.' There was a Burmese doctor bound for his homeland, a Sudanese heading for Khartoum and an Egyptian returning to Cairo. The *crème de la crème* (as I reported to Aunt Henrie later) was a slightly faded American female traveller, bound for Kandy (Sri Lanka) in search of, 'culshure and a kinda spiritual peace.' She had 'done' Africa in a month, India in a fortnight and, after three weeks in Britain — thoroughly sickened by close contact with the decadent locals — she was seeking rest in Ceylon. Judging by subsequent reports that year of saffron-robed monks beating in each other's heads with stakes, she may have been sadly disappointed.

She had a weakness for whisky. Lugging a bottle of duty-free 'Vat 69' out of her cabin one evening, she invited us to help her finish it. She was last seen singing at the phosphorus in the water, near the captain's cabin. Halfway through 'Stardust', a very small cadet, doubled out from the bridge and squeaked at her, 'Master's compliments, and if you want to sing, would you go to the other end of the vessel!'

We were all thoroughly sick of the *Salween* by the time we had joined the south-bound convoy through the Suez Canal. The Red Sea in July is the nearest thing to hell, I thought at times: there was a following breeze blowing, at about the same speed as the ship's passage. Apart from the cloying heat, a cloud of smuts hung round us, drifting like grimy snowflakes onto anyone desperately coming up from below, to escape the horrors of the cabins. It was nothing, though, as compared to our next experience.

We tied up at Port Sudan, to unload railway sleepers; we were there for five days and four nights. It was so unbearable that we were not surprised to hear two persons had apparently collapsed and died, while we were alongside. One was a member of the crew, and the other was working on the wharf. The temperatures were much the same, day and night. Even at midnight on deck the metal stanchions and rails seemed glowing to the touch. We wandered the ship, pillows stuck wetly under our arms, looking for some part of the deck where there might be a breeze. There never was, although just before dawn there was some respite, and then that fearsome sun obliterated once again the damp blackness.

On shore, Sudanese in gleaming white robes and loosely tied turbans mopped their shining black faces. Half-naked tribesmen with huge horny bare feet stared at us arrogantly and demanded, 'Baksheesh!' of the American lady when she had summoned up enough energy to attempt to take a photograph. These fearsome-looking people were the descendants of the 'Fuzzywuzzies', immortalized by Kipling as the only opponents ever to have broken the British Army's traditional defensive formation of a 'British square.'

Towards the end of our enforced stay came a nicely worded letter addressed to me: it was from the Mayor of Port Sudan, a Dr Mohamed Ali. He had been trained as a medical student by my father and remembered him with affection. Would I care to visit him at the Club and talk of old days? Indeed I would.

Dr Mohamed Ali was large, avuncular and very British, except for his Sudanese colour and features. He spoke in warm tones of my father and how he had been missed by the Sudan Medical Service. As we chatted, he pressed on me another whisky-and-soda, pausing only to fill his own glass and to switch on the BBC Nine O'Clock News. He called me, 'Old Boy,' and invited me to a cigar. I liked him very much.

Aden, at last: the ship was one of a number tied up, refuelling in mid-harbour. The crushing heat was alleviated by the sparkle of the moving water and the constant buzz of one of the world's busiest ports.

Against a background of the well-known jagged crater (the town of Crater sprawled therein) and the wide sweep of desert further round the bay, there were vessels of many descriptions, going about their business. There were two great passenger liners, three times as big as the *Salween*, busily letting on and off lines of tourists, into the waiting launches. There were bulky tankers, scruffy tiny coasters, graceful Arab dhows, self-important little *sambuks* (smaller Arab fishing boats) putt-putting in between the ships moored in line.

A scholarly-looking man shook me by the hand and motioned me to the smart government launch lying alongside the *Salween*. The Hon. Alec Cumming-Bruce from the Secretariat in Aden was kindly looking after me; his had been the signature on the first letter I had received from Aden, before leaving England. Alec ordered the launch crew to cast off and we headed towards the pier, already crowded with streams of tourists, eager to spend their money in this duty-free mecca. Laden with packages ranging from sewing machines to cameras, watches and clothes, others came staggering back with their bargains, anxious to be absorbed into the air-conditioned womb of their floating home.

The launch came briskly to the jetty; one of the Water Police reached out a helpful hand to steady me, as I stepped over the gunwale. I lurched for a second as I secured my first footstep resolutely onto Arabian soil. I had arrived, and not for me the disorderly shambling of the tourist crowds — a car was waiting. The Arab driver, hand to his turban, ushered us to the back seats and we drove at speed towards the Crescent Hotel where I was to stay for the few days of kitting out and of introductions to some of the people with whom I was to share my career. Alec dropped me with most of my cases at Reception, told me to get settled in and he would collect me later that afternoon for a spot of shopping, followed by dinner and a film show, later on. 'Here, have a look through this,' he said, handing me a book, *Welcome to Aden*, 'It'll tell you something about the Colony.'

Old fashioned, but cool and welcoming after the humid hassle outside, the Crescent Hotel had been part of Aden since the 1920s. My room had a very high ceiling; it was large, with an enormous fan languidly revolving to raise a whisper of cool against the heat barred by shutters. I found my way to the bar where I ordered a long lime-and-soda. It was early noon. The bar contained the first air-conditioning I had ever come across and I was one of a surprisingly large number of men congregated along its length. I listened idly to the conversation.

It seemed to be mainly mercantile — when ships were expected, turn-round time, that sort of thing. Gin or beer flowed. The scene had more than a tinge of the Mombasa Club about it; the line of plump, red faced convivial drinkers, uniformly dressed in white, did nothing to remind me that I was on the edge not only of my new life, but of Arabia Felix. Then someone was talking of a demonstration, 'Those bloody Yemenis — it's a pity they don't ship them back where they belong.' A murmur of agreement. I went up to my room and collapsed on to the enormous double bed.

A small gecko eyed me nervously from behind the standing mirror, decided I meant no harm, and concentrated on its ambush of a dozing mosquito. I found the guidebook and glanced at the inside cover: 'Interested in sausages?' I read, 'Enough are eaten by the British Forces in Aden each year to make a line 120 miles long.' There were some more useful facts, perhaps.

At the last census held in 1955 there were 36,910 Aden Arabs, 18,991 Protectorate Arabs, 48,088 Yemenis, 15,817 Indians, 10,611 Somalis, 3763 Britons, 721 'other Europeans', and 831 Jews. Interesting, the last, but I recalled that one of the oldest Jewish populations in the world had been based in the Yemen, to the north of Aden, apparently dating from when King Solomon had sent for the Queen of Sheba. I read on. 'Those whose stay (is longer) are likely to find life in the Colony rather restricted, both spacially and socially.' The heart of the Colony was in Crater, the home for most of the polyglot of Adenis listed in the census. Its narrow streets made up a dusty slum where little shops fronted the ramshackle houses, the available space taken up by a flowing tide of humanity, and of those omnivorous goats, some of the nannies in milk clad, unexpectedly (but quite sensibly, really), in satin brassieres, to prevent their kids from suckling.

The shops always seemed to be open; and those inhabitants not beckoning in the passing tourist were usually sprawled asleep on *charpoys* (beds of rope and wood). These represented the majority of Aden's population; I was also to become familiar with the names of local trading houses and merchants whose rich dwellings, often built high upon steep crags above Crater and overlooking Steamer Point, where they caught a breeze and enjoyed a view, contrasted with the cramped tenements in those crowded streets below.

The Aden guidebook I had been lent featured the most prominent names; that of Besse, a French Levantine family the founder of which had made a fortune mainly from certain monopolies at crucial times of war, was known to me. My mother's younger brother Archie had worked for 'Old Man' Besse between the wars. In a foolishly romantic moment he had proposed marriage to Besse's secretary and found himself summarily dismissed. Antoine Besse had eventually endowed St Antony's College at Oxford. There were the Parsee firms of Cowasjee Dinshaw and Bhicajee Cowasjee (the full page advertisement for the latter jumped at me out of the page 'Wines–Spirits–Provisions–Watches–Tobacco & Cigarettes–Jewellery in Silver, Gold & Cultured Pearls–Toys of all types'). I closed my eyes.

It must have been about 5.30 p.m. that Alec called for me, this time in his own car. 'Some shopping?' he asked; I had already mentioned my need to buy some tropical clothing — bush jackets, shorts, long cotton trousers, that sort of thing. The estimable Messrs F.P. Baker & Company in Soho had already suggested that I stock up with their tropical clothing. One glance at the strange vast garments and the accompanying prices had me politely refusing. But Steamer Point offered just what was needed.

It was humming with life. A fresh load of tourists had been caught up in bargaining with the polyglot collection of Arabs, Indians and Somalis manning those little shops. The Arabs and Somalis were mostly engaged in enticing the shoppers into their establishments with a mixture of hearty, bullying and jocular blandishments. Cross-legged Indian tailors sewed intently, elderly Singer sewing machines whirred and clattered, powered by the thin legs of their operators, expertly manoeuvring both the treadles underneath and the rolls of material being fed through, above. It took perhaps 15 minutes for me to be measured and questioned as to what exactly I wanted; cloth was brought out to be fingered and argued over (this by Alec on my behalf). 'You should be here still the day after tomorrow; they'll be ready then. No, don't pay now.'

We retraced our steps to Bhicajees, where I was advised with what to stock up — tinned food, cases of Chianti, some gin, whisky, beer. It seemed an awful lot to me, but remembering my mother's stories of privation in the Southern Sudan, I kept silent. 'Mukalla's officially dry,' said Alec kindly, perhaps noticing my doubting looks (did I really need to take enough to stock a bar?). 'But you'll get this lot through, seeing you're staying at the Residency. May have to pay some duty though.' Having signed for these expensive essentials (gin at East African shs. 6/– a bottle, whisky a bit more) it was back to Alec's car and on to the Club.

Even to my untutored eye it was Victoriana virtually unchanged, except the punkahs had recently been replaced by fans — the dusty gloom of billiard tables and easy chairs with holes cut in the mahogany arms to hold drinks; it was shabbily comfortable. There I was introduced to a number of pleasant but anonymous individuals, each with a glass in his hand, and we dined off lamb chops, tinned vegetables and tinned fruit, washed down with Pilsener beer.

Now it was dark and we wandered outside to a cool patio sort of area, with chairs laid out in rows. An outdoor screen had been erected. We settled down comfortably, a last order for drinks and the films started. I never did remember what they were, but it did not matter, either to me or to my hosts. I happened to glance along the row. Everyone appeared fast asleep.

It was a hectic five days in all, about which I recalled little — calls on British officials in the crowded Secretariat building, files heaped on desks, drinks in the evening as part of endless rounds of hospitality, swims at the little bathing beach of Gold Mohur carefully netted against sharks. On my last evening I was taken to Government House, to be presented to HE the Governor, Sir William Luce.

Immaculate guards stiffened to attention as the car swept past the sentry boxes and up to the entrance. HE made me feel very welcome; he was ex-Sudan himself and so the first inquiry was after my mother's health and a few reminiscences of my father, though Bill Luce would have been fairly junior when my father had left the Sudan. 'You'll enjoy working with Colonel Boustead. He has only a few weeks left before he leaves, you know.' Colonel Boustead was the Resident Adviser and British Agent of the Eastern Aden Protectorate. HE smiled at me in kindly fashion, tall and elegant in his light tropical suit. We sat relaxed, fresh lime-and-sodas to hand, in a circle of easy chairs on the wide verandah; there was now some colour in the background with the evening light, after the anonymous opaqueness of

the day's heat. Behind and below us was the sparkling blue of Aden
harbour. Another great ship glided into view. In the foreground three
or four servants stood motionless, their backs to the lines of white
pillars at the edge of the verandahs. 'I hope you'll call by again when
next you're in Aden,' said HE pleasantly, 'And now,' he got to his
feet. We scrambled to ours, and made our farewells.

That evening, after having sorted out my kit ready for an early start
to Aden airport the next morning, I once again concentrated on the
scribble of notes I had assembled on my hurried and confusing passage
of the past five days. Colonel Hugh Boustead: now there was a name
with which I had been familiar ever since I had been able to relate to
my parents' talk of the Sudan, my mother's in particular. He was
another old friend of theirs, a larger-than-life character whose exploits
read like the heroes of G.A. Henty's novels of my boyhood.

Hugh Boustead had begun his career in the Royal Navy, as a
midshipman. In 1915 his ship had been off South Africa, from which,
bored with the lack of action, he deserted to join up with the Transvaal
Scottish. He saw distinguished service on the Western Front, was
commissioned in the field, decorated and given a free pardon, for
desertion, by the king. His army service included a turbulent period
with the White Russians; later he commanded the Sudan Camel Corps
(and served as a district commissioner in the Sudan Political Service).
During the 1939–45 war (along with the famous explorer Wilfred
Thesiger and that strange man, Wingate) he was much involved in
supporting the Ethiopian Emperor Haile Selassie in his fight against
the Italians. As a younger man he had boxed for the army (his
damaged knuckles accounted for his indecipherable hand: his writing
resembled a kind of cuneiform); he had been a British Olympic
pentathlon champion and he had attempted to climb Everest, on the
1933 expedition.

Colonel Hugh was to be my first real boss. I had been given some
cursory detail as to what my first job was to be — Assistant Adviser
Residency was the title, 'dogsbody' the role. The title itself had a
strange, almost romantic, ring about it and I was totally unaware of the
routine nature of the appointment. No one in Aden I met seemed to
have had very clear ideas about the Eastern Aden Protectorate's
workings, or if they had, I was so ignorant that I could barely have
absorbed what I might have been told.

During those last hours in the Crescent Hotel the Aden stay suddenly seemed an irrelevant interlude; I longed for the dawn, with all the impatience of a schoolboy at the end of term in perhaps exactly the right context: there I was, totally absorbed, one day at a time, with the preoccupation and the self-confidence of arrogant, callow youth.

The elderly looking Dakota of Aden Airways took off promptly. We were a varied group that had boarded; I was the only European passenger. There were immaculately-robed gentlemen, prayer beads passing busily through somewhat nervous hands as their owners doubtless called on Allah for a smooth takeoff and an even smoother landing. Neatly swathed green-topped headpieces indicated their owners were *Seiyeds* (descendants of the Prophet Muhammad), with at least one visit to Mecca to their credit. There were their wives, or someone's wives, shapeless bundles of black robes, with just the occasional glimpse of a hennaed palm of a hand and sometimes the flash of an eye. There were babies being held everywhere. At the rear of the aircraft, just aft of the strapped bags, bales and suitcases and tin trunks, were two goats tightly wrapped in sacks; their lustrous eyes perhaps revealed just a hint of their concern at being separated from their free-roaming kin on the Aden streets.

I sat back in the narrow seat, gazing through the square window at the broken brown landscape, clearly visible below. There were two hours or so of flight, over some of the most inhospitable terrain I was yet to encounter on the ground. For the first time I began to feel I was heading out of my depth. At last I sensed the real isolation of being among strangers indifferent to my presence. Over the roar of the two engines came the shrill cries of infants dandled by their mothers. The Aden Airways steward offered me a warm orange drink and a biscuit. The aircraft bucketed suddenly in an up-draft and my stomach lurched. I focused my eyes sternly on Harold Ingrams' *Arabia and the Isles*. The aircraft droned on and on.

# 5

# A Touch of Local Colour

THE grim-looking territory over which we were flying changed little as the aircraft droned and quivered its way out of Khormaksar airport, flying at a height of not more than 8000 to 10,000 feet. This was the Aden Protectorate or, more accurately, the Western Aden Protectorate (the WAP), bordered by the Eastern Aden Protectorate (the EAP) and my destination. To the right, and stretching along our flight-path was the undulating coastline, in some places narrow sweeps of yellow beach, at others black headlands and jagged lava-seeming flows edging into the thin line of surf. To the left it was rocky, barren; the terrain varying only in the degree of jagged peaks or, by contrast, deceptively flat plateaux of rocky wilderness, stretching into a hazy blue of seemingly endless ranges. Every so often this moonscape would be interspersed by the winding courses of flood beds of such exceeding dryness that, adding to the moonscape effect, they appeared to have been scoured by anything but water, so barren was the aspect.

Occasionally a thin vehicle track could be seen, clinging like a thread of white or yellow cotton to the tattered and worn shift of one of its itinerant desert wanderers. Tiring of this majestic but somehow depressing view, I turned to the simple map I had with me: there were only a few names of towns or areas shown — Aden — Mukalla — Hadhramaut — Wahidi — Baihan; not much else. The map was clinically neat; it covered, I supposed, an area of about a quarter of a million square miles. I noted it was over 600 miles from Aden to the furthest point shown, the north-eastern corner of the Dhofar/EAP

41

intersection. Much of the border bore the simple but intriguing legend, UNDEFINED.

I had read that to the east, in particular, the Bedouin tribes continued to utilize their traditional grazing territory, impervious to whatever line there might be on the map and restricted only by neighbourly feuds and the odd government outpost. In the west, it seemed that the WAP border, though still disputed by the Yemen, was nominally recognized by the tribes on the British side of the frontier. Such trouble as occurred along the Protectorate border was caused by the Yemen, rather than by the Saudis, however much the latter might have brooded about the British presence to their south.

The 65-year-old Imam Yahya of the Yemen, self-proclaimed suzerain of Aden, a despot of the old school, had ruled his kingdom 'absolutely' (I saw a postcard being sold in Aden of a'typical Yemeni public execution in progress) since 1919. Until then, the Turks had been in nominal control, having invaded the Aden Protectorate in the 1870s and again in 1915. It had been the willingness of the various tribal rulers to accept British protection from the Imam's attentions that had led to the rulers' undertaking to recognize British sovereignty over the Aden Protectorates and, by a remote extension, to the appointment of this latest green recruit to Her Majesty's Overseas Service.

The history of the EAP and WAP, I had read, was just a matter of a few decades. The early political officers had been men of some courage and individuality. Men such as Jacobs, Belhaven and Ingrams had used their own initiatives and made their own contacts among the suspicious tribes, rent by blood feud and xenophobia, who were living in that barren territory over which I was flying.

Harold Ingrams was the great father figure of the EAP. During the 1930s it had been his efforts that had secured what came to be known as 'Ingrams' Peace' among the Hadhrami tribes. By a patient process of negotiation, aided by powerful local figures who were anxious to open up safe trade routes crossing the vast area below me, men could walk safely among their fellows. Their women could once more till their fields. Kerosene was no longer poured down neighbours' furrows, to kill off their trees. Routes from the interior to the coast were reopened; village schools, government courts, and a network of local government centres were established.

Stationed in key areas of the EAP were Ingrams' successors, those colleagues I was on my way to join. Political officers in both Protectorates were essentially advisers to the local Arab rulers (though they carried out their duties very differently in the WAP, as I was later to experience) with the added responsibility, as British representatives, to keep a watchful eye on tribal machinations, to enhance British prestige and, via the British Agent, to keep Her Majesty's Government informed of anything that might affect British interests.

Tact was the order of the day. Fluency in Arabic was just part of the job. (A quick flashback to my efforts to learn Arabic at Oxford. Where, I wondered, would my judges' daughters' flashing eyes fit in?) The other essential in being an effective political officer seemed to be an ability to enjoy a lifestyle that was essentially in tune with the indigenous population. Well, we'd see.

On occasion when there was a breakdown of law-and-order, it was sometimes necessary for the political officer to back the local Arab administration by calling for military help. Maybe all that was required in the Eastern Protectorate was for a platoon of the Hadhrami Bedouin Legion (HBL, the force of about 1400 men raised and trained by the British) to support the local state militia; or perhaps a larger contingent of the HBL would go it alone. On other occasions it was appropriate for the Royal Air Force to be asked to provide a show of military strength, from Aden. Often without further aerial sanctions this was enough to save the local recalcitrant's 'face'; in he would come to parley with government and, perhaps, to leave a small son hostage with the authorities, to be schooled at the Bedouin Boys' School in Mukalla, to learn the way of peace and progress, maybe to join the HBL in due course.

I must have dozed off at this point. I opened my eyes as the Dakota began to lose height. Now there were signs of habitation. The plane banked and I could see the airstrips ahead, alongside a cluster of small buildings that gleamed blindingly white in the afternoon sun. This was Riyan, a Royal Air Force station manned by just a few expatriate personnel, a remnant of the old imperial flying-boat route to India, and now the main gateway to Mukalla, capital of the Quaiti sultanate and headquarters of the Resident Adviser and British Agent of the Eastern Aden Protectorate.

It was about 3.00 p.m. and on the ground the dusty scene was bathed in a mellow yellowness of slanting light. It was still hot, but the stickiness of that afternoon by the Arabian Sea had nothing in common with the miasmic blanket-stifling heat of Crater-clogged Aden. There was a light breeze blowing; it enhanced a definite feeling of escape from all the hurly-burly of the last few days.

Any feelings of euphoria were interrupted by the down-to-earth presence of a bulky figure dressed in white — enormous shorts set above squat dependable legs. This was Pat Booker, a straight-forward Scot with a dry, cynical manner and (as I was to discover) almost the odd man out, in an isolated community most noticeable for its colourful diversity of approach and behaviour. Pat was Assistant Adviser Coastal Areas, a role to which he was anxious to return, 'Now that you'll be handling all the Residency stuff.'

Our long-wheel-based Land Rover had been backed with some difficulty, up to the Dakota. A harassed local official was engaged in heated altercation with passengers over the contents of their shiny tin trunks. Two depressed-looking local policemen in ill-fitting khaki pushed owners away from their possessions. Torrents of unintelligible speech passed back and forth; babies cried and were shrilly consoled by their shrouded mothers. The packaged goats eyed the scene with resignation: the Adeni steward loftily surveyed the jumble of packages and bundles from the vantage of the aircraft's steps. The two British pilots busied themselves inspecting various protuberances on the wings and tail of the machine, which I saw had a towing hook, denoting it had probably been used to manoeuvre gliders over Arnhem. Three or four RAF aircraftmen, stripped to the waist and burnt dark brown, chatted among themselves as the Dakota was being re-fuelled.

Pat motioned to the Residency driver who extracted my copious gear from the heap of baggage being squabbled over by its owners and the customs official. Pat spoke briefly to the latter, pointed to me, and the small wizened man in his over-sized uniform nodded. 'I've told him that it is all personal belongings of yours.' Pat took the wheel, I sat alongside him and the driver perched on my heap of cases. The road was very corrugated and I feared for some of the new china I had had packed away (In fact I lost only a cup).

The blue background towards which we were heading opened up into a defile between jagged hills. To our right rose a dominant massif, the

44

southern edge of the plateau I had been seeing from the aircraft, more-
or-less continuously, for the past hour. The road became very stony and
the dust rose. It narrowed to the point where Pat had to slow suddenly
to allow an old man and his donkey, piled high with sacks of charcoal,
to plod stoically past us. A ruined fort hung in an unlikely manner on
the edge of one of the crags.

Now the road opened out into almost a metropolitan thoroughfare. It
was hardened through constant use and the salt in the soil, giving a
semblance of tarmac. We were in a valley opening widely to reveal
white dwellings, long barracks and lime-whitened stones. The
Hadhrami Bedouin Legion's headquarters were to our left. We came
down towards the sea, competing for road space with local taxi-trucks
crammed with humanity. Lines of camels, laden with firewood and
escorted by wild-haired men, plodded stolidly seawards. The camel
escorts each carried a rifle over a shoulder and great silver *jambiyas*
(curved daggers) at their waist-fronts. Mostly they wore loin cloths,
leather ammunition belts and, apart from a headband or two, that was
it. They were coloured as blue as their scant clothing. 'Bedou,' shouted
Pat, over the engine, 'That's indigo. They rub it all over them. They
say it keeps out the cold, up on the Jol.' The latter was that great stony
plateau which I had already noticed, bordering the coastal plain.

Now we could sight the sea: to the right of us was a suburb of
Mukalla, Sherij. There was only a handful of Europeans living
there —the two bank staff, one married, and one Residency official,
with his family. To left and right of us there were camels, couched and
chewing, their owners bargaining with townsfolk for the loads they had
brought in — charcoal, firewood and lucerne, grown further up near
one of the precious sources of water. The Land Rover nosed its way
through tumultuous humanity to pass under a very oriental but
unmistakable city gate. We were in the main street of Mukalla, capital
of the Quaiti sultanate.

To our right lethargic sentries in khaki turbans guarded the entrance
into the Sultan's palace. I caught a glimpse of a curious hotchpotch of
a building — a mixture of a Victorian railway station, a large gazebo
and a crow's nest. Our vehicle turned left, into the Residency
compound. We alighted under a porticoed entrance of a handsome
building with all the hallmarks of being the British Residency, quite
apart from the Union flag that flapped energetically in the afternoon

sea breeze. The Residency was gleaming white: it presented a dependable double-storied visage of authority, enhanced by the small cannon. The HBL sentry came smartly to attention, his motor-tyre sandals shuffling together and his .303 rifle slapped into his shoulder. He was dressed in a sort of long white nightshirt, embellished by a red cummerbund over which was his ammunition belt, his *amama* (head cloth) held firmly in place by his *aqal* (head-rope) from which flashed his silver HBL badge.

Pat handed me over to the jovial figure who came down the steps to greet me; he also wore huge white shorts but no knee stockings. Willie Wise, ex Royal Naval reserve, combined an amusing stutter with a relaxed panache. He was acting Deputy British Agent, as he informed me on the way into his office. We walked through the doorway, the large painted metal coat of arms above the entrance informing the world that this was a British consular agency: there was a sharp blast of a whistle from above. Willie turned. 'That's how the "Old Man" summons his deputy, or his messenger, or his servant. Follow me, I'll introduce you.' He led the way up the wide wooden staircase.

'Come on, Willie, old boy. I want—,' the smallish nut-brown figure stopped abruptly as I came into view. The brilliant blue eyes set off a smile of sheer charm; my new boss came forward to greet me. Colonel Hugh Boustead, '*Al Mustashar*' ('the adviser') as his myriad Arab friends knew and greeted him, treated me as if I were an old friend. 'Well, young Michael. I expect you and Willie have been talking like 14 typewriters?' His opening query threw me into some confusion. 'Well no, sir.' I began to explain I had only just arrived, but no response was required. Colonel Hugh had turned to Willie with some administrative query.

The *mustashar's* idiosyncratic phrases had their amusing consequences, not least because his Arab staff, keen to perfect their English, copied the idiom of their boss. This had once resulted in Lady (Margaret) Luce, accompanying her husband the Governor on an official tour, being greeted by an affable Arab aide, as she emerged from the women's quarters of some local notable, with 'Ah, Lady Luce. I expect you have been talking like 14 typewriters?' The Colonel himself had made absolutely no effort to improve on the appalling Arabic he had picked up in early Sudan days. One phrase in typical 'Bousteadian' (addressed to his Sudanese servant, Fadhl Osman) was,

'*La taamal muddle ya Fadhl!*' ('Don't make a muddle, Fadhl!') It was to strike me some years later that the *mustashar's* Arabic, while more amusing than most, in fact was quite typical of the sort of military Arabic spouted by some British military officers serving with Arab units; they had supposedly been to a language school (unlike Colonel Hugh who had picked his up while with the Sudan Camel Corps). It was, '*Marawahid tamaam, Wakil-Qaid!*' ('Excellent, Major' — this in pidgin Arabic) and then, 'Carry on, please.' The difference between Colonel Hugh and some of those seconded military was that he continued to communicate with whoever was there, Arab or British. They, by contrast, enjoyed very limited communication with their Arab colleagues; it was to be the source of much trouble, later on.

The conversation with Willie over, Colonel Hugh blew briefly on his whistle again. The messenger appeared, saluted and took instructions for the Resident Adviser's (the RA's) vehicle to be made ready to convey him for his evening walk along the beach. The RA then blew for his servant; he ordered a tray of tea which was brought and served in elegant Residency crockery, the gold crown prominent on each piece. He questioned me closely about what I had been doing. Mixed in with our conversation two or three Arab visitors were shown up, for brief consultations. Two were well dressed townsfolk, quickly at ease in the RA's company.

The third was an elderly tribesman who stood at the door, until the RA invited him to sit down, unselfconsciously running his hand over a Balinese carving of a young girl. The bust was a reminder of the strong connection there was between that part of the world and Indonesia, to where many Hadhramis had travelled to earn a living, returning to their homeland on retirement.

The RA bounded down the steep stairs; I panted in his wake. The sentry on duty called out the guard and Colonel Hugh stood at attention as the quarter guard presented arms. This over, he chatted amicably with each of them. Broad grins indicated he had amused them, but I was far too ignorant then, to get any indication of what was being said. I awaited him in the middle passenger seat of the Land Rover, the official Union flag on the bonnet. The RA swung in along-side me and an HBL orderly tumbled in behind, his rifle nearly catching me on the head.

The vehicle moved slowly through the street, crowded with walkers, some plainly just enjoying the evening air, others hurrying to whatever urgent appointment awaited them. The RA talked to people in the crowd as we progressed; elderly tribesmen thrust grimy pieces of paper at him through the window. 'Petitions, old boy,' said Colonel Hugh briefly. 'They want to get a son into the HBL, or the Bedouin Boys' School.' He handed the petitions to his orderly in the back.

We were now on the beach having crossed the 'camel park', the RA still pausing to talk to passers-by. We headed west over firm, glorious golden sand for what seemed like miles. Suddenly the Colonel reached behind me and appeared to cuff the driver over the head. The latter gave a (mock) yelp of terror, and I saw he was grinning broadly. '*Waqqaf, ya majnoon!*' ('Stop, you madman!') ordered the RA, and we executed a sharp about-turn and alighted. I stared at the town of Mukalla, in the light of the late afternoon sun. It looked a very long way away. This was the start of my first Bousteadian walk: I was to enjoy it very much, though prominent visitors from the UK had been known to plead heart trouble to avoid it. I got into the habit of life-long regular walks myself, thanks to Colonel Hugh.

The vehicle started to move off and to maintain a quarter mile of distance between us. Colonel Hugh broke into a smart gait, I had to walk quickly to keep apace. The orderly slung his rifle and kept his distance, a few yards behind. To our right, the blue, blue sea broke and hissed in a series of irregular waves. It looked inviting; my shirt clung damply to my back after the contact with the vehicle seat. 'See those patches on the bottom?' asked the Colonel, pointing. I could: there were dozens of them. 'Stingrays. They come during the summer from the cold water further out. Careful where you bathe.'

It was actually the most beautiful of beaches and, except for the noisome spread of sardines drying in the sun, was seldom used for anything other than the odd vehicle and camel train. But it did provide the favourite recreation of the small British community. As we strode out steadily towards the town, the Colonel never drew breath, for he was either firing a series of questions at me, or telling me of his plans for the next few weeks, during which he would be touring the most accessible parts of the Eastern Aden Protectorate, to say farewell. He thought it would be useful if I came along as his ADC. I was thrilled at the prospect, though apprehensive at facing the dour Pat Booker, who had so relished the thought of my taking over the Residency office. Colonel Hugh told me something of the British community in the EAP.

There were upwards of 25 Europeans, most of them based in Mukalla, and, except for the bank staff, all government employed. There was the Deputy British Agent and his wife, Willie and Janet Wise. There was Pat Booker, and his nice, prim Scots wife Catherine. There was a dapper Military Adviser to the Resident Adviser (MARA) George Coles, with his glamorous wife the Hon. Bridget. George was very relaxed; he was so relaxed that others — not themselves noted for their speed of action — noticed it. A piece of doggerel was circulating about the time I arrived. It read:

### Stand at Ease — Stand Easy
> To have an in-tray like an MARA
> Is a heaven that's not often gained,
> It is said that a mouse once use't for a house
> And lived there six months until brained ...

It continued (in part)

> The moral is simple, to maintain your dimple
> And laugh and grow fat all your life,
> For comparative wealth and disgusting good health,
> To be able to keep-up a wife,
> Do not try to be gay as a noble RA ...
> But put up your tent as a milit'ry gent
> And idle your troubles away.

There was a Fisheries Officer (about whom more later) and his wife, and a doctor called Cen Jones who, as Health Adviser in the Protectorate, also ministered to the Residency community. We had an irrigation man; we had two or more military men at various times who helped train the local state forces and who ran the HBL (I was to have very close dealings with both of these); and there was a man who knew all about running cooperatives. A couple of mechanical experts lived in Mukalla and in Saiun respectively. The latter was the capital of the Kathiri Sultan and in the Wadi Hadhramaut, which was where two other political officers (one married) were stationed. Other than the personnel referred to, there were political staff positioned in the Northern Deserts area and in the Wahidi State. The expatriate population increased with the temporary appearance of oil prospectors, locust hunters, the occasional exploring type and, of course, visitors from Aden and further afield. We were a far-flung lot.

In essence the resident British population was there to support various state administrations that by dint of some British aid, colourful local improvizations and (on the part of the locals) a deal of graft and influence, ran their various fiefdoms. It was a curious mixture of the twentieth century and of *The Thousand and One Nights*, as I was about to discover.

# 6

# Riding Down to Duan

Riding down to Duan
Isn't, kindly note,
Always quite as jolly
As the Colonel wrote.
By oriental village
With oriental smell,
Sat inexperienced traveller
Who thought the journey hell.

Striding up one mountain,
Swaying up the next.
'Crouch, you little b******!'
Cries the Colonel, vexed.
'All young fellows these days
Your bodies are a mess;
But at eating and at sleeping
You're a definite success!'

Hours and hours of fuddling
On quasi-concrete floors,
Patriarchal figures
Complain without a pause.
Temperature has risen,
Enthusiasm sours.
Colonel is surrounded
By gesticulating bores.

51

When the day is over,
When the talking's done,
Colonel's at the table
With this poor mother's son
Scribbling in the darkness,
As if he's gone insane;
*Mustashar* dictation
From a 40 horse-power brain.

'Don't panic,' says the Colonel,
'Midnight's drawing in.'
Inexperienced traveller
Tries hard to raise a grin.
After sundry whistles,
Peace at last will fall.
Inexperienced traveller
Unconscious with them all.

THIS was my attempt to summarize that memorable journey; I tried to employ as many of Colonel Hugh's little figures of speech, in recalling the flavour of the moment. In the meantime, I was to stay at the Residency until we had returned from tour: the barn-like house allocated to me (originally constructed for a predecessor of exceeding fecundity) was to be temporarily used as a single men's quarters. I did not like the idea of having to share my off-duty existence with anyone, so was in no hurry to set up house. The continued luxury of regular meals provided by someone else and the services of the efficient red-turbaned Residency staff compensated for the occasional *mustashar* explosion of feverish activity, which had me rushing in circles, at the Colonel's directions, with no very clear idea of what he wanted me to do. I began to learn the routine, just by keeping in earshot and observing all that went on. It was not hard to keep myself informed: the Residency seemed to shake with noise and movement.

Against a background of imperious whistles there was the constant interchange of conversations, upstairs (where the RA had his own small office and living room) and in the large downstairs office (later to be taken over by Colonel Hugh's successors but currently occupied by Willie). Then there was the HBL quarter guard, which either seemed to be turning out to present arms, or was being changed, both with considerable bellowing of orders and accompanying back-chat. There were the messengers (the 'peons') flap-flapping between the Residency offices and the main administrative complex, set further down the compound.

These contained the offices of Assistant Adviser Residency (to be me), Assistant Adviser Coastal Areas, Pat Booker, and the Military Assistant, George Coles. The latter had the services of a Jordanian, one Abdullah Suleiman, styled Bedouin Affairs Assistant to the RA, and caparisoned as a lieutenant-colonel of the Arab Legion. I never did quite understand the significance of that gentleman's contribution, but he looked good.

Also in the main office complex was the finance section, headed by studious gold rimmed clerks, one of whom carried the enormous companion key to the Residency sub-treasury safe (in which was stored the EAP's supply of cash, at that time East African currency notes). Years later, when I was in charge of the other safe key, I used to speculate in jest how I would dispose of the £1 million in used notes that was deposited there at the time, if I were to knock the weedy Mr Barahim over his head and relieve him of his key — impractical, I decided.

Also to be under my control was the Passport Office: the Residency authenticated the bright red passports issued by the Quaiti State, its subjects having the status of British-protected persons. During the hadj, the pilgrimage season, I might find myself signing the inside covers (on behalf of the Resident Adviser and British Agent) of up to a couple of hundred passports a day. This exercise was responsible for my illegible signature that puzzled Australian colleagues, years later.

The remainder of the Residency office to be in my charge was a large administrative section, which included the handling of non-classified correspondence and the overseeing of our well-equipped stores, which included not only an extensive range of camping gear, but an assortment of national flags for the most unlikely official visits, including Panama and Canada.

The only other office of note within the Residency complex was the RA's personal one, headed by his efficient and discrete Goan clerk, Mani. Abdullah Safi was the peon responsible for affixing the perfectly applied red seal on classified covers, with the brass coat-of-arms bearing 'The Residency Mukalla' with impressive clarity. As the classified mail was closed in Willie's office it took on the effect of a time-honoured ritual. There was Abdullah Safi, his sallow Indonesian features intently focused on obtaining just the right consistency of red wax, before applying the seal. Looking down in apparent approval, from vast signed and heavily framed formal portraits, were their late Majesties George V and VI, with their respective consorts. The big ceiling fans went thump-swish-swish and the gardeners' voices, as they watered the bougainvillaea, provided the necessary oriental background to the imperial dispatches. I could imagine my grand-father's head messenger attending to just the same kind of routine, 50 years previously.

Before I set out with the RA on his last trek I was encouraged to explore the town of Mukalla itself. Visitors had always found it very beautiful and it had been well described long before I came along. A large hill dominated the town proper, with subsidiary hills each crowned by a ruined fort, and with crowded houses pressing down to the water's edge. Later I was to explore these forts, dating, so I was told, from the first visits of Vasco da Gama and other early Portuguese voyagers to India; I found ships' guns, with the arms of the Hon. East India Company embossed thereon.

The main street always teemed with humanity. Those casual strollers I had observed on my first evening were crystallizing into more than just strange passers-by. There were lordly *Seiyeds* conversing languidly; groups of sight-seeing Bedouin, wide eyed at the strings of electric light globes bedecked to announce a wedding; there were fast moving, sweating black porters, often each carrying a heavy sack of grain, or cement, up from the jetty. There were local townsfolk, merchants, teachers, usually wearing the ankle length *futa*, the cotton sarong with its distinctive pattern, and the white cap usual for those parts. They might be seated at a cafe, drinking the tiny cups of the coffee husks and ginger that was popular in those parts, or enjoying the 'Stim' soft drink, of lurid colour and sickly taste. Other citizenry would be walking, sometimes in a family group if it were towards dusk, the women fully veiled and the children often in their best clothes on the Friday, on their way to a festive gathering. The street stalls sold everything, as did the dark little shops that were typical of what I had seen in Aden and along the East African coast.

The noise was constant — a babble of voices, laughter, imprecations. Radios wailed the latest record of Umm Kalthoum (the buxom female Egyptian singer famous throughout the Arab world) and everywhere the sound of Cairo's Voice of the Arabs was complemented by the handsome vulpine features of Gamal Abdul Nasser, whose portrait hung in each shop and at times in specially illuminated frames. Just in case I had failed to notice the ubiquitous features, swarms of small boys would pop up in front of me, shrilling, '*Ayesh Gamal, Ayesh Nasser!*' ('Long live Gamal, Long live Nasser!'). It was not so much threatening as annoying — rather in the context of the busy flies that might briefly distract the visitor from his perambulations.

It used to be possible to acquire the old carved chests made of teak from the Malabar coast of India which, until they became popular with European visitors, cost next to nothing. There were ancient muzzle loaders (the Arabs regarded them as junk) and even, on occasion, pieces of Ming porcelain. Further round, by the harbour and near the bank, was the little shop of Kako, the Indian jeweller. Unpretentious for a man with so much wealth passing through his hands, his was the only premises where I have seen a drawer full of gold sovereigns (into which I enjoyed plunging my hands). Much of the gold work was gaudy and spoilt by the copious use of red glass, but later I was to buy an American $10 gold piece (an 'eagle') and a beautiful Mexican 50-peso gold coin, both adapted to hang round my future wife's neck.

The colourful harbour with its lines of fishing boats was dominated by the exquisitely shaped mosque in the background; it was too shallow to allow any large vessels to come alongside, and the cargo was unloaded into lighters and discharged onto the wharf where it was guarded by Rahman Khan's customs' men, two of whom I had seen at Riyan. Rahman Khan was warm hearted, with a reputation for honesty, which did not endear him to the local population. He used to receive me in a room crowded with merchants haggling over the state duties to be paid. He would argue gently with his Residency visitors over what was owed. We only got taxable items in duty free if the RAF flew them in.

Further on, through the town, was the road to the Fisheries Officer's house. Mark Veevers-Carter was his name and, with his red beard and cheerful mien, he enjoyed a reputation for being something of a modern-day buccaneer. He certainly displayed a very laissez-faire attitude towards the assistance provided by Her Majesty's Government for the local fishing industry. Indeed, his rather original attitude to all aspects of bureaucracy was best confirmed when I was later deputed to preside over Boards of Survey that reported the disappearance of entire fishing craft. It was not as if he were badly off: he was married to Wendy, daughter of Clarence Day, the wealthy author of the book and TV series *Life with Father*. The expatriate community viewed them both with considerable affection. They threw rather original parties, as I was to discover quite soon after my arrival.

Beyond Mark's house were the rocks from which I and other members of the Residency Club fished in the evenings, they in their long *futas* hitched up, everyone squatting on the jagged edge, intent on the lines twitching in the surge below.

But this was all some time ahead. I was ready to tour with the *mustashar*. Colonel Hugh had had a Mercedes saloon fitted with outside wheels to negotiate the fearsome tracks that led to the interior. The fact that each time the car lurched over a bump the tyres hit the wheel housing, with a sickening thump and a smell of burning, worried the *mustashar* not at all.

We were accompanied by a platoon of HBL soldiers, large tents, and the Residency staff, the most prominent (in every sense) being the fat, sleek shape of Ahmed al Sameen (literally Ahmed 'the Fat One') perched resignedly on the kitchen boxes. A couple of HBL Land Rovers, and at one stage two 'Ferret' armoured cars, completed our convoy. Just prior to leaving Mukalla I had acquired the services of an ingratiating Yemeni cook, Abdo Hassan, who bowed each time he caught my eye. His English was about equal to my Arabic, at that stage; kitchen communication was rudimentary.

It was about two weeks later that I was able to record my impressions of that memorable tour. What follows was written to my mother:

*Riding Down to Duan*

On Trek
Wahidi border

5 August 1958

It is about to pour with rain and there is a real chance that the river will cut off our retreat, so I may be here for days. We were due to return to Mukalla, about 165 miles from here, tomorrow. We had a heck of a time to get here, through very mountainous country, with a ghastly track winding its way up the slopes. I travelled with the Colonel (the flag flying, it being his official trek wagon) and behind us came a pick-up [truck] with kit and a couple of local officials who seem to hate having to come out into this barbarous part of the world, especially with an energetic type like *Al Mustashar*. The last vehicle is a lorry load of Bedouin Legion, armed to the teeth and looking very pictur-esque in their kit.

For the first two nights we slept in the open and have been very comfortable. My servant has been pretty well trained and I may be lucky to have him. There have been insects every night, so a net has been useful. But where some of these said insects live is incredible. They can't rely on passing government officials to keep their strength up, yet there is not a scrap of vegetation anywhere, except in the occasional wadi [valley]. It is most impressive country with the flat plateau, which is a few thousand feet high, cut by great gashes in the surface plunging down a couple of thousand feet or so, quite suddenly.

We have been meeting the Bedouin tribes of this area, who are normally difficult to find as they live up in the hills, employ-ing black men to farm for them in the few arable waddies there are; they only come down to collect the dates, and that is the time for us to meet them and hear their grievances. The entry to each settlement is fun; when they hear the motors they rush towards us firing their rifles in the air in a very dangerous way, to show their pleasure. They are fearsome characters to look at, each armed with a more-or-less contemporary firearm, sometimes bound with silver, and huge daggers tucked in their waistbands. We sit down with them and the *mustashar* tells them what he thinks is best for them, and he hears their woes, then we all end up drinking some nauseous brew of coffee and ginger, or something. But I much enjoy it. We have had a couple of local feasts where we wear local dress, *futa* and sandals, the latter which we remove when we sit, as is normal silver, and huge daggers tucked in their waistbands. We sit down with them and the *mustashar* tells them what he thinks is best for them, and he hears their woes, then we all end up drinking some nauseous brew of coffee and ginger, or something. But I much enjoy it. We have had a couple of local feasts where we wear local dress, *futa* and sandals, the latter which we remove when we sit, as is normal.

Before coming on this trek, I went with the Colonel to Shihr up the coast from Mukalla, where there was a religious gathering, and where I met the Quaiti Sultan, covered with pearls and gold, and his small son dragging an enormous sword as big as himself. The little boy is only nine and he was obviously bored during the proceedings, as he sat picking at a large ruby set in the hilt of his sword, all the time.

As you can see, life is very agreeable and I hope it stays so. The Colonel is regarded with much affection and respect wherever he goes and I can see it will be a great loss when he leaves here: they are an unruly bunch, always shooting at each other — and sometimes us.

It was hard being the only other European on such tours. Colonel Hugh had entirely the right idea of ensuring the expatriates did not huddle in their own groups and leave our Arab hosts to theirs. It was in Wadi Duan, at the first evening meal to which we had been invited (on the flat roof of the large house of the local Arab province governor, at a settled edge of the Wadi Hadhramaut) that he showed me how things were done.

We had alighted from our vehicle, the escort carrying a hissing 'Petromax', its glare throwing into sharp contrast the white *futas* of our urban-based hosts and the crowd of curious tribesmen who had been bidden to say farewell to the RA. 'Now old boy,' said the Colonel crisply, 'You go and sit with those fellows down there. Tell them your father was a doctor in the Sudan. Ask them about their camels. You know the sort of thing,' and he pointed to the far end of the large roof. He made his way to the head of the spread, taking the bright light with him. I looked where he had pointed: there was a hurricane lamp, its badly-trimmed wick giving off just enough light to reveal a semi-circle of silent tribesmen, sitting in a tightly compressed line, legs either tucked under them or knees pressed to chests. Light reflected from bandoleers of brass cartridges, off the silver of curved *jambiyas*. I caught the occasional shine of fierce eyes staring at me. I walked hesitantly towards them. I was terrified.

'*Salaam aleikum*,' ('Peace be upon you' — the normal polite greeting) I ventured, in a no-doubt Oxford accent. No one responded. I looked in desperation at the circle of humanity. Someone moved sideways, I eased into the gap, contorting my frame into the impossibly small space. I glanced to both sides of me, tried a smile, got no response. I stared ahead, trying to remember something, just a word or two, other than anything to do with judges' daughters. It was no good. We all sat in a heavy slough of unease (or so it seemed to me). I felt miserable. Was it for this dreadful lack of communication I had come out here? Was I disgracing the reputation of the *mustashar* — of the British government?

Suddenly — oh joy! In the flickering light a large communal dish of what looked like rice, with lumps of what appeared to be meat on top, was placed in front of me. I knew that the Arab prefers to get on with eating when food is before him; no polite small talk for him. Bedouin in any event relished the opportunity of a good feed, after their usual sparse existence in the hills. With a ritual mutter on either side of me my neighbours each reached out for a handful of rice. I did the same, plunging my right hand into the glistening mound. I had to bite my lip to avoid shrieking aloud in agony. It was rice, and it was searingly hot.

I withdrew my injured fingers and contemplated the next stage. Let the rice cool and I would have a go at the meat placed on top. I could not quite see what it was, but at least my teeth were sound. All I had to do was detach (again, with my right hand, the left being used for the ablutions and 'taboo' in polite society) a small portion of the meat, and I could chew — easier said than done. My fingers struggled with the bit I had selected, but I just could not detach a portion. Nothing for it then, but to transfer the whole chunk to my mouth and let my teeth do the separating. I managed the transfer surreptitiously, but — horrors! It was (I discovered later) a whole goat's heart, attached to a windpipe.

I chewed that mouthful for the next hour or so and made no impression at all. I tried exciting manoeuvres with my tongue against the palate; I forced sections between one gum and slewed my upper jaw to get a grip. It was no good: it remained the consistency and taste of inner tube. At least though there was no opportunity for me to attempt a conversation. As for spitting it out. I might have disgraced the whole British Raj, for all I knew. And I did care.

It was when we had shaken hands and had met by the vehicle that I was able to dispose of my evening meal. 'You were a bit quiet tonight, old boy,' said the Colonel. I explained. I thought he was going to have a seizure, he was so amused. He told me that the heart with its attachments was always placed before the guest of honour (at that location, me) and the host would have ceremoniously at some stage cut the heart in two and offered me half. I should have just as ceremoniously pretended to have refused it; he would have insisted while I pressed him to have the other half. The wind pipe played no part in the ceremony. What my host actually thought of his guest's behaviour, I did not like to contemplate.

I was quite happy ever after to enjoy all subsequent Arab meals; I became expert at using my right hand, as a gathering and severing instrument, and of course my Arabic was soon so fluent that chatter before and after the meal became a pleasure. That of course was part of the political officer's role, one incidentally that many military men, as well as certain diplomats posted to Arab countries, had difficulty in emulating.

We were never offered sheep's eyes and someone told me that it was probably a fable invented at a time when a pompous politician was visiting an Arab country at the cool time of year. The local British host told an Arab sheikh who was throwing a feast for the visitor that the latter really enjoyed sheep's eyes. He then told the visitor that it was incumbent on him to eat what was placed before him. In fact, it was common to have half a head placed before one, with the expectation one would enjoy the brains, the tongue and the cheek meat. But the eye? It really never appealed.

# 7

# Getting into Gear

M Y return to Mukalla from the *mustashar's* farewell tour was dominated by the rain which continued unabated. The RA began to worry about meeting the remainder of his busy schedule, back in Mukalla, of parties and of formal farewells. He signalled for an aircraft to lift him out, and a Royal Air Force Dakota en route from Muscat was diverted to rescue him. The weather was threatening, with sullen cloud swirling about the high ground, but suddenly, after a couple of low passes, the aircraft made a hazardous landing on the short and rocky airstrip that served the Wahidi State's mountainous terrain. There we were, camped somewhat despondently, for we doubted it could land in the chilly rain.

I went forward to the aircraft, as it taxied to a halt, appearing through the mist like a visitor to *The Lost World*. This was real tribal territory and the locals gathered to farewell the Colonel had seemed as well armed as the HBL. To our surprise, as the fuselage door opened, a somewhat incongruous figure, wearing the crowns of a major, climbed ponderously down the steps. He was portly, middle aged, with not much hair but with a massive moustache that submerged his face in foliage, intermingling with the 'mutton chops' that just allowed space for his eyes. This apparition advanced effusively on Colonel Hugh. His name was Pat Gray and it transpired he had been employed in a depressingly unsuccessful military capacity in Muscat; this was his chance to meet Colonel Hugh, with a view to his being appointed as Commandant of the Hadhrami Bedouin Legion. He had therefore hitched a lift with the RAF, and during the return flight to Riyan was able to impress on the Colonel his suitability for the appointment. Pat

Gray was of South African origin and for a substantial period served with the Arab Legion, in Jordan. While he must have had considerable experience of soldiering with Arab troops, I was to find that he relied significantly on being a 'character'. His Arabic was poor, for a man of his Middle Eastern service, being of the *'Marawahid tamaam'* variety, referred to earlier and, in my eyes at least, he in no way could be compared with the professionally serving British Army officer. He is remembered for his personal bravery, but he lacked a sense of humour — and he had little time for me. I was to come into close contact both with Pat and his 'grande dame' of a consort, Edith, once they were established in Mukalla.

The Royal Air Force hurriedly took off before the clouds closed in, and I returned to the vehicle convoy, to accompany it back to Mukalla along the coast. We bumped our way down the rocky track from the airstrip, past the ancient village of Azzan, through the modern 'capital' of Maifaah (the modest settlement where the Sultan's administration with his political adviser was based) and along the sandy track that led to the coast. Leaving the impressive stone walls of Naqab al Hajr, an early Himyaritic centre from the incense route (I was to be based in Wahidi myself, later, and could describe it appropriately, then) — we reached the coast. There was Bir Ali, a depressing little fishing village close by the ruined citadel of the ancient port. We turned towards Mukalla and rattled our way through the drizzle until we were on the banks of the Wadi Hajr, which was usually a sandy river bed. One's driver would pause, change gear noisily, and abruptly would roar in low gear to avoid getting stuck in the sand. A tossing, whirling flood greeted us: a yellow torrent of turbulence made further passage impossible. We camped by the bank and contemplated what next to do. We had no alternative but to await the fall in water, but in the meantime it should be possible to find a way across, on foot.

With an escort I waded through the shallower but soft and sticky wadi mouth and walked upstream again to opposite where our vehicles were halted. A muddy Land Rover came down the bank from our side and halted; a stocky figure in white shirt and shorts with burly bare legs climbed down. This was Karl Schlatholt; he worked as an agricultural/irrigation officer. He was a brusque German whose accented English bore all the idiom of the self taught. He had been in the German Navy during the war. When his vessel was about to be impounded he had made his way across the Red Sea to come ashore on the Yemen coast, from which he had been taken into the employ of the Imam Yahya. His ability to 'fix things' mechanical created an ongoing demand for his services, until he and his wife had ended up in the Eastern Aden Protectorate, doing a practical job for the Agricultural Department.

Karl drove me to the neat little Mediterranean villa he had built himself, apparently entirely out of concrete; the beds and chairs were all constructed of concrete, with gaily-coloured cushions and mattresses. There was a primitive but effective system of air conditioning: the never-ceasing wind that blew through matting hanging on the outside had water dripping through it. It was a real little oasis in the wilderness of Maifa Hajr, quite some hours out of Mukalla. Karl and Giselle lived there all alone. He had rigid black-and-white views about the effete British dealings with the locals. I felt he would have fitted in well in the old Tanganyika, when Imperial Germany ruled. However, they were a hospitable couple, and I stayed with them until the convoy was able to ford the wadi, and without further incident I reached Mukalla.

Colonel Hugh Boustead departed on schedule, to work as development adviser for the Sultan of Muscat and later for the Sheikh of Abu Dhubi, where he ended his active days with a knighthood, looking after the Ruler's horse stud. I was so lucky to have had him point me in the right direction.

I settled into my routine in charge of Residency office work. I took afternoon classes in colloquial and written Arabic from the unctuous office assistant whose loquacity, I learnt, was only matched by his matrimonial excesses, even by local standards. Not only had he four wives (it was exorbitantly expensive to maintain each lady, according to her station) but each wife was expecting a child, concurrently as it were. Mohamed Bafaqih confided in me that he found his time in the office infinitely more restful than at home.

I walked miles and I swam regularly, with an eye on those sinister black shapes on the bottom; I took long walks with my 'Holland & Holland' 12-bore shotgun during the winter months and, even with my indifferent aim, was often able to bag one or two from the migrating flights, heading south from Iran.

An Element of Luck

The water courses near Mukalla were usually dry, in spite of those
torrential rains which had greeted me. The wadi mouths shrank and
were cut off from the sea by sand bars, which only broke to release the
intermittent flood waters. The brackish shallows of the temporary
lagoons harboured prawns and large crabs that came easily to a scrap
of meat dragged on a string. The prawns were caught by local fishermen who were happy to make a sale to the British community; prawns
were regarded as *haram* (unclean) by the locals who classified things
that crawled in the sea, as well as birds that swam, as being forbidden
by Islam. The baskets of fresh prawns and crayfish for the asking
meant permanent glut in the season — prawn curry, prawn
sandwiches, prawn with everything — and thereafter a life-long
indifference on my part to those delicacies.

For such a relatively small community there was always something
social going on: there were countless dinner parties, luncheons with
vast curries. There were formal gatherings at the Residency, to meet
visiting VIPs; I helped entertain two famous 'Arabian identities', the
explorer van der Meulen and the American who had helped to make
Lawrence of Arabia famous, Lowell Thomas. I had read van der
Meulen's book, *Aden to the Hadhramaut*, and was curious to meet
him. I knew of Lowell Thomas and was less interested in him;
however, both were a disappointment. They expected to be treated as
celebrities. They could not stand each other and Mukalla was too small
a community to house them both. The two old gentlemen sat stiffly and
in silence. On a more relaxed note, there were beach parties, and there
were excursions to the RAF Officers Mess (with its two members) at
Riyan, to watch films. There were amateur cine shows; Cen Jones the
doctor had an interesting one, hardly in the tradition of recording
beach parties and the like. He had filmed it of one of the infrequent
public executions in Mukalla.

The official death penalty was rare in the Aden Protectorates
because, under Sharia law (it was nothing to do with the British) to kill
someone was regarded primarily as an offence demanding recompense
for the deprived family or tribe. Provided there was no specific
cause — such as the murderer being a professional killer, or being
guilty of some gross breach of hospitality, such as shooting a sleeping
guest — the courts would decree that blood money, or compensation in
kind would be levied against the guilty man and, possibly, his family.

However, where the death penalty was inevitable because of the circumstances, or because the aggrieved party had made it clear that 'an eye for an eye' was appropriate, if only to prevent a blood feud, then the execution was held in public, with the executioner being appointed by the government. He was of non-tribal stock and, in the footage taken by Cen, was one of the Sultan's retainers of African slave origin.

It was a shattering film, mainly because it was unexpected. It started with the usual home movies-type shot, of friends picnicking on Mukalla beach. Then, suddenly, there was the condemned man (quite ordinary looking and inoffensive, which was also shocking: do all killers look as ordinary?) having been paraded through the main street of Mukalla, being tied to a stake. He had said his farewells to the onlookers, been allowed to make his final prayers and was having his chest solemnly sounded by a government doctor (to pronounce he was fit enough to be shot) before a large square of sticking plaster was attached over his heart. The executioner took up position only a few yards in front, and fired one round of his .303 rifle at the man's chest. There was no sound track to the 8 mm film, but the effect of the white-washed stake — to which the condemned man was tied — suddenly turning bright red was drama enough.

Amateur movies may have been unexpectedly spectacular, but shortly after there was my memorable effort to celebrate Halloween. It started with an invitation to the whole expatriate community to get into fancy dress (theme: something to do with the devil) and spend the evening at Mark and Wendy Veevers-Carter's. All accepted, save the Bookers — Catherine feeling, 'It was not right to tempt the devil so.' Besides, I do not think she approved of the Veevers-Carters, but she asked everyone to have a drink with them beforehand, so she could view the costumes.

What to wear? I knew — a flash of inspiration — I would go as a werewolf. I had a supply of tow, that fibre used to clean the barrels of a shotgun. I would shred it and stick it thinly over my person, using glue from the souk (market). It was an excellent idea, up to a point; the disadvantages emerged later.

It took me hours to get dressed, with the assistance of an Arab friend, the local Passport Officer Issa Musallim. I had an animal skin round my waist and that was it. No glasses (werewolves did not suffer from short-sightedness) and I had to leave them off at the start, so they did not get glued on by mistake. I sipped at a long glass of whisky and peered myopically at myself in the glass. Not bad: I had kohl round each eye; long, henna-tipped claws of cardboard were tied to each finger and toe. My helper, a bit unsteady on his feet, was enthusiastic. An hour later I shambled my way next door, for those drinks at the Bookers'. As I went in through the entrance and started towards their stairs, to the party above, I met their Arab cook descending, with an empty Gordon's gin bottle (we also used them to store water) in each hand.

I was mystified at my reception: he slumped to the floor, shrieking and waving the bottles at me. I soon realized that for some reason he was hysterical and I went over to him to calm him. As I bent over him he fainted. I tried to shake him awake. I saw his eyes open. I smiled and greeted him. He shrieked again and his eyes rolled into his head. I shrugged — must be unwell, poor fellow — nothing that I could do. He needed a doctor. I would see if Cen was upstairs. He was.

So was my hostess. As I entered the Bookers' living room Catherine was coming towards me, a tray in her hand. She dropped it and what was on it fell and broke. I bent clumsily to help retrieve the fragments. 'It doesn't matter,' she said acidly. 'We don't use them much. They were only wedding presents.' I felt unwelcome and went over to the corner where Cen was eyeing me. 'Magnificent!' he said. 'Not so bad yourself, Cen.' I thought his get-up was terrific. He was wearing a skin-tight costume of black satin with all the bones painted in luminous paint. 'But what's that dreadful noise down there?' he enquired. I suddenly remembered the Bookers' cook who must recovered consciousness. I hurriedly explained that the poor fellow had some sort of unexplained fit. Cen got up and went to him.

I was later told that the cook was just coming to again when he opened his eyes and found a skeleton bending over him. He went to hospital for the rest of the night. From then on our hosts' zest for entertaining us faded somewhat — no cook and a shattered wedding present. We thanked them and piled into Residency vehicles for the trip through the town, towards Mark and Wendy's. There we were greeted with much wit and jollity, accepted drinks and soon the gaiety was restored.

*Getting into Gear*

I was bobbing for apples on strings, next to the assistant bank manager; Cliff Leslie was dressed rather obscenely as a baby devil, with a forked tail protruding from his black nappy and a sparkler tied to the end. Someone lit it, quite innocently. The next thing there was a 'Whooshhh!' I was on fire from the waist up. The tow, impregnated with gun oil, had caught a spark.

It lasted a few seconds. I ran yelling round the large room, flames shooting six feet into the air. Then they were out, the last bit extinguished by Janet with her cushion. She was dressed as an old lady — 'They say I'm an old witch in the village' — with football boots on, which made it hard for her to keep up with my passage. She must have swung out as I rushed by.

They had great problems putting me under a general anaesthetic while Cen and his assistant, Dr Tayib, were trying to clean me up. I came to every so often under that bright light, with sharp pains lashing my shoulder and Dr Tayib's reassuring voice, 'Breathe deeply, Mr Crouch. Oh, breathe *deeply*!' The glue had burnt well, too; at least I was spared the trouble of trying to get it off. I was scorched nearly all over, but only severely so on one shoulder and on both ears, which crisped and blackened like two overdone cocktail eats, for some weeks. After the first excruciating 24 hours, during which I vomited with the pain each time the oozing bandages were changed to avoid sepsis, I was flown to the air-conditioned sterility of the Queen Elizabeth Hospital in Aden, for a fortnight. I was perched naked in a freezing cold room, on one relatively unburned buttock, and was injected four-hourly with penicillin (until I developed a severe allergy); and I grew several new skins a day that split, until the fierce red had calmed to baby-bottom pink.

My Mukalla epitaph was twofold — I won the prize for the best costume (I never wore fancy dress again) and two elderly *Seiyeds*, it was reported, had been overheard discussing the accident. The conversation (in Arabic) was apparently as follows:

'The Christians (God rot them!) had a party — one of them (God spare him!) was injured.'

'Heavens! [or equivalent] — what happened?'

'He was drinking whisky and smoking cigarettes at the same time.'

And so, while my skin strengthened and my confidence did likewise, my role of Assistant Adviser Residency blossomed. At last I started to earn some of the £800 or so a year Her Majesty had awarded me. Much of my official life was mundane; after all, I was the Residency 'dogsbody'. There was endless correspondence to be followed up and replied to; there were all those passports. There was a huge file running into eight volumes or so that involved Hadhramis in Indonesia claiming compensation for land sequestered by the Indonesian authorities. Embassies had entered into the debate with enthusiasm, and it was up to me to keep the paper war moving. For a change from the clerical routine, a colleague's wife, hysterical in her demands, shrilly bullied me until she obtained extra items of issue furniture. Then there were convoys to be organized, there was camp equipment for the RA to be replaced and there was, 'Residency Tennis Court, the provision for' (as the official file title had it).

Apparently the Residency had tried for years to obtain sanction from Aden for the use of official funds, with the chief secretary's blessing. Ultimately Willie had written the most heart-rending letter about the need for a court — the shark-infested sea, the lack of anything but HMG transport (which was not available for recreation, of course not!) the break down in officers' health (I am not sure beriberi did not come into it somewhere). To no avail — the final response was by signal, 'You break my heart but the answer is still NO.' So prison labour it was to be: only a few inmates from Mukalla's gaol were sent to help me lay it out and a fine court we constructed. It was my personal legacy to Mukalla, really.

Christmas 1958 (my first away from family) was celebrated with a carol service. Just before the new year when my colleagues all seemed to be temporarily unavailable, a cunning Arab clerk placed in front of me an order for my signature, giving a holiday to all staff and to the HBL, on New Year's Day. I asked rather dubiously if this was OK and was assured that it was normal practice. I signed and found it was not: I had awarded a new public holiday to everyone; I was aghast. The RA thought it rather a good idea though, so it stayed. I made the best of my impromptu initiative and disappeared down the coast with a colleague and two shotguns. Luncheon was roast duck and green peas (tinned), washed down with dry Monopole '57.

Official visits took up time. I was responsible for the arrangements at the Mukalla end. My first was when we had a Royal Naval frigate in, just before that new year. As they arrived they fired a 13-gun salute which was meant to be answered by a sultanic salute, from the gun normally used to call the faithful to prayer each Friday. It was a very ancient piece, apparently almost out of fashion in Nelson's time. It was meant to fire a nine-gun reply as the ship cruised to her moorings. There was a terrific bang which made things on my desk rattle: small children cried with fright, dogs barked hysterically and a cloud of frightened pigeons circled the town. It took many minutes for that gun to fire the full reply, by which time the frigate had steamed past the town and had to do a big circle back.

On a subsequent occasion an American Admiral called: we had understood it was to be an unofficial visit and this time it was on a Friday. We were relaxing over a midday drink at Willie and Janet's, holiday-clothed and pink gins to hand. The *USS Ducksberry Bay* came into view and, as she did so, there was the boom of a gun. Chaos reigned while the acting RA struggled into a white uniform and I, in a hastily donned suit, was sent to the jetty to greet the Admiral and escort him formally to call on the Resident Adviser.

I arrived, out of breath, to find some laconic Americans in Hawaiian-styled shirts. Yes, it was an unofficial visit; they did not even carry a gun, for the vessel was a seaplane tender. It was the Admiral's flagship in those parts so she could negotiate shallow creeks (the Admiral was a duck shooter). The gun? It transpired that it was the Mukalla Regular Army having three-inch mortar practice further up the beach.

Generally such visits went very well: the sailors always provided a football team to take on the locals, the Royal Navy entertained us royally on board, after drinking heavily of our supplies on shore. It was slightly less of a two-way affair with the Americans. They gave us chilled fruit juice aboard and drank copiously of our alcohol ashore.

Other visitors were to include the occasional exploring type, anxious to make his or her mark on uncrossed (or unwritten about, more likely) territory. I had been warned they could be 'difficult'. I was to meet two of these: the first, the well known Barbara Toy, a determined Australian lady (who was still going strong into her eighties, only a year or so before this was written). She was a perverse mixture of 'helpless little me' and someone who was extremely competent at getting her own way. She spent some time in Mukalla, Maifaah and Saiun, before she was able to join a pilgrimage convoy via north-eastern Yemen. In the book on these particular exploits she was uncomplimentary about what she saw as the unnecessary hassles of her travelling as a lone female in a single vehicle through dangerous terrain. I think we tried extremely hard to help these sorts of people, if only to speed them safely on their way, without having to send a bevy of troops to look after them, when they had got into trouble through their own initiatives.

The other traveller with whom I was personally concerned was a young man who arrived in Mukalla by sea from East Africa, with a little wire-wheeled vehicle in which he intended to motor back to Britain. He was forced to stay as my guest for quite some days while the monsoon abated, allowing him to take passage to Aden with his little car, by dhow. After eating my food, draining my drink, and upsetting my cook he departed with two of my shirts. I was later to see him in Aden Prison, quite by chance, awaiting deportation to Britain. He had been unabashed, shaking me enthusiastically by the hand, as an old friend.

# 8

# Following on Figgis

Towards the end of the last six months of my stint as Assistant Adviser Residency I was becoming increasingly impatient: I had come to appreciate that being based in Mukalla posed a severe limitation to any aspirations I might have, of making a meaningful contribution as a political officer. The Mukalla routine itself was an essential learning experience and I had already made some life-long friendships. There were also understandably those other colleagues with whom I was to have less in common, but whose actions and influence was to impact on me and my future. It was important also not to get caught up in the petty social disputations that beset any small community, the cliques and the jealousies of little competing groups, inevitably headed by opposing wives.

The arrival of Edith Gray to Mukalla was a case in point. She fancied herself as 'the senior lady', as consort to the commanding officer of the HBL. Pat Gray started to call himself 'Lieutenant-Colonel' (a British military rank, of course. Pat had been, I believe, a substantive captain in the South African military) until formally reminded he was actually Commandant of the HBL, but Edith understandably continued to regard herself as 'the Colonel's lady'. Neither of them could abide the Residency's occupants and they collected around them recruits to their camp. The eddies and swirls of power politics were rather fun for an unattached male like me to observe, though one soon tired of the machinations. I dined in both camps and kept my counsel.

Initially, though, it was the job itself that was starting to pall; I was still Residency dogsbody, however skilled I became in the niceties of Residency administration. The weekly routine continued, with only the occasional incident to remind me that working in the Residency office was different, say, from working in the British Bank of the Middle East, whose assistant manager had added his spark to the Halloween party. Perhaps I enjoyed a variety in the routine. For instance, I had an official interest in the climate.

I was responsible for the weather readings. Our annual rainfall was unimpressive — until the meteorological assistant started to report a daily recording akin to that of the monsoon period in Assam. The two ancient Arabists, van der Meulen and Lowell Thomas, who happened to be in Mukalla at that time, were greatly intrigued. Shortly after, however, the Met. man came to see me, in a very indignant state. 'Sir, Sir. Some man. He had pissed in the bottle!' Well, he had too and the clerk in the time honoured routine of his fellows had merely checked what turned out to be the urine level daily, until the aroma was apparent. Who had taken the trouble to adulterate the samples was never discovered.

Then there was taking tea with the Sultan. During this final period of my time in Mukalla I was one of the official Residency party that called on His Highness the Sultan, to celebrate his Accession Day. It was about my only opportunity to don my white uniform in Mukalla. I had dressed rapidly and eyed my reflection up and down in the mirror. With my father's dress sword tucked at my side, my white gloves and that enormous helmet, for practically the only time in my Arabian service I felt I was the latest in some family's imperial saga — India–Sudan–Mukalla. The brief glow lasted all of a minute; I gained quite a new perspective once I had joined the others. We looked uncomfortable and faintly ridiculous, except for Willie whose years of naval service would have accustomed him to being dressed in a white tunic done up to the neck, and squinting into the hot afternoon sun.

Being one of the few such formal occasions on which I dressed up, being overwhelmed at the time with the tedium of just sitting for hours in some discomfort and letting my thoughts wander about my colleagues, it now seems an appropriate opportunity to introduce this unlikely cavalcade of characters, against a suitably Ruritanian background of strange exotic uniforms, swords and — just dressing up. If, initially, I concentrate on the more bizarre of my colleagues, it is because it is with them in Mukalla that later I came most to associate a period of my career, when I was eventually posted to the remoter parts of the EAP, and consequently dependent on them.

## Following on Figgis

The format of the sultanic festivities themselves never seemed to change, so it does not matter at what stage of my Mukalla sojourn they occurred. We were seated in red plush chairs in a row, along the frontage of the palace, being entertained by local performers, in the presence of the Ruler. His Highness Sultan Awadh bin Salih was seated in the middle of the row, in full cloth-of-gold regalia. He had a squat turban planted unevenly on his head, reminiscent of one's favourite aunt playing the part of an oriental potentate in the village hall production of *Chu Chin Chow*. He gazed vacuously at the performers, picking at his face with a bejewelled finger. The Quaiti sultanic family owed some sort of allegiance to the Nizam of Hyderabad, whose traditional bodyguard contained an element of Quaiti (mercenary) support. The Hyderabadi connection seemed to work both ways. The Sultan's household was itself of mixed origin; tribally his family was Yafai from the Western Aden Protectorate but, more recently, there must have been a strong Indian mix.

To the side of the Quaiti Sultan (on such meaningful occasions as the one I attended) was the Resident Adviser. The successor but one to Hugh Boustead was Arthur Watts, whose unsoldierly bulk was not best set off by his white uniform. Otherwise there was nothing untoward about Arthur, who conscientiously played his part throughout those hot afternoons, showing every sign of being absorbed by the succession of performances taking place before him. To me, if not the Colonel exactly, Arthur represented a degree of normality.

It was somehow different at an earlier ceremony of this kind that I happened to attend. Colonel Hugh's successor, Alastair McIntosh, looked ill at ease in white uniform. His neck was too short for his helmet, so the back part rested on his tubby shoulders; from the rear he presented an armadillo effect. From the front, his animated good natured features were those of an attentive hamster, with small twinkling eyes, his little moustache moving up and down above two prominent front teeth, as he conversed inaudibly.

Alastair would already have lunched well and liquidly. I had been told that on an earlier full-dress occasion he had pinned his medals to the wrong side of his tunic, humming to himself as he squinted in the mirror. He had apparently been an organ scholar at Oxford (one account had it that he had also been studying for holy orders) and bound for a brilliant career in Palestine, under Sir Harold McMahon.

Eventually he had arrived in the Aden service and worked (and drank) his way to the role of RA. One story of him was that when stationed in Aden he had been used to playing the organ at the Garrison Church. The congregation was seated one Sunday at matins: Alastair arrived late, somewhat red in the face; seated at the organ he burst into the introductory bars of a hymn that did not feature in the order of service. The choir made a brave effort: some sang along, others stuck to the scheduled tune. Alastair turned round furiously to the congregation. 'Sing you b******! SING!' Apparently he was not asked to play again.

The substantive Deputy British Agent was Johnny Johnson, an ex-Chindit. He wore his war-time ribbons with a dash, though he was overweight in his tight white uniform. After the ceremonies he had enjoyed drawing his court sword, for my amusement. The effect was somewhat surrealist: at some stage the blade had snapped off, not far below the hilt. With his slight stammer and twinkle, he was fun to listen to.

Johnny had been stationed for years, in Upper Aulaqi country, miles out in the blue, and probably left too long on his own. He must have been a contemporary of the near-apocryphal Figgis who, also marooned on his own for too long, had taken to wearing a kilt and swiping at all and sundry with a fly whisk. One day, so I was informed, Figgis had sent an 'operational immediate' signal which said simply, 'Bedouins are b*******.' He had been called for, given a medical examination and sent on leave. Johnny counselled me (when I was to be posted on my own) never to get myself into that condition of unhealthy introspection (what the French, or at least PC Wren with his *Beau Geste*, called *cafard*) but just to add the words, 'Figgis was right,' to the end of any routine signal. This would be picked up and I would be called for and sent on leave.

Johnny was a good man in his job, a mine of information; he was brave, resourceful and intelligent, but, alas, he did drink like a fish. It was such a waste. He eventually died of blackwater fever. He enjoyed teasing the Hon. Bridget Coles (whom he considered put on airs, though she never did to me) about her father's alleged carryings-on, when the latter was governor of Bengal and Johnny a junior army officer.

Three other cronies of Alastair's were posted to the EAP during Alastair's term of office there; one of them would have been seated with us on those hot afternoons outside the Sultan's palace, though dressed soberly in a suit. He was Charles Inge, a veteran from the Western Aden Protectorate who had been a political officer at Dhala, on the Yemen frontier. He had an intelligence role, which apparently necessitated many hours of sitting with Alastair in the Residency.

Continuing the ongoing preoccupation with the demon drink (as some of my father's more censorious relatives might have put it), a one-armed ex-serviceman was posted to Saiun who made his own brew from the local dates, so I was informed. Lionel had also made his own wine when he had been on the WAP border, pressed from Yemeni grapes which he trod in his bath. Both brews were described to me as 'an acquired taste'. But it was the famous Archie Wilson who really sealed the Residency's later reputation, at the time I was posted out of Mukalla.

Archie was another good-natured man, at least to me. I was aware of one thing about him, for certain: when I knew him he never consciously made a meaningful decision. He was tall, granite-hewed of feature, often sporting a beard and a monocle, and smoking a huge curved pipe. He had come to a service that plainly attracted characters of his ilk, but even so, he must have stood out wherever he had served. His war career ('worst DSO in the whole show!' Archie told me, without further explanation) was apparently remembered for a drunken duel in the centre of Beirut, when Archie took on an equally inebriated American major. They were both in tanks at the time. His military career ceasing shortly thereafter, Archie joined the Desert Locust Survey (DLS).

The DLS had consisted of rugged individuals (Willie Wise had been one of them for a time) who were stationed and travelled in remote parts of Arabia and the Horn of Africa, where the desert locust bred after rain. There were many stories about the DLS. One was that a message was received at headquarters from a lonely locust spotter which read as follows. 'MANY LOCUSTS STOP COPULATING STOP WHAT SHALL I DO QUERY.' Reply sent 'STOP COPULATING KILL LOCUSTS.' By forewarning the authorities, poison bran could be distributed, thus obliterating many of the locust swarms at hopper stage. Humorous stories or no, it was a useful organization that undoubtedly prevented many of the locust plagues that were to ravage one third of cultivated Africa, 20 years after the organization was disbanded.

The DLS attracted many such as Archie who liked to while away the hours with a bottle or three. Someone, perhaps not Archie, was sharing just such a lonely posting with a kindred soul; they used to sit under a large tree, passing the time convivially. The colleague died and the other, greatly sorrowing, had a pipe let down to the grave under the tree, where the deceased's remains were interred. As the survivor poured himself a drink he would tip another down the pipe, doubtless with a 'Cheers, old boy!' Archie was a bottle-of-whisky-a-day man: I personally never observed him as becoming loud or unsteady with drink; and I was to see plenty of him.

Years later an old friend of mine described what it was like to arrive overland in Mukalla, call at the Residency one evening and be asked to stay. Alastair, by then practically speechless but brimming with hospitality, Charles and Archie were there. Alastair insisted on a bridge four being formed, after the appalling evening meal had been cleared away (the Residency cuisine had deteriorated when Alastair, as a bachelor, left the menus to his staff. The establishment was known unkindly then as 'Dysentery Hall'). My friend was no bridge player and Alastair, under 'normal circumstances', was rather good. At some stage of the evening a young successor to me in the role of Assistant Adviser (Residency) had been dragooned into replacing a member of the four. This youngster had played no bridge at all until then. The evening's rubbers were what the Arabs used to describe as a 'fantasia' — of total incomprehension, dropped cards, mumbled incoherent instructions and the steady clink of glasses.

But back to the Sultan's celebrations: the afternoon had passed in a dull and slow scenario of sticky heat and dust, as endless speeches were read, in such flowery Arabic as to be totally incomprehensible; small sullen schoolboys acted out vaguely anti-British pageants, based on Saladin's ousting of the infidels from Jerusalem (it was always the fattest and most unattractive of the actors who played the part of the craven Christian armies and who was mercilessly beaten until he yelped). Sweating athletes of African origin competed for prizes, every so often taking part in competitions that featured white flour being plastered to dark countenances, to the vast amusement of the crowd. At last the Residency limousine, flag hanging listlessly, would drive up, the RA would make his formal departure, and his party would stride off with an alert briskness, for the sort of refreshment that would obliterate the taste of small pink cakes and warm, sweet drinks of 7-Up.

In case I should give the impression that the British presence was entirely in the hands of inebriates, it must be clearly recorded that there was a hard core of hard-working officers whose presence helped to keep the world sane for impressionable youngsters like myself. Some I have already mentioned earlier, without the urge to remember them for some aspect of aberrant behaviour, or of indifferent work standards. Of those I met after Colonel Hugh's departure, I have referred to the most senior, Arthur Watts, his successor as Resident Adviser, who attracted much criticism from those in the know for various perceived deficiencies. I only knew him as a supportive boss when I was most to need it. He had risen from a humble start as an RAF serviceman posted to Aden and had developed a remarkable ability for learning various dialects of Arabic and some esoteric aspects of Arab culture.

Then there was the exceptional Jim Ellis, best described (however clichéd the phrase) as a 'gentle giant'. He had been around, in most parts of the EAP since the early 1950s having previously been a military man in one of the more romantic units of what became the Pakistan Army, and George Coles's oh-so-effective predecessor-but-one as Military Assistant to the Resident Adviser. Jim's memory was encyclopaedic, his personal acquaintances legion and his energy incredible. Many aspiring authors turned to Jim Ellis for succinct and accurate summaries of some obscure aspects of Eastern Protectorate history. He continued to entertain his friends, years after he retired.

There was Ralph Daly who, along with a friend of mine from Cambridge and North African archaeological days, John Lanfear, had been running the Saiun office, in the Wadi Hadhramaut. John later died from a brain tumour. With his Sudan background, Ralph provided an essential element in both Protectorates for a sound tradition of steady administration. However dull that might have sounded to the more mercurial of our colleagues, many of whom I was to meet later in the Western Aden Protectorate, it was the essence of what distinguished the EAP Political Service from the swash-buckling existence on the Western Aden Protectorate frontier. Life in the Wadi Hadhramaut was about development of the Pump Scheme, the improvement of the major road routes in and out of the Wadi and all that the Sudan Political Service had stood for, in assisting the local populace to do the best for themselves, with the limited resources available.

John Weakley, just junior to me, also went initially to Saiun and succeeded Ralph. His common sense and solid hard work contributed to keeping a sense of proportion going amongst those of us who at times wondered whether to booze heavily was to belong. John and Joyce quietly maintained a steady routine that reminded those of us that such normality was achievable, in spite of the excesses of others.

Others like Johnny Johnson made their mark on the EAP at a time when they were left too long in remote situations with a bottle of whisky for company. Jock Snell was one. He was an ex-military man and Jim Ellis's successor as MARA. His star was waning when I came on the scene, but, as its commandant, he had done useful things with the HBL before the force came under the sway of Pat Gray. When I knew Jock he had just remarried; I associated him with being an unlikely 'newlywed' and a friendly red-faced, sandy-haired, hard-drinking and hard-smoking (coughing) relic of the days when Ellis and Snell between them 'ran' remote chunks of the EAP. Jock Snell was to crop up again in Aden years later, when my life had taken a distinctly distasteful turn.

Sharing my barrack of a house in Mukalla were two other single men. Tubby Dawson ran the mechanical side of the HBL and only moved out on marriage. The other occupant was a nearly speechless water driller, Derek someone-or-other from the North Country, who sat motionless on my settee with one of my glasses in his hand, thinking deep and personal thoughts. He would stir, caress his straggly beard and utter, 'Erh.' I would look up from my book. 'Yes, Derek?' But that was it — no follow-up. I tended to avoid spending much time in Derek's company.

The evenings were not usually a problem. As a single man I would often be invited out to dinner to make up numbers. Or perhaps it would be David Eales who came to share my meal. David was on secondment from the Middlesex Regiment. He was charming. And he was a sponger. He had never been known to buy a drink for anyone and he certainly never entertained anyone to whom he owed hospitality. He was known locally as the 'MMIME' (Meanest Man in Middle East). He had apparently been an ADC to the Governor General in the Sudan, at one stage, where he had been involved in a traffic accident on the way to the airport in which his passengers were killed. His career was blighted; he was now appointed as a training officer to the local forces, and later as Deputy Commandant of the HBL. He was saving hard to buy first an ancient Rolls Royce (this he achieved) and secondly a Piaget watch. Poor David — he came to a horrible end. When I first met him, he was excellent company, and hostesses forgave him for his incredible meanness, a failing which was undoubtedly to be responsible for his tragic death. But that was some years ahead.

There were only two remaining characters in the Eastern Aden Protectorate cast who impacted on me at that period of my life: one was Mohamed Said Nagi, the only Arab Assistant Adviser in either Protectorate. He must have been a sort of token example of promoting a representative of local talent into what came to be seen in retrospect as an untenable role, a real lackey of the British, poor man. Mohamed Said was posted to Wahidi when Colonel Hugh and I called there on that memorable first tour. He was later regarded as one of the hopes for the newly emergent Federation with which I was to be concerned much later. That was his nemesis: Mohamed Said was to be assassinated with the rest of his ilk.

In the Northern Deserts served one Dick Gannon, another ex-Arab Legion man and a stickler for what he regarded as the way 'things should be done'. I respected his obvious knowledge when I met him as he passed through Mukalla. He seemed to be very tense; even with my inexperience I wondered how his temperament would cope with the vagaries of life in the loosely structured service of those who followed in the Figgis tradition. I had not too long to wait.

It all came about very quickly, with just a few days to pack up my house, engage a new 'cook' (Hassan was most reluctant to serve among people he regarded as barbarians) and to take over from an embittered and sombre Dick Gannon. Up to then the talk had been of my possibly relieving Mohamed Said Nagi in Wahidi. Mohamed Said loathed being there (secretly I think he was rather frightened of the Wahidis); he was a true townsman who missed the café chatter and the urban intrigue. But Northern Deserts it was to be, and without delay. Gannon had fallen into disfavour with the HBL — so much for being an ex-military man himself and ex-Arab Legion to boot. It was his abrasive personality as much as anything; it was reported that he had almost been left to die of heat exhaustion when his vehicle stuck in the sand

and his escort refused to help him extricate it. Apparently he had sweated and raved and shoved so hard, he had collapsed. He was brought to, but his future was decided; he was on the plane home.

The slow two-day bumpy haul up the Jol (the plateau massif), via the Hadhramaut and out towards the three flat-topped hills of Husn (fort) Al Abr (the wells), gave me time to reflect on what I had to assume in the way of responsibility and know-how. So much for my yearning to be given a 'proper' job. It was now mine, with a vengeance. The map showed a long stretch of barren wilderness (a 1500-mile return trip to the further end of the 'parish' from Mukalla). It was cut by the quarter-million square miles of the Rubl Khali (Empty Quarter), the gigantic sand seas running in a NE/SW direction and rising to heights of hundreds of feet. It bordered three countries and it contained six permanent water points, which were looked after by garrisons of HBL. The wandering and semi-settled Bedouin tribes, each male of whom carried a rifle, followed the rains where possible, to fodder their camels and sometimes their goats. Blood feuds often broke out, camel raiders from the Yemen were fairly frequent, and arms trickled in and out of the Protectorate over the Saudi border. The eastern section ran across the top of a large chunk of no-man's-land, Mahra country.

And stuck somewhere in this vastness was an oil company.

# 9
# Lifestyle of a Nomad

THE oil company was to be in the news, due to a tribal confrontation in the Al Abr area. It was Petroleum Concessions Ltd (PCL), an exploration subsidiary of Iraq Petroleum; a near-village of 100 persons or so, it was supplied by air from Aden and was currently established near my nominal headquarters-to-be, Thamud — just a name on the map at that stage. PCL was merely a distant priority at that time; I had had to ensure I was properly kitted out before I was into my new desert lifestyle. There was a major advantage to having been in charge of the Residency stores and vehicles. My transport was to be a new long-wheel-based Land Rover and a Bedford 25 cwt utility truck. In the stores I had kept my eye on a splendid lightweight three-partition tent and even had it unrolled and repacked under my eye, to check all guy ropes and pegs were present (I had sour memories of that first archaeological expedition to Libya with flapping half-erected tents). Canvas wash basin and bath, standard wooden table and chairs, rugs, safari-type bed and mosquito net were supplemented by two metal-and-canvas deck chairs so that it was possible in the evening to put one's head back, as one stretched before the camp fire. This had completed my basic furniture and accoutrements, not forgetting a couple of pressure lamps, six hurricane lamps and battery-powered lights, including spare bits and pieces to keep them all working.

I was using my parents' pre-war metal trunks for kitchen items and my crockery was moulded of a sort of new shatter-proof plastic (which shattered just the same). Canvas water bags, tarpaulins and two 44-gallon drums strapped in the Bedford (one petrol, one water) ensured I was reasonably self-contained for a few days, at least. I wore a cotton bush jacket and long trousers (lots of pockets for storing petitions, peanuts, letters from home and spare glasses); my feet were usually bare, except in winter (washing socks was a bore and one's feet were healthier exposed), and thrust into leather sandals. On my head I wore, for entirely practical reasons, an Arab head cloth and rope; I could fasten the cloth securely round the whole of my face, tucking the edge into my spectacle frames. This was reasonable protection against exposure (especially important when the Land Rover might have been totally stripped down) but even so, those little areas on the cheeks where the cloth gaped were susceptible to the desert sun. (Years later I still have a number of basal skin carcinomas regularly removed.)

Also part of my baggage was a modest armoury; I had never belonged to the almost arrogant school of political officer who disdained the carrying of personal arms, and despised those who did. I had become used to a pistol in Mau Mau times; this time I was equipped with a .38 Smith & Wesson revolver, with' PROPERTY OF THE US GOVERNMENT stamped on it. It had an interesting history: originally acquired by a British officer working for MI6 during the war, it had been used to arrest the Vichy Mayor of Algiers, when the Allies moved back into North Africa. Subsequently it had been taken to England where its owner, guilty that it had not been surrendered, begged me to take it with me to Arabia. I wore it discretely under my bush jacket. I had had Shaikhan, the Residency tailor, sew a cloth strip to my khaki trousers under the bush jacket into which I could slip the revolver; it was easy to access and did not get tangled while I was sitting in a vehicle. I was to be very relieved that I had it, on at least one occasion: it probably saved my life. Without making a big 'thing' of it, people knew I had it with me and that would perhaps have urged restraint on the ungodly; I had no intention of relying solely on personal charm, character or presumed goodwill to keep alive.

My .375 Holland & Holland rifle was also with me, plus an ammunition belt I had had made up in Mukalla, to accommodate the large rounds it fired. Once I had taken over the Northern Deserts, the rifle was handed over to my personal orderly to look after and to carry. The third firearm was my 12-bore shotgun which sat in its case, behind my seat in the vehicle. Sand grouse, gazelle, even a bustard (all shot for the pot) provided a refreshing change from the diet of tinned beef, tuna and vegetables, supplemented by rice and the occasional fresh delicacy brought up from the Hadhramaut.

I had rather a large entourage; apart from the youth who was learning to cook (and to make my bed without leaving greasy thumb prints on my pillow, from the last tin of tuna he had opened) there were my two drivers and an assistant, a 'garage boy' who travelled in the Bedford. There was a section of HBL with all their gear transported in the Bedford (occasionally supported by an extra HBL vehicle if the security situation warranted it) or if I needed access to a mobile radio. The HBL section performed the mundane duties of getting the tent/s erected, and of mounting a guard at night. They helped with perhaps killing a goat or skinning a gazelle; they liaised with the local Bedou. With some exceptions, they were useful and cooperative and I was pleased to have them along.

Often a soldier would be related to the Bedou we met and that could provide additional access to a source of news, and certainly enhance goodwill. Apart from the HBL escort my principal link with the locals was via the local HBL commander and my personal orderly. Sometimes it was an HBL soldier who was detailed to stay with me, but of all the pleasant individuals attached to me, I came to prefer a splendid man from the Sear tribe living near Al Abr. He was Abdullah bin Ndail. Abdullah was perhaps a bit younger than me (he was not sure). He was tall, compared with his fellows, and he had a splendid black beard. He looked quite fierce but in reality he was a bit of a softy. He wore the .375 ammunition belt with a swagger and handled the rifle itself as though it were made of gold. He was much in awe of the kick it gave into the shoulder when it discharged; the deep roar of the exploding round gave the .375 the local name of *Al mudfar* (the mortar).

Abdullah was an amusing gossip, as we drove along or walked for exercise at the end of a long day. I enjoyed this, picking up the odd titbit about a local character or perhaps an item concerning one of the HBL officers. I perfected my particular brand of colloquial Arabic, mainly by having to respond to Abdullah bin Ndail. Not that I had any option unless I wanted to remain silent. There was no one, for hundreds of miles either side of Al Abr who spoke English, unless I counted the Junior Assistant Adviser, Kharusi.

Mohamed al Kharusi was a well-born Zanzibari of impressive size (he once beat the Royal Naval boxing champion) who was based at Al Abr with his charming wife and family. Until he was moved on, he lived in what came to be the rest house, and quarters for me when I was working in the western end of Northern Deserts. When I first met him, I found him invaluable; he knew so much. He suffered though from that affliction common to so many expatriates in our service; he was an alcoholic. Living in Al Abr one might have thought he would be isolated from booze, but Al Abr was on the main vehicle route to and from Najran in Saudi Arabia and it was inevitable that he should get his hands on a bottle. When that happened he might disappear from sight for days on end, his occasional roars and the accompanying screams from his wife emerging from his quarters to remind me that he would appear one day with a dreadful hangover. I tried to keep my distance and a sense of proportion on those occasions, often by visiting a nearby Bedouin encampment for the night, and enjoying a meal with them.

The wells at Al Abr were a magnet for the tribes, which were obliged to keep their animals within convenient reach of the water and therefore camped nearby. Sometimes Abdullah bin Ndail's family was with them. Having secured the necessary invitation to visit, the HBL commander and I (we tended to move round his area together) would motor out, to arrive before dark. We would be met formally, sometimes with a fusillade of shots (I did try to discourage this) and be invited to join our hosts on the strips of gaily-woven rug, usually outside the black tents where the women were preparing the evening meal. If we had timed it right, a full moon would rise on cue.

The greeting ritual was always the same, though the actual wording depended on the area. It went something like, 'Peace be upon you!' 'And you!' 'Are you all well? The crops? Your animals?' to which the response was, 'Praise be to God!' 'Has anyone died?' 'Don't say so!' and after a few more questions and answers in this vein, out came the story of local catastrophes, of lost (or stolen) camels, or government's inhumanity to these poor, suffering innocents. The conversation would then vary between attempts by our hosts to enlist a commitment to take on their neighbours, or the tribes over the border, or an exchange of information. All the time, there would be refreshments brought: cups of sweet tea, ginger-and-coffee husks and little nibbles of camel milk whey. The goat's kidneys might be offered as an aperitif, only lightly cooked.

Then it was time to eat properly: the usual chunks of meat piled on the rice was about all; only in the towns did one expect the elaborate little side dishes. A bowl of greasy but tasty soup would be passed around, one's host encouraging one to eat and drink more and more: '*Kul! Kul! Shrb! Shrb!*' ('Eat! Eat! Drink! Drink!') and one would politely hold one's right hand over one's heart indicating one was full, perhaps with a refined belch and a *Alhamdullilah* ('Praise be to God'). A bowl of greasy warm water was brought round, with a bar of meat encrusted soap (some of my hosts merely rubbed their greasy fingers in their matted hair) and, shortly after more coffee or tea, I would get to my feet and there would be mutual protestations of thanks and of general goodwill. Back to camp and a usually comfortable night, with just the odd desert noise to disturb that overwhelming silence once the roaring lamp had been extinguished, the fire died down and the soldiery's chatter completed as they rolled into their blankets and fell into slumber.

If there was no moon, the sky overhead was so full of stars that it was surprising I could pick out the jerky movement of a satellite crossing the firmament. 'Look, an "artificial moon",' Abdullah had said casually in Arabic on an earlier occasion. He was remarkably relaxed about it all, for a man who had lived in the remote Al Abr area all his life.

Depending on the season, one arose at first light or just after the sun had provided some warmth, for it could be very cold, first thing, with ice forming on water left outside. A hot cup of tea was the start; a wash and shave. I always tried to keep up the niceties, perhaps unconsciously aware of the dangers of 'not bothering', of the temptation not to summon the effort to change one's clothing as often as one might and, eventually, relaxing into a poor attempt to copy the locals, instead of being a highly-paid (by local standards) foreigner required to hold one's own, often under trying conditions. We became very close, my Arab companions and I but, in their eyes as well as my own, it was important that I lived as a European.

How one spent the day again depended on the season. If it were very hot, one aimed to confine one's travel to before 10.00 a.m. and to after 4.00 p.m., lying up during the rest of the day, or meeting with the locals. In the winter one could move as one pleased, always with the proviso that one had made camp well before it was dark, so that the oncoming chill of the evening was combated by a roaring fire, a hot meal and a properly made-up bed, inside a tent that had been erected on a suitable site (not too far from ground that allowed a decent cover to squat, but, in certain areas, not too close to terrain that might allow anyone unfriendly to creep up on me).

Then there were those days when a hot wind would blow, perhaps on and off for 48 hours. Visibility fell to a few feet, the sand and thin dust would get into everything (the food, one's bed, the vehicles' engines) and there was little one could do except wrap one's head and await the wind to drop and, with it, the dry, searing heat. When one emerged, it was into a world that had been purified, the sand or stony surface left cleansed, with ripple patterns of sand pointing in the direction of the departed wind. Once the sand had been shaken out of one's belongings, it would be time to continue with the schedule of touring, of meetings and of discussing what needed doing, to keep Northern Deserts functioning (if that is not too grand a word for my peripatetic administration).

An hour or so east of Al Abr there were the ancient wells of Zamarkh and of Minwalkh, each with its soldiery in a little fort, keeping an eye on the locals as they ceaselessly drew the water from the depths, the stones lining the well edges deeply grooved from the ropes of generations before them. The pretty young women of the Sear and Kurab tribes wore only vestigial veils, if they wore any at all (their sisters of the Mahra to the east were heavily shrouded). These girls would be hauling water and as they took turns they would smile sideways, '*Ya achoie, ya Nasrani.*' ('Oh my brother, oh Christian.') Not for nothing were the Sear women of one section known as *Ahl Franzoia* (the French women). I learnt to swap jokes with the grave old men, and not to smile too openly at the vulgar chants of young Bedouin soldiers clearing stones off an improvized landing strip, or engaging in other repetitious chores.

Depending on where it had rained (and someone told me it rained in the same place twice, every 14 years) would be the odd camel grazing, the females in milk with their udders neatly tied up to prevent the milk being drained by their young. The owners might stop us for water, using the sign of cupping a hand and gesturing at their mouths. We would halt and exchange the time of day, filling their goatskin water bags, and in return were offered a brimming basin of foaming camel's milk, drawn while we waited, and passed round politely, each person raising the grimy bowl to his lips with loud sucking sounds. Camel milk is low in butter fat and tastes equally good with chocolate, or even better warmed with a little whisky.

The journey continued, as described when I wrote to my mother in a letter dispatched via an oil company aircraft and therefore guaranteed delivery in a week or so, rather than the more usual month's delay.

My dear Mother,

I am over 700 miles from where I last wrote, sitting on the balcony of the fort. My lamp is flaring away cheerfully and there is a crescent moon sinking. Cheerful Bedouin are having a meal below and all is well, though noisy, with the world.

It has been an interesting trip! Moved from Al Abr to Thamud, getting caught in a terrific sand storm as I crossed the corner of the Rubl Khali. We were damn lucky not to get lost as visibility was a few feet and even the 150-foot high dunes on each side were invisible.

I arrived at Thamud, my nominal HQ for Northern Deserts though I've spent more time in the west owing to the convoy trouble (of which more, later). In Thamud I had three days' talk with the chief of the tribe in whose territory the oil company will be working next season. All very amicable but the chief (or *muqaddam* as they call him here) could only think of oil profits before we have discovered it! Anyway, I think I have got the *muqaddam* on government's side, which is essential as discontented Bedouin sniping at the camp would be a darn nuisance.

At Thamud I made a very exciting and, I think, unique discovery: a local Bedouin talked vaguely of a strange stone; I went to see it and found it to be (I think) an ancient 'mile' stone (Himyaritic?). There have been plenty of Himyaritic bits and pieces found further west, but Thamud is in the middle of nowhere. The markings are very distinct and I hope someone can identify them. It suggests that one of the incense routes to Palestine, or Rome must have come down that way.

From Thamud I proceeded to Sanau (100 miles) which was quite the most tiring part of the journey. It is in Mahra country, where the locals all have long narrow faces, little glittering eyes and protruding teeth. They screamed for two days at the tops of their voices, about nothing in particular, every so often rushing outside and firing rifles in the air in excitement. The main incident of note was that a Mahra boy fell off a camel and got a four-inch slice in his head. There was a great chunk of skull showing which didn't look cracked. I had to treat him, and I hope he doesn't die on me or else I'll probably have to pay blood money or something — very gory.

It's another 175 miles to Habarut over pretty rough country. They've had the best rain for 40 years and so there was a green sheen over the ground. Unfortunately the floods washed away half the fort. But there's actually running water in the wadi, and mosquitoes.

To my dismay I ran out of reading matter at Sanau; I have since been reading old letters and the book Henrie sent me, *The Catcher in the Rye*. You might tell her that not only did I enjoy reading it the first two times, but that I have now read it six times and am still fond of it. It is such a different world from here, reading about a crazy mixed-up American adolescent.

I haven't spoken English for days and today have been trying to talk Arabic with some Dhofaris — amazing how different it is. I expect to be back in Al Abr in four to five days and will send these letters off to be posted by first vehicle available. God knows when you will get them [as it turned out, there was an oil company aircraft]. As it happens, I am nearer Hugh Boustead in Muscat than in Mukalla, so it's a pity I can't ask him to help with the mail!

The vast distances, the screaming locals and lack of anyone to lean on is a bit disturbing at times. It's true I am in wireless contact but signals get distorted. Anyway, I'll see some non-Arabs in the near future. Pass my news around, won't you, as I haven't written much to other people. I'll write again when suitable.

Much love,
Michael

*Lifestyle of a Nomad*

The 'non-Arabs' to whom I referred were of course PCL's oil employees and it was to my own 'oily boy's' caravan to which I repaired, to recover from yet another overnight stay at Sanau. The latter was particularly trying; the water contained about one quarter magnesium sulphate and stank abominably. It also had the same effect on my insides as it did on the camels', which scoured perpetually. There were no latrines in the nasty little fort. I had to leave my vehicle permanently at the fort's entrance, so that when I emerged urgently, I could jump in and roar off to the nearest outcrop of white gypsum, where I could squat, and return to the fort before the Mahra managed to catch up with me, importuning fiercely for whatever was on their minds. The countryside was truly ghastly, but there was a deposit of worked Neolithic flint blades scattered everywhere. There must have been people using that water for thousands of years. Ugh!

Sanau was quite the worst of the HBL forts in which to stay overnight. Thamud and Habarut (what was left of it) were luxury by comparison, but nothing could compare with the PCL caravan. It was kept permanently for me. It was small, dark and air conditioned. There were wonderful showers nearby and a mess tent with luxurious supplies of top-class food and drink. There I could put on clean albeit crumpled clothing, stretch out in the cool and chat about European things. The oil company geologists, the drillers, were not much interested in Northern Desert affairs. To them this was just another bit of god-forsaken wilderness with funny looking natives. Their talk was of football pools, and when next they would be going on leave, all mixed up with comments on 'fault lines' and other mysterious geological terms. There were, however, two drillers who got a kick out of visiting the fort at Thamud; Johnny Vale had even taken the trouble to learn some Arabic. I enjoyed their company, particularly. There was also Abdullah Hassan Jaffar who was the Adeni liaison officer who worked for PCL. He was an oily (how apt) smiling gentleman with a broad pock-marked face and stout figure. He, too, openly loathed being away from the bright lights, but the company obviously paid him well. He was a dangerous man as far as I was concerned. He took it on himself to have dealings with the tribesmen, many of them in secret, with money changing hands on a scale that not only could I not have matched, but which cut across the government policy I was trying to carry out. Luckily my sources kept me more or less informed of what went on.

Abdullah Hassan was later murdered in Northern Deserts, no doubt by someone who was irritated by being cut out of a nefarious deal. As it was, I had had no time for tears, when I heard: my Northern Deserts job was difficult enough, without accommodating his machinations. There was even a basic British altruism here: our priorities were quite different.

# 10

# Under 'British Protection'

T HE Northern Deserts area of the Eastern Aden Protectorate was the closest the British presence came to any form of direct administration, outside Aden. There were two main reasons for this and they should be seen primarily in terms of British interests: firstly, it was a frontier area, running from the Yemen in the west, to Dhofar in the east, along a *de facto* line separating Saudi Arabia from the EAP. With the possible exception of the Sultan of Muscat (the Dhofari tribes in any event disputed the border) neither of the other countries accepted the frontier as being a substantive one. The tribes were constantly ready to assert rights to areas claimed by their neighbours; such claims were backed by the particular EAP state (Quaiti or Kathiri) and even the neighbouring Western Aden Protectorate state/s, to which a particular tribe might owe a nominal allegiance. Tribal claims did not necessarily follow the frontier. A British presence made sense, if only (metaphorically) to knock heads together.

The second reason why I found myself reporting to the Resident Adviser direct in Mukalla, rather than advising a local state administrator, was that the British government had its own reasons for maintaining a presence in an area where there might be oil, and where British influence in South Arabia was seen as possibly crucial to the western presence in the Middle East, particularly after the failure of the Anglo/French/Israeli efforts to take back the Suez Canal. So much for the broad sweep of British policy (if that is not too grand a way of referring to the British presence in Northern Deserts). Boiled down to essentials, I personally had two principal concerns: the first focused on security, my own, the oil company's and the local population's, in whatever order seemed appropriate at the time. My second preoccupation was to do with water, and the lack thereof. But it was oil company

91

security that first took up my waking thoughts and much of my time, at least initially, and I found it a frightening responsibility, until I had some real understanding of what needed to be done.

Shortly after I arrived in Al Abr a convoy of PCL vehicles, with heavy stores and replacement caravans, had been ambushed by Bedouin, on the high ground, north-east of Al Abr, firing at the convoy for a day and a night, on and off. The tribesmen were apparently disgruntled at vehicles moving through their territory, doubtless motivated by a mixture of xenophobia and jealousy at the search for oil taking place in the Thamud area. There was also no love lost between a particular clan of the Sear, causing the trouble, and the Manahil around Thamud.

Having over-nighted at Al Abr, and been introduced to Mohamed Kharusi (who was resolutely sober on our first meeting), I briefly consulted the few hand-over notes left me by the shattered Dick Gannon (he had really got in bad with the HBL. The local word was that three attempts had been made on his life. I worried briefly about how to avoid his fate, and then forgot it for the moment). The notes told me nothing useful (at least he had paid the desert guards): I had about 100 miles to cover, through the rugged foothills abutting the stony plains, over an appalling track that writhed its way upwards, from behind the well and fort at Zamakh. We drove with caution, expecting either a broken spring or some shots across our front. With me, I had a platoon of HBL and the company commander from Al Abr. It was July, hot, dusty and supremely uncomfortable, though the setting sun was behind us, illuminating the strangely curved hills that had begun to loom on either side. There had been no sign of habitation, other than an isolated settlement of medieval dwellings earlier, perched at the side of small, parched fields. This was the headquarters of one of the Sear's chiefs, a small gnomic gentleman, of great wisdom, called bin Jerboa (son of the Jerboa). I was to return to meet him later.

I was reluctant to drive too much at night because of ambush danger, so we camped about 50 miles from the spot and left there at 3.00 a.m., to arrive at the convoy by dawn. There was no trouble when we arrived, but as we jolted into sight of the stranded vehicles, my eyes semi-closed against the rising sun's rays, an RAF Meteor jet greeted us. It had been sent from Aden to recce before the wind got up and obscured outlines, and the kidney-shaped hills shimmered in the haze. It had swooped along the track from behind us. The first I was aware that we had a visitor was when it overtook my vehicle, just a few feet above us. A large black shape deafened us with a terrible roar; my driver swore and clung to the wheel as dust and stones enveloped us: just ahead of us the Meteor soared vertically into the air and waggled its wings as it came over for a second pass. We shook our fists and pointed to the direction where the dissidents had gone to ground and it darted off to take photos. The Royal Air Force enjoyed providing ground support, but got a bit carried away, on occasion. A fighter aircraft took over, later in the day.

I drafted a letter with the help of the HBL commander. It was addressed to the local *muqaddam* and I asked him to appear at a meeting in two days' time and to bring in those guilty of firing on the convoy, as hostages. They had been responsible for a considerable volume of fire over the two days the convoy had been baled up; luckily, though, casualties were light; a Bedouin travelling with the convoy had his arm smashed and a pet gazelle belonging to one of the PCL drivers was killed.

The beleaguered convoy was eventually shepherded through, and I settled in to await any response from the local bandits and to prepare for the next PCL convoy due in the area in just a few days. The Residency would take no chances that there would be another ambush in the area: the HBL was sending a company escort, which included armoured cars and the Commandant, Pat Gray plus David Eales, no less!

The local *muqaddam* showed no signs of appearing. The second convoy lurched into sight and suddenly the barren landscape was alive with HBL, and Pat Gray, who was disappointed that there had been no second attempt to stop them. But, as I wrote to my mother, 'it would have to have been a very rash chap to try popping off at the convoy, in spite of our soldiers being such bad shots. We also had a jet fighter come screaming over which terrified our side as well as theirs, by doing a victory roll over us at about 100 feet.' I continued, 'Eventually the vehicles moved through, a very impressive sight, with about one and a half miles of enormous trucks towing trailers.' Pat left with them and David Eales stayed with me, as a military contact in case I needed further armed support.

93

The dust had settled: it was then my business to start closing the account for the past, with our recalcitrant friends who had still not showed themselves. My notes having had no effect, I was joined by the local state official, a Quaiti provincial governor who sported a moustache almost the equivalent of Pat Gray's spread. Naib Badr al Kassadi was alert and displayed a sort of impish humour that helped to pass the long hours of waiting. He would arrange his long *futa* in elegant fold around his loins, squat on the rug and light up the latest in a series of rank, 'roll your own' cigarettes that at least kept the flies away, if you sat down wind of him. In between his stories, he too sent off messages into the blue, requiring the offenders' presence. He got a response: it was a rude one. By then I had been sitting on my own personal rock for a fortnight.

We retired to consult with the wizened bin Jerboa at his dingy edifice, some hours away. Bin Jerboa appeared to think there was nothing to be done except teach this lot a lesson. Normally it would have been arranged for the RAF to have put a couple of rockets through one of the forts, just as a sign that enough was enough, the inhabitants having been given enough notice to remove themselves and their livestock; but in this case it was decided that something more lasting was required. We thought that the actual destruction of property was important as a meaningful gesture in a violent society, and to avoid possible future loss of life. Besides, the track to Thamud was too important to risk further interference, and it would be impossible to provide an appropriate escort for each convoy in future. I was instructed to blow up the three empty *husns* (forts), *'pour encourager les autres.'*

Local gunpowder took time to organize but it was quite satisfactory in the end: the *husns* were made entirely of mud and one blast in each resulted in total disintegration. The crops were untouched. The final stage in the saga was to warn all around that any of the offenders were to be arrested, if seen, and brought in for trial. The sanctions taken were effective; bin Jerboa set the scene with his endorsement of strong action and, most important, there was no loss of life.

Security continued to be a priority in the west. I took a six-vehicle patrol along the Yemen end of the border; it was also the HBL's company commander's first visit to that area and we were well armed; anyone we met from the other side would be likewise. We drove first over featureless plain, well into an area that could have been Yemen (or, more likely on the Saudi side of the 'line') where there had been a scuffle three months previously. It concerned raiders from the Dahm tribe in the Yemen who were making off with Seari camels. The HBL patrol caught up with them and in the exchange of fire one of our drivers had been killed. The HBL score was six of their camels; and the leader of the raid, the son of a prominent Dahmi head. His loss was counted as ignominious by the Dahm and it was put about that the life of a senior HBL officer (or even that of a British political officer) would make the score even.

The place where the affray took place had not been visited since then. There were the mounds, on the flat surface, of the six dead camels, mostly desiccated by the sun and wind; there was no insect life. There was the corpse of the dead man, partly covered by sand. I would not have noticed it until a cheerful desert guard with me (from a tribal section at fierce odds with the Dahm) scrabbled in the sand. To my horror he pulled out, with a creaking noise, a gaunt human arm: it was slightly decayed in places, still with the finger nails intact and most of the skin. At my protest the desert guard dropped the remains and they were properly interred, on the right side, facing towards Mecca. The body had originally been left as it fell, as warning to any of the Dahm who may have returned.

I had to restrain the desert guard concerned from levering himself into the back of the vehicle before (I insisted) washing his hands thoroughly. This was probably the first time he had performed this exotic ablution: he and his fellows used sand for the formalities of the daily prayers, when they could be so bothered.

We moved off across the most lovely area of smooth desert. There was a light breeze for once, the sky was deep blue and the HBL soldiery were chanting something rhythmical. There was uneventful running for 80 miles, to the south, a billiard table surface and just the occasional·line of tracks to show where someone had made a journey. We had crossed the Jol Madram 'highway', on which the huge trucks undertook the journey between the Hadhramaut and Saudi Arabia. These trucks had to pass via Al Abr: there was a cursory arms and quarantine check, unless we had been tipped off that a particular vehicle had been smuggling arms or other contraband. Then it was not unknown for the great vehicle to be almost totally stripped down (as much a deterrent to would-be smugglers as the hope of finding anything) while the 40 to 50 passengers stood by, fuming.

The second preoccupation of Assistant Adviser Northern Deserts was to keep going various expensive tube-well pumps that had been installed on wells drilled by PCL for its own operations and existence. They determined the sites of the various camps they established within the concessions granted to explore. Once the exploration moved on, the wells were left, each with an 'operator': the Bedou would flock to the vicinity of these wells that produced unlimited good water, from a great depth. Often the wells were located at considerable distances from the traditional water sources. From PCL's perspective this was for very good reasons, of security and being close to the prospecting areas.

When I was usually days away myself I would receive a despairing signal from the nearest HBL garrison that the pump had broken down. Unless it could be fixed urgently, I was assured that thousands of stock and their Bedou owners would perish. It was then a question of transporting a mechanic hundreds of miles from the Wadi Hadhramaut Pump Scheme workshops in Saiun, to make repairs — always, it appeared, in the nick of time. One of my first tasks was to prepare an estimate of what it would cost to keep all pumps serviceable. The figure I came up with was ignored as laughable and I contemplated 'doing a Figgis'; I kept my morale up by persuading the irascible Donald Guthrie, the pump mechanic in charge of the Saiun workshops, to tour the various pumps and leave a little technical knowledge plus some basic spare parts, at each site. Don had a rotten trip; he was given the Gannon treatment by his HBL escort. When they stuck in dune country, the HBL took exception to being told to help. It took Guthrie and his mechanics five hours to dig themselves out; when they got back from under the vehicles, they found the escort not only had brewed themselves tea on a fire made from Guthrie's wooden tent pegs, but they had drunk it all.

Later that year (October 1959) saw me over on the Dhofari side; I had been escorting a couple of British Army surveyors taking the route along the northern border that followed the Rubl Khali sand sea. It was an extra 100 miles. I was looking for signs of the Arabian oryx and we spotted them (old and new spoor) and not a camel print in sight. It was the remotest area I had ever visited, a thin crusty terrain with just the occasional dried watercourses, a few shrubs bravely existing in the lea of the prevailing wind direction. At night the place came alive with desert foxes, insects galore, fat little jerboas and other mice. As soon as it was light there came the transformation of the landscape into deserted vastness — the background dunes bright red, even purple, in the morning light.

Towards that evening we saw them, a cloud of dust moving very slowly: a pair of oryx. They were white, with black stripes and long, slender horns. I reported briefly to my mother so she could inform the Fauna Preservation Society in London that there were still oryx around — enough, maybe, to consider rescuing a nucleus before a Gulf Arab hunting party or an oil exploration group moved into the area. It was almost too late by the time such an expedition was organized.

There was also chat about Wilfred Thesiger with one of my escorts, Mabhout bin Hassanah, who had spent a brief period with the famous explorer (he knew him as 'Umbarak bin Miriam') when he had walked through these parts only a decade or so earlier.

Back with PCL the British election results were announced, with a Tory victory. One of the English-speaking Adeni Arabs approached me, 'You have heard the results, Mr Crouch?' I thought he would be regretting Labour's loss. 'I hoped Labour would not win. They would give Aden to the Yemen, and that is not our idea of freedom!' This apparent pro-British stance was enhanced by enthusiasm at the visit of Sir William and Lady Luce who flew into Northern Deserts and toured with me out of Thamud, Lady Luce looking very chic in blue jeans. After the guard of honour they met the officers of 3 Coy HBL for a cup of tea, the latter perfect gentlemen as always, as though they were quite used to entertaining the Governor and his wife on the fort's ramparts. Then it was off to PCL where the company had laid on the sort of spread one would expect in a London hotel — a whole salmon, caviar. The Luces talked drilling as if they were interested in nothing else, their hosts squeezed into tight formal shirts, gleaming with goodwill.

After a brief break during that winter season (in Kenya) I continued my Northern Deserts existence in much the same mode. I had my successes: both involved the Dahm camel raiders from the Yemen. A patrol I dispatched caught 17 of them, in the act. A week later 30 others were cornered with their loot and they fought a pitched battle from behind their couched camels, with the HBL and a lucky youngster, Stewart Hawkins, who had been spending time with me perfecting his fluent Arabic, from university in the UK. Their leader was shot four times by the HBL and the rest surrendered. I had to put the dying camels out of their misery and we took our prisoners back to Al Abr. Our wounded man expired and I was given his black Yemeni goat-hair coat with the bullet holes in it: we arranged a big meeting of the tribes to settle the camel score.

John Lanfear from Saiun sent me the following signal:

> There was a young PO from Hotham
> Who had an affray with the Dahm;
> The result of this frolic
> Was a bad dose of colic
> From a surplus of lead in the diaphragm.

To which we replied:

> Oh Assistant Adviser Saiun —
> Do not envy our life in the dune.
> Let us assure you,
> Your parish adore you —
> You're expert at being a buffoon!

Tribesmen continued to fight over water and animals; pumps broke down, hostages were taken into custody and there were some unpleasant incidents involving the HBL. The first concerned an HBL driver who got hold of someone's rifle and apparently shot himself stone-dead, in the head. It caused no end of trouble because whether it was an accident or not, one option (that of suicide) was quite unacceptable to the dead man's family. They set out to prove he had been shot by someone and that had everyone accusing everyone else around. The HBL arranged a court of enquiry and I had to inspect the corpse while it was being washed, in case there were allegations as to the bullet passage. It was horrible: there is not much left of a skull after a .303 round has exited, having entered from six inches away.

The second HBL incident occurred much later, well after I had had the pleasure of another visit by David Eales (who was now Deputy Commandant) inspecting his HBL garrisons. He was accompanied by

98

an Austrian anthropologist who was studying the Mahra and was now looking for some practical experience. His communications were somewhat limited by a thick accent and a frank dislike of all that he was experiencing; it turned out that this earlier hatred palled into a mild distaste by comparison, once he had been in Sanau fort for a few days. He was already suffering internally from various Mukalla germs: Sanau's generous laxative effect nearly disposed of him.

It was May 1961, desperately hot in Al Abr and I was due to escort a British Army major who was an expert in travel by star-fixing. I had collected him from the Western Aden Protectorate Federal Army outpost at Ataq. I had been well looked after in the officers' mess there; the CO was one Adrian Donaldson, ex-Black Watch and a ranker who had risen to great heights by being an excellent soldier, Arabic speaker and capable with it. I drove the major with his astrolabe back to Al Abr and the next day, after the fierce heat had abated somewhat, we set off for Thamud in just my two vehicles, the usual small escort of HBL on the back of the Bedford, my visitor travelling with me. It was his first venture into such desolation; we were to camp by the edge of the sand sea, at a feature called 'Khoshm al Jebel' (the Nose of the Mountain) and he would take sightings after dark. At this point we were only a short distance from the Saudi border.

I had noticed that the Bedford seemed to be making heavy weather of negotiating the small dunes near where we were to stop, and I commented as such to Abdullah bin Ndail and the driver of my vehicle. They exchanged glances, and then out came the reason. It was carrying smuggled ammunition bought in Ataq by my escort, for sale to the Manahil and Mahra further east. What was I to do?

I could hardly ignore it. The Bedford would not make it through the sand (which was one of the reasons my driver had decided to speak out; he knew the truth would emerge, when we had to unload the Bedford before digging it out. The HBL responsible would not allow me to find the load and it would be relatively easy for them to dispose of me and fade over the Saudi border). I decided to return to Al Abr and hand the escort over to the HBL commander there. I explained what I would do to the British major (who was beginning to regret his visit to the Empty Quarter) and to Abdullah. They both looked to their arms.

I stopped the vehicle and ordered the soldiers off.

Unsuspecting they stood where I directed. I then told them that I had reason to believe they were smuggling ammunition and that they were all under arrest. I ordered them to take off their ammunition belts and lay their rifles down. By then I had my .38 in my hand. There was a momentary pause and then they did meekly what I said, the sergeant leading the way. The drivers and garage boy unloaded case after case of new .303 ammunition, which was stowed back in the truck. Abdullah covered the soldiers and they climbed back on the Bedford which started back to Al Abr, ahead of us, the soldiers' rifles in my vehicle. We arrived in the early morning and I called out the HBL commander, explained what I had done, and asked him to let HQ HBL know. I then went to bed, having informed Mukalla myself by signal of the situation.

We awoke early the next morning to the sound of shots whistling over the rest house. I summoned the HBL commander who informed me that his men were angry at their honour being besmirched and were going to teach me a lesson. There was nothing I could do at that stage except keep my head down and inform Arthur Watts in Mukalla of the situation. I reported despondently that I thought I had 'done a Gannon.' He replied promptly to the effect that he saw no similarity in the two situations and that I had behaved well.

With the RA's unofficial commendation to support me, I was able to repair the damage that had been caused, in confidence and with surprising ease. The HBL company commander was replaced, several HBL other ranks were court martialled and dismissed, but Pat Gray never forgave me for, as he saw it, besmirching his beloved force's honour, by daring to draw a firearm on its members.

# 11
## The Wilds of Wahidi

IT was time that I was moved on: gone were the days when a single man was to be left on his own for an extended period in Northern Deserts. Although the longer one stayed, the more one learnt of what really went on, there was also the danger of my becoming blasé, careless in what I did and how I looked after myself. 'Remember Michael,' Johnny Johnson cautioned, only semi-humorously, 'A dead political officer is a damn nuisance.' Yes, of course, but apart from the trouble caused, I saw myself almost as a professional coward, only willing to take risks if I felt reasonably in charge of the situation; and the more I thought I was in charge, the less, in reality, I probably was.

It was therefore opportune as my second UK leave loomed to accept promptly the notice of intent to move me to the position of Assistant Adviser Wahidi States. First, I had to arrange a handover to Richard Etridge, a younger man than myself but one who gave the impression of knowing it all already. I had driven into the Wadi Hadhramaut to visit my colleagues in Saiun, something I always looked forward to after the relative privations of Northern Deserts and the isolation from my own kind.

Assistant Adviser Northern Areas and his family lived in the luxury of a white villa in the green serenity of the Saiun gardens, the great palace of the Kathiri Sultan looming above the town. Each house was equipped with a *jabiya*, an indoor pool in which one could cool off, before the water was pumped out onto the gardens. Little birds were everywhere, the fields were bright with lucerne and the witch-hatted peasant girls cut the crops with their small sickles. All seemed stable and prosperous, an Arab culture with a strong Indonesian influence. There had been six sterling millionaires living in the Wadi, of whom most had made their fortunes trading in the Far East.

101

Yes, it was very different from Northern Deserts, though it was as hot. Midsummer temperatures radiated off the wadi walls and the dry heat was often in the high forties, or even low fifties. In the winter it could be nearly as correspondingly cold. Once Richard Etridge had got over an attack of pneumonia, which required a prolonged period of convalescence, I drove him coughing and spitting to Al Abr; and, having toured the whole of Northern Deserts with him, I left him. It was a much smoother handover than an earlier one, before I took my first home leave. My first handover was supervized by Arthur Watts, personally. I had had to leave Northern Deserts in the temporary care of Archie Wilson. I had enthusiastically prepared handing-over notes (included as the appendix to this book) but I need not really have bothered. Archie had no intention of getting involved in the problems of Northern Deserts. His only executive action was to organize a large goatskin water carrier (which hung on the vehicle door to keep the contents cool as it sweated moisture) suitably strengthened, to accommodate a carton of beer cans.

It had been an inauspicious start to Archie's suzerainty, at least from Arthur's perspective; Arthur was a man of moderate, even somewhat precious, habits, and he would not have chosen Archie to relieve me, but there was no-one else. It was near Al Abr: it was winter, it was cold, and the sun was just up. Arthur and I emerged from our respective tents and made our way to the nearest dunes, to relieve ourselves. As we passed Archie's tent, there was a hiss of a beer can being opened; Archie was sitting in the tent entrance, shaving round the edge of his beard with a cut-throat razor. His pipe stuck through the froth of shaving soap, his monocle was in his eye and there was an open can of beer at his side.

'Good morning, Archie,' said Arthur, reprovingly. 'A bit early for that first drop of alcohol, surely?' Archie had screwed his monocle well in. 'Good morning, old boy. I have two things to say. One: beer is not counted as alcohol; two: it's not my first, it's my fourth.' Archie liked to be accurate in such matters. Later he was to have a couple of gins and tonics, and a bottle of whisky would be opened at about 10.00 a.m. Years later I was to recall seeing him dressed as a Scottish laird on the back cover of *Country Life*, advertising scotch whisky; he had just the right features — solid, convincing.

My leave was thoroughly self indulgent. It was my second visit to the UK since leaving Oxford for Aden and even more memorable than my first, for which I had purchased a white MGA Mk 2 sports coupé and enjoyed the hedonism inherent in the ownership of such a machine. For the first and only time in my life, I had taken the MG down the recently opened stretch of the (then) sparsely used M1 motorway, at a speed of 117 miles an hour, just for a short distance.

This second leave was momentous, for two reasons: one, I was invited to Buckingham Palace to escort an old friend of my mother's at the disbanding ceremony of the Third Battalion of the Grenadier Guards. Morning dress (expensive at the end of a leave) and tying a tie in a stiff collar added to the problems of crossing London by tube, dressed for the occasion. However, to be photographed by American tourists, as Aileen and I entered Buckingham Palace by the side entrance, and the subsequent moving ceremony of the guards marching off to muffled drums, made it 'an occasion'. Elderly well-dressed gentlemen blew their noses loudly with emotion, and the Royal Family moved sedately through the select crowd assembled on the palace steps, above the formal gardens at the rear.

The second reason for remembering this leave, however, was that Lynette Waudby had completed her nursing training at the Middlesex Hospital. She was a Kenya girl; her grandfather had pioneered his farm site from virgin land at Molo, before the First World War. Our families had known each other there, but without any sort of contact between Lynette and me, at that stage. Now it was different: this was London. At the end of my leave she went off to be an au pair in France, and I returned to Aden, promising to keep in touch. Later she joined the Colonial Nursing Service and I wrote spasmodically to her in Nairobi. I was very busy in my new role; so was Lynette; news of her filtered through from friends who had been on leave and met her at the Equator Club.

So, on leaving Northern Deserts, my life was to change quite noticeably. Although I had one more tour to complete as a single officer, it was in quite a different role, an advisory one, for a start. The countryside, tribal ethos and relative stage of sophistication was a change. Wahidi was a mainly mountainous area, sandwiched between Mukalla and the Western Aden Protectorate (WAP). In my time the tribes coexisted, more or less, united in dislike of the Aulaqi tribes, to the west.

It was an area full of Old Testament history, of ruined ancient settlements, and of the remains of once mighty trade routes, winding alongside the sheer drops into gorges. One of the early incense roads must have started at Bir Ali, a noisome fishing village where the forbidding black lump of Husn al Ghorab (Cana) still showed signs of its early stone structures. From there the road went through Naqb al Hagar, still with many of its great walls partly standing, each mortarless stone so shaped as to fit exactly its fellows.

The find of the Himyaritic milestone near Thamud had sparked my first archaeological interest in South Arabia (I was to retrieve this stone to the Residency compound in Mukalla, to avoid the Manahil tribesmen's sharpening their knives thereon). Between Thamud and Sanau I had crossed the 'Ubar' track, a quarter-mile-wide indentation in the stony plain, running north/south, from the rugged mountains of Mahra into the gigantic sand seas of Saudi. It was plainly made by the tracks of thousands of pack animals carrying, presumably, loads of incense to the markets of Phoenicia. The locals had told me that the fabled city of Ubar (Ophir?) lay under the sands, which would part only briefly to reveal it. (The latest expedition claims to have discovered Ubar, but I think it is doubtful. The site mooted is too far to the east of the Ubar track, which would certainly have led to somewhere significant.)

But this was Wahidi and the signs of those who lived there long before the Arabs invaded were everywhere to see. To the north, at Al Abr, there had been the graffiti of waterers at the ancient wells, scribbling in their strange script. Near the ancient ruins of Shabwa (a no-go area, except to its inhabitants, because of the surface seepage of oil, which guaranteed a fight between everyone for ownership) little boys would try to sell me small alabaster heads of long-faced, ringleted high-cheek-boned (almost Slavonic, definitely not Semitic) people. There were charging bulls of bronze and seals carved in onyx, probably by the Queen of Sheba's people.

So far, I have referred very casually to the 'Himyars'. Pre-Arab history fascinated me enough to want to learn, just a little more specifically, about what had apparently transpired before the present inhabitants of this desiccated country had arrived. These people have been traced to about the fourteenth century BC, when they traded with Egypt. They are also likely to have had connections with the Babylonians, with the Chinese and with India, because it was on the shipment of their produce, as well as on the frankincense extracted from a shrub or small tree growing only in Southern Arabia, that the Mineans, their successors the Sabeans and the final pre-Arab inhabitants, the Himyars, depended.

They seem to have worshipped the moon, along with the sun. Perhaps the most likely reminder of this is the elaborately curved sheath of the silver *jambiyas* carried in some parts; the slightly curved dagger blades were contained in a sheath that curved right back on itself, in an elaborate sickle shape that had no obvious use (it must have been even more uncomfortable to wear than the straighter weapon worn by the Hadhrami tribes).

Where there is reference to the Queen of Sheba it is probably a reference to 'Saba' (the Sabeans) and to Shabwa, those remains just north of the Wahidi state. I got into the careless habit of just referring to the 'Himyars', because that is what my Arab colleagues did. Any ruins were 'Hamyari'. The exciting thing about all this was that it was possible to stumble across ancient remnants all over Wahidi and to feel that this had been part of a land that had been running its own affairs almost since the very start of civilization. It was Old Testament come alive.

Further up from Naqb al Hajr, the Himyars had cut channels through the living rock to divert the wadi floods onto fields, long since obliterated. The river bed had sunk 20 feet since then, so the channel entrances loomed above the vehicles. To the right, upstream from Maifaah, the state capital, was Sultan Nasser's home village of Azzan. It was the fabled base for one of the Three Kings who had travelled to the far north of Arabia, following that star.

Wahidi had a rudimentary administration to advise, from a basic office, complete with three clerks and filing cabinets. In this seat of government I was kept busy with the intricacies of inducing a group of medieval despots to accept the responsibilities of modern administration. My Arab colleagues were colourful, charming, courteous and conniving. Old bin Said, the one-eyed state secretary, who ran the sultanate on behalf of his feckless relative the Sultan, combined all these attributes, to a positive art form. His passion was intrigue over a good smoke, and his 'hubble bubble', his water pipe, went everywhere with him.

He was a great charmer; he called on my mother in Hampstead and they carried on a vivid conversation, with much hand signalling and flashing of gold-filled teeth. Lady Johnston, the wife of the incoming Governor/High Commissioner, Sir Charles, was enraptured with bin Said. He had breakfasted with his hosts and been served with a runny poached egg, which he had managed to eat, neatly and with no fuss, off the gold-and-white crockery, using only the fingers of his right hand. 'See Charlee, he has managed it,' said Lady J triumphantly (she was Russian and ebullient and a good counterbalance to her more staid husband, to whom she once remarked in my presence, 'Charlee. That is a teepical HE-type remark!'). I liked them both; they stayed with me in Wahidi and Lady J (as we called her) had been very ill, from some stale meat served at a banquet in the Aulaqi state. It was an occupational hazard for them, and the Wahidis were quite smug at the thought that it had been their disliked neighbours who had poisoned her.

Old bin Said was later killed, along with one of my successors in Wahidi, Tim Goschen, when a bomb was placed in their aircraft, but that was quite some years later. In my day we were preoccupied with purely local politics and with the business of getting through each day in as civilized a way as the limited amenities would allow. The main bonus was that I actually had my first permanent residence, albeit fairly primitive, without either having to pack it all into the back of a vehicle, or share it with an incoherent driller. The second was that I had two other expatriates in Maifaah, a positive crowd after what I had been used to.

One was the Agricultural Officer, Don Willcox, who was pleasant enough company but of a disposition that led him to seek out undesirable social liaisons. He was later murdered in London, on leave. The other European was Vincenzo Carozza, the huge mechanic: one of his tasks was to service the electric generator that provided power to my quarters and to the agricultural station (Maifaah had no electricity). The generator went off at 9.00 p.m., leaving us to the still, hot summer nights of barking dogs, sandflies, and small trickles of sweat soaking the sheets as one attempted to grab some sleep before the sun rose.

Vincenzo coped with the night-time heat by putting his sheet in the kerosene refrigerator. When he could take no more of the tiny incessant bites and itches, he would rush to the fridge, tear out the frozen sheet (to the accompaniment of tinkles of frozen sweat on the kitchen floor) and wrap his vast body before crashing onto his bed. Muffled roars of rage some 20 minutes later and Vincenzo would jump up to stuff his sheets back in the fridge. It made for restless nights; I could hear him all the way across the compound.

I had a battery-run extractor fan reversed, so that the moist air blew over me, for at least part of the night until the battery had expired. Otherwise, I would take my camp bed and maybe sleep on the wadi walls overlooking the small township. But summer was not the season for sleeping for more than a few hours at a time, any more than it had been in Northern Deserts. I toured a lot.

More usually it was by vehicle. Part of my role was to help improve communications through the sultanate to encourage the movement north of trucks from Mukalla and Aden on the coast. This was not only to link up with the traffic that served the Northern Yemen and the Hadhramaut, but to provide goods to those communities in the Wahidi hinterland that had hitherto had to rely on camels. I had access to sufficient funds to ensure that part of the ancient incense route was rebuilt. I imported a *muallim* (a master builder) from the Hadhramaut.

With the help of local labour we painstakingly extended that tortuous route right up to the high plateau, where for centuries the camel had been the only means of bulk transport. Now lorries could inch their way up the road that seemed to cling like a scar to the edge of the gorges. Huge blocks had been dragged from quarries many miles away and thousands of years ago; some had been washed aside and needed to be painstakingly realigned into position. Others were in place and provided the foundation for the careful cobbling that had been perfected by the famous Said al Ingleez, the road builder from the Hadhramaut (part of his 'highway' into Saiun is still used, today). The new road was opened about one year later, before I left Wahidi at the end of 1962.

It was quite an occasion. Wahidi had opted to leave the Eastern Aden Protectorate to join the Western Federation (of which, more later) and I, as adviser, had gone with it, into the WAP. The Sultan and his uncle, bin Said, used the occasion of the road's opening to welcome dignitaries from the West. I reported it to my mother.

The visit itself was fun. The aircraft landed at 8.30 and as it touched down there was the usual oriental extravagance, with four bullocks being slaughtered simultaneously, and blood everywhere, and tribesmen firing off rifles just above our heads. The party split up; Ralph [Daly] took most of them to Maifaah. I drove the BA [Kennedy Trevaskis, the British Agent of the Western Protectorate, based in Aden] with the sultans of Lahej and Wahidi to the road. That went off very well; the road has now reached about 6000 feet after climbing the most impressive pass and, as we stood at the highest point, about 14 charges of blasting powder went off along the route with great puffs and chunks of rock whistling up.

Then we returned to a lunch spread out on an awning near the workers' camp. I had taken all my carpets and cushions from the house and spread them about, and the VIPs sat on them. A particularly artistic arrangement was made of Granny's tiger skin spread out over a couple of camel saddles, and HH the Sultan of Lahej was reclining on it. He was most impressed and was amused to learn that my grandmother had shot it; it definitely made the day!

Other areas of the Wahidi State were only available on foot and the best time to walk was during the summer, away from the sandflies of Maifaah, up in the cool highlands. I took a protesting Assistant State Secretary, deputed by bin Said, to keep an eye on me, an equally voluble cook who hated roughing it, and a crowd of stoical soldiers, plus a dozen camels. I walked 100 miles in one week, through rough and impressive country. We climbed thousands of feet onto great bare slopes that then plunged to ribbons of green in deep valleys, with shady trees lining pools of water and not a soul around.

The water was tempting, but luckily I had been warned. It not only contained a number of the endemic bilharzia strains and so I was careful to avoid contact, but there was malaria, which was to bring me down with two severe attacks that dated from that time. Closer to more accessible areas it was possible to teach the villagers that those little wriggling things in the well or stagnant pool turned into mosquitoes, which made them *maridh* (ill). Giving them a small tomato tin of kerosene to settle on the surface, or a handful of those splendid little fish that fed on larvae, was simple and it worked. But bilharzia was a problem: it could only be treated at a hospital, or at least a medical centre, where a course of injections could be monitored. The trouble was that sufferers from bilharzia soon had their symptoms alleviated after just a few injections and they preferred to return home, with the treatment incomplete. The patients were unconcerned; it seemed no more than a common cold to them.

I was probably the first (and last) European to have done the trip after the explorers of the 1930s. The first few days were hard on the feet, particularly the Assistant State Secretary's; he started off in a pair of two-tone leather town shoes and had to revert to a camel for most of the way, only striding on his own feet when we were greeted at our destination.

The object of our journey was a remote part of the Wahidi domain, Yebeth, which had been visited by a member of the ruling family ten years previously. We received a great welcome with the usual fusillade. There were copious meals, which I worked off with strenuous walking. We would set off ahead of the camels and baggage, and then meet up with the next settlement to discuss matters of common import until our baggage caught up. I enjoyed a hot (canvas) bath every night and I returned, brimming with the feeling of having accomplished something out of the ordinary.

Other visits to the outer Wahidi areas were by vehicle, with some care taken over where we slept and at what time of day. It was not that it was exactly dangerous; it was just that the simmering animosity on the Wahidi/Aulaqi border suggested that it would be easy for an 'incident' to create an embarrassing moment involving a passing political officer, for which both sides would blame the other. The genuine welcome I received in that area, near Habban, was partly because Kharusi's successor in Al Abr came from near there; he was Ali Misaed Babakri and he had been awarded a Military Cross for his role in an incident with the Saudis, over the Buraimi Oasis. Ali Misaed was a subaltern in charge of Arab levies and it was his personal bravery that had saved the situation. Subsequently he rather tarnished his reputation by going into exile as an erstwhile supporter of the

South Arabian League (an anti-Sultan/anti-British Egyptian-backed group). He asked to come back, was forgiven, and had joined me in Al Abr. He was later described as having 'the heart of a lion and the brain of a sheep'. But he was a strict Muslim, which was a refreshing change from the Kharusi regime.

On that day I met Ali Misaed Babakri MC in his family home; I was treated like royalty. After the usual *feu de joie* we were welcomed into the fort-like house high on a hill, into a most luxurious room, 'all decked with Japanese and Chinese silks. The food was magnificent,' as I reported to my mother. But I was beginning to look forward to some proper restaurant food, in Aden.

It was all part of a plot. Earlier on I had suddenly written off to Lynette in Nairobi and asked her to be my guest for a fortnight in Aden, after Christmas. My letter was sent off on the weekly Dakota and I expected a reply in a few weeks. The first response was a cable: it said 'IGNORE LETTER COMING AFTER ALL.' Then the letter arrived, full of polite reasons why she had to go on safari. There were floods (so no safari) and she had agreed to come. I had to arrange with my new headquarters in Aden that I might visit them over the Christmas period, on urgent business.

With just a driver, an orderly and my cook, we drove about 150 miles to the beach track. through the cotton-growing area of Abyan to the sophistication of bitumen, air-conditioned shops, and stout men in white slacks leaning against the Crescent Bar. I met Lynette as planned. I drove her up the steep road round Crater and, half-way up, I heard myself asking her to marry me. We were unofficially engaged from then onwards and, after it had been officially announced, we had a ten-month separation before we could get married. But first there was the time in Aden together: it acquired a strange Alice-in-Wonderland aspect to it, due entirely to a dinner party Alastair and Archie gave for my fiancée.

110

# 12

# Oryx and other Occasions

A DEN was a wonderful place in which to get engaged, especially over the festive season. The various service units all seemed to have their regimental bands plus the trimmings — mess silver, elaborate parties and get-togethers. It was quite the thing for girls to come out for the cool season, joining the many families accompanying their husbands. In time-honoured fashion the visitors were known as 'The Fishing Fleet'. We had ten days available together (I had to spend a brief period meeting my new bosses and colleagues and introducing myself to the WAP headquarters) to enjoy ourselves at the beach parties, drinks parties, dinners and balls. It was heady stuff for me, fresh from my lonely posting with no one the other end except Don the Agricultural Officer and Vincenzo the mechanic. Here I was, my fiancée at my side. Everyone made a fuss of us.

Alastair and Archie, having terminated their respective tours in the EAP, were then sharing a house in Aden. Alastair very kindly asked me to bring Lynette to meet them; he would give a dinner party in her honour. His house, known as 'Bait [house of] Lake' (named after an earlier Protectorate identity and founder of the Aden Protectorate Levies who had lived there) was one of the old types. It had fans but no air-conditioning. I had stayed overnight in Bait Lake previously, in great discomfort, when returning from my second UK leave. My aircraft had landed in the late evening; it had been September and water was dribbling down the inside of the house walls from the humidity, at midnight. The fan in the spare room had been sequestered by the cook and, in desperation, I had wandered about the house trying to get a drink of water. The refrigerator gave me a fierce shock each time I tried the handle and every tap in the house was also 'live'. But this dinner party was during the cool time of year, so no discomfort on that score.

Alastair met us at the top of the steps, his podgy face set in a very hamsterish smile of welcome; he was really most hospitable and I appreciated the gesture. He swept Lynette into a chair next to him and fell asleep. Guests arrived and were seen to their chairs by Archie. After drinks, dinner was announced. Alastair jumped to his feet, gestured to Lynette to take his arm and he led her into dinner. He sat her down to his right and fell asleep, this time with a glass in his hand.

I was way 'below the salt' so could not offer support or advice. Course after course came; the servants would remove Alastair's plate ceremoniously and replace it with another one. Alastair slumbered on, his glass of liquor gradually tilting in his hand. Conversation would pause as guests awaited the glass slopping over. It never did; Alastair's hand would right itself. At the end of the dinner chairs were pulled back. Alastair jumped to his feet, planted Lynette on his arm again and led her into another room. He marched her up to a record player, put on Elgar's 'Pomp and Circumstance' and asked Lynette to dance with him. They managed two rounds of the floor, much to her credit. He then abruptly released her and fell into a trance, close to the record player.

With some relief, Lynette floated towards us. Archie, monocle well screwed in, watched her approach, with kindly concern. 'Well, my dear,' he began, 'How are you enjoying Aden?' Lynette started to reply when Alastair opened his eyes. 'Shut up!' he bellowed. He relaxed into sleep again. Shortly after the guests took their leave.

Our ten-month engagement would have been particularly hard for me to endure had it not been for the continued variety of my duties. Now that I was on the staff of the British Agent, Western Aden Protectorate, it was appropriate to take stock of a regime different from that in the EAP. It was, for a start, a federation of states. The Federation of Arab Amirates of the South was brought into existence in 1959 (the second year of my appointment to the EAP) as an initiative that would strengthen the bonds between the traditional rulers by creating an entity that was recognizably an embryo state capable of running its own affairs in due course. It also represented an effort to generate local support for those who had been under verbal attack from Colonel Nasser and the rest of the Arab world that saw a British-supported

112

presence in the Middle East as an anachronism, especially after the Egyptians' triumph at Suez in 1956.

The Wahidis had perhaps previously looked towards their fellow EAP states — the Quaitis, Kathiris, even the Mahris (though that was a state in name only: the titular Ruler, Sultan Issa of Socotra, had not hitherto dared to set foot on 'his' mainland). The hope was for oil, but PCL had made no commercial discovery. And so the Wahidis looked westwards, towards the Federation. There the Wahidi Sultan could expect to be made head of a ministry and there were funds to develop this British-inspired entity. Eventually, of course, it was intended that not only Aden would join the Federation (as it did, with unhappy consequences); there were optimists who also saw the EAP states being part, though that only transpired after the British had left.

The British staff of the Western Aden Protectorate Office (WAP Office) was different (in how it operated and in its outlook and priorities) and, having been schooled in the EAP ways of Hugh Boustead, it was a difference in attitude and in approach with which, subsequently, I was always to find it hard to live. It struck me on my first visit.

The WAP Office itself was situated at the new Federal capital of Al Ittihad (the Federation), a site between Aden and Little Aden (where BP's refinery was operated). Ostensibly the scene was similar to that at the Residency in Mukalla, with a core of expatriate staff and numerous Arab visitors. However, to sit in at a typical meeting, as I did once Lynette had departed for Nairobi, was to make it clear that the emphasis was apparently overwhelmingly to do with the enhancement of security, by keeping tribesmen and their rulers 'sweet'.

This was done, in the main, by providing supplicants with chitties entitling them to be issued with so many rifles and boxes of ammunition, free, from special government stocks. 'Give him "two and two",' was a typical phrase I came to recognize over the next few years. It was true that there were only a few areas of the WAP where there might have been an emphasis on development, rather than on keeping the peace, by what was known by my WAP friends, British and Arab, as 'keeni-meeni' (best translated as 'jiggery-pokery').

In this idiom and economy of arms and ammunition, on which the WAP Office relied, it was possible even to pay for pumps and other agricultural items by issuing a "two and two". The more progressive of my WAP colleagues undoubtedly did so; the others? It was just a means of keeping importuning tribesmen at bay, and even of arranging some underhand operation through a tribal intermediary.

I returned to Wahidi, thoughtful yet still unaware of quite what the implications were, of being a political officer in the WAP. Certainly I had determined not to issue one round of ammunition while I was still posted at Maifaah, whatever pressure bin Said and Sultan Nasser might bring on me. It was Brigadier (later Major General) James Lunt who had strengthened me in this resolve, when I had arranged facilities for various of his Federal Army troops on their first operation in Wahidi after we had joined the Federation.

'The two things that most impressed me ... were the roads, which I thought first class [he had been up my incense route] and the fact that no-one was carrying a rifle. I knew the moment I had crossed the border into Lower Aulaqi because there, by the roadside, were a couple of tribesmen, armed to the teeth!'

It was interesting how popular Wahidi became with the British military, mainly because it was new territory. It was a large area in which troops could exercise with a reasonable expectation of not being shot at. The Special Air Service was next: I wrote, during its visit in July 1962, when it was hot and humid:

Following on the first lot of army visitors, squadrons of the SAS (the crack boys of the army) started arriving in Wahidi in force, for a week's exercise. We were invaded by all routes: we found almost naked brown-skinned types under every bush in certain areas, all looking at the Wahidi landscape with a certain jaundiced eye. Among them was a squadron of Rhodesians, many of whom seemed to consist of tough Boers from South Africa. All of them were driving a most extraordinary collection of scruffy Land Rovers and were engaged in getting stuck in any available sand. I have had most of them in (about 100 of them) at various moments, to give them a beer or a cup of tea.

I have since had a fantastic amount of (fresh) rations just given to me. They seem to like living out of tins and any rations they get from Aden they just waste or give to me. I have 27 packets of sausages, for instance, which I shall have some difficulty in eating, I think, as next week I go off on a tour of

Western Wahidi and shall have to leave most of the stuff going bad in the fridge. However, it is pleasant to have visitors, even if they do rather overwhelm one. I have been asked to put up the Colonel of the regiment for two nights from tomorrow and the following day the C-in-C [Commander in Chief Middle East Command] pays a flying visit. So, as you can imagine, it has been a tiring period and I shall be glad of some peace and quiet.

Also helping to pass the time before the wedding in November were matters definitely non-military. I had acquired about £1600 to put towards the provision of a piped water scheme for Maifaah. Hitherto all the town supplies were carted by donkey, or by human porter power, to fill whatever tank each house might possess. I personally had a wash-hand basin and a canvas shower, but the lavatory (the 'zooli') was, as it was throughout the EAP, that old stand-by, the Elsan. John Lanfear in Saiun had a rather grand one mounted over the 'Hadhrami long-drop', the primitive system whereby the night soil was deposited down a shoot and collected to fertilize the fields. John's Elsan had been ceremoniously painted by his artistic wife, Gillian, with a discrete coat of arms to grace the vice-regal posterior when the Governor visited. It was John's successors, the Weakleys, who coined the little jingle:

> When the wind's in the east
> The zooli's a beast.
> East or west—
> Elsans are best.

The preoccupation with things lavatorial was only because it was an indication of where the EAP's priorities had been. Such niceties were left to the last until the more important things in life were assured, such as a roof over one's head and an ability to move about, in safety. In the WAP, on the other hand, the lavatorial facilities were usually superior to those further east, but the security ...

An irrigation man came up from Aden to supervise the laying of the piping. The cement and pipes had been brought overland from Aden and the project aroused immense interest. It really was very basic, but the thrill of transporting water over even a short distance, and to have it issuing out of a shiny brass tap into a cement basin, in the centre of town. Now there was progress indeed. Bin Said performed the ceremonial first gush.

I spent about six weeks out of Wahidi, after my return from Aden. It was all to do with the reports I had sent from lonely Thamud, regarding the last sightings of the Arabian oryx. The Fauna Preservation Society, at my urging, had started to assemble an expedition that could look for the last survivors of the once great number of oryx that had roamed the Arabian peninsular.

When I had first reported on their number there must have been some 40 remaining in all (probably the world's last surviving population in the wild) and alive only because of the remoteness of the area (the north-eastern corner of the EAP) and the fact that there was no oil company nearby. The danger came from expensively motorized parties of Arab notables from the oil-rich Gulf states, sweeping through the Rubl Khali and shooting down anything they saw: gazelle, bustard, or oryx. During the latter part of my time in Northern Deserts I received a report that a recent raid had shot all but a mere few; and *The Daily Mail* newspaper in Britain, which had pledged £5000 towards a rescue expedition, withdrew its support.

With the help of the World Wild Life Fund, the International Union for the Conservation of Nature, the Kenya Game Department and sundry others, another expedition was assembled and I was released by the high commission in Aden to be the deputy leader. I had first-hand knowledge of the area; I spoke the language and I had the contacts. It was a measure of the confidence the WAP Office had in capable and ruthless old bin Said that I was allowed to leave my post for so many weeks without a replacement; I could not seeing it happening anywhere else in the WAP, where it was judged necessary to post a political officer.

One of the expedition members, Anthony Shepherd, wrote a highly entertaining account of 'Operation Oryx' (*The Flight of the Unicorns*, Elek 1965); I merely added to the official account in letters to Lynette and my mother.

The expedition is now over. I flew down in the spotter plane a couple of days ago, to Mukalla, to await the arrival of the road convoy and the servants, whom I have to see paid off and borrowed articles returned. I didn't have any time to describe the expedition to you when I did write, as when we were on the job it was pretty all-absorbing and tiring. We had done about a month in the field, though we didn't have all that time looking for oryx. The final figure of oryx caught stands at three (two bulls, one cow) and one casualty, a bull that died shortly after capture; we found one cause of exhaustion was a .303 bullet in the rear quarters.

The heat was killing, very dry: work after 10.00 a.m. was an impossibility. This meant getting up at 3.00 a.m. each morning to be on the spoor by sunrise and so we never really caught up on our sleep. My health was generally good, though I had a couple of days of malaria and one day of a blinding headache. Grimwood [Major Ian Grimwood, chief game warden of Kenya and expedition leader] broke two ribs during the capture of one animal and we all suffered from Sanau water which, in addition to its strong Epsom Salts content, also had a good flavour of petrol and rust, after the long journey to our camp from the well.

Members of the expedition on the whole got on very well with each other — a change from the last expedition [Libya] I was on. Grimwood is one of the toughest men I have ever met. He smokes between 100 and 120 cigarettes a day, spent three years on the Burma Railway and treated his broken ribs with complete unconcern. We all got on very well with him, though there are natural differences of opinion.

I spent much time in the aircraft, which I did not relish (the chances of getting lost in such a large area were all too apparent) but I had to do the various chores of flying into a fort and arranging spares, of doing a quick trip to Mukalla to pick up some essential. I was very glad when the expedition dispersed without any mishap; the plane is so small and we invariably travelled overloaded.

The oryx are being flown out tonight by the RAF and should be in Kenya tomorrow, with the party. I have all the chores to clean up, this with an impatient Ralph Daly in the WAP asking me when I am due to return — next week, I hope.

I forgot to tell you about the most engaging member of our party, 'Herbert', an Arabian hedgehog whom we found wandering along one morning, before it was hot, in company with his wife. She never uncurled and, I'm afraid, ended up in the specimen tins. He, on the other hand, from the moment of capture, never curled up and spent much time investigating the Land Rover and people. He has enormous bat-like ears, is slightly bigger than the English type, and is a most attractive little animal. Herbert took readily to food and drink in captivity. He has his own travelling crate, alongside the three big oryx ones, which causes some amusement.

My attachment to the Wahidi States (in reality it was one state but there was a treaty with another old fellow who claimed part of the sultanate) ended with something of a military flourish. August 1962 had been particularly steamy in Maifaah; tempers were short with the lack of sleep, and it was a pleasant break to participate in a military patrol, to the north of the Wahidi State, where there had been some unrest. Both I and the neighbouring political officer, from the Aulaqi sheikhdom next door, came along. The patrol was done in a big way, at least in local terms: there were over 100 infantry, armoured cars and guns towed by specially-powered Land Rovers (how versatile that useful make of motor vehicle was in the pre-Toyota days). There was no military action, although there nearly was a fire fight when some tribesman saw the convoy and fired a rifle twice in a panic-stricken way (all tribesmen seemed to have guilty consciences and he must have thought we were after him).

As soon as we heard the first shot there were soldiers taking up positions, armoured cars rushing towards the origin of the shots, and each big gun with its muzzle cap off and a round up the breech. With some difficulty I stopped the colonel in command from starting a full stage offensive; the tribesman was apprehended without any further to-do. It was perhaps a symptom of the willingness of certain military to get set to, without a proper appreciation of the true situation. I cannot recall that particular colonel's name but, allowing for any previous engagement in the WAP (which might have prompted him to order an instant return of fire), I do remember him as being of the 'black or white' type of soldier, 'enemy or friend', who was incapable of comprehending the many shades of grey that lay between treating a tribesman with relaxed friendliness, at one end of the scale, and

118

recognizing that an aggressive assailant was about to renew an attack, at the other.

It was reassuring that the British Army turned out enough of the thoughtful, Arabic-speaking type of officer to make the political officer, on occasion, almost a supernumerary to the important decision of whether to open return fire, or not. This was the period of the British Army's last real operational service, as a matter of routine, under 'frontier conditions' and it was a training ground for some superlative military men whom I, as a mere civilian, could recognize as top professionals at the time, and who went on to make their mark as such. Names such as Colonel (later Brigadier) Roy Watson and Adrian Donaldson (already mentioned) come to mind, as well as a certain captain in the Federal Regular Army who had just sailed a yacht to Aden from the UK, one Peter de la Billière (later General Sir Peter de la Billière, of Operation 'Desert Storm' fame).

I handed over Wahidi to my successor, having weathered a series of heart-warming farewell parties from various Arab friends throughout the state, and flew off to Nairobi to be wed. The ceremony was in the same little Limuru church I had attended with my parents in those halcyon post-Khartoum days, when thoughts of personal tragedy were absent and there was no Mau Mau looming on the horizon. Singing at the ceremony was the Limuru Girls' School Choir, courtesy of my bride's status as an Old Girl, rather than of mine. I should have liked to have got some last wear out of my formal uniform (particularly as my best man, Tony Boyle, was ADC to Sir Charles Johnston and could have shone in white and sword alongside me), but Lynette put her foot down and I could see her point. Her beautiful dress was of off-white, and to appear to be the unsuccessful version of the contemporary advertisement, 'Persil washes whiter than white,' was plainly not an option.

We were booked to spend a fortnight in Beirut, which we had selected as an alternative to Malta. My nervousness had nothing to do with the subsequent picture conjured up by the bloody events in the Lebanon; Beirut was a haven for holiday-makers then, and an investment centre for the entrepreneurial Arab world. It was more to do with the fact that, in spite of a specific request to the contrary, the Nairobi travel agency had booked us via United Arab Airlines (the Egyptian flag carrier) to overnight in Cairo and from there on to Beirut. I had been cautioned in Aden about visiting Egypt; the pressure was beginning to be felt on British institutions and on those British officials who were connected with political affairs in Aden.

We flew out of Nairobi and landed in Cairo at midnight, and were herded into a hall filled with screaming humanity. A sinister man in dark glasses identified me from a list and motioned to me to follow him. Filled with foreboding I left my bride sitting on our new cases, seemingly to be abandoned. I was ushered into a small room, with three other officials, two of whom were similarly wearing sun glasses (at midnight? I was increasingly alarmed; it was a disguise). The questions were in English, and the conversation went something like this.

What was I doing in Cairo? I explained: we were *en route* for Beirut, our '*shahr al asil*.' (Silly of me, I realized, as soon as I had stopped being ingratiating.) Oh, so I spoke Arabic? Just a few words I had picked up. No reaction. Then — was I carrying foreign currency? (That was it then. I'd be held on the common charge of currency smuggling.) How much? About 15/6d, to pay for a taxi when we arrived in England. Did I know it was an offence to enter Egypt with undeclared foreign currency? Yes, I did. That was why I had declared it.

I offered to hand it over and immediately the atmosphere changed to near farce, as each official present felt through his pockets for the appropriate Egyptian change, pocketing the British coins. I rejoined my worried bride who by then was fearing the worst.

Beirut was heaven — a small hotel with a glimpse of the blue sea. We toured as far as Damascus for the day, pausing for a couple of hours at Baalbeck, where the remains of the Temple of Jupiter were a reminder to me not only of what I had helped unearth at Cyrene in Libya some eight years earlier, but of an elaborate frieze I had seen depicted on one of the postage stamps put out by the Yemen government. It was one of Yemen's ancient treasures and depicted the work of an artist who had apparently been taught by the creator of the temple at Baalbeck in the Lebanon.

Back in Aden later, James Nash, a WAP colleague, was to show us what he had under a green baize cloth in his hall. It was that very same piece of frieze, looted from the Yemen by a hopeful tribesman after the fall of the Imamic regime. In WAP-honoured style James had signed a chitty for 'two and two' (or whatever he considered was the going rate) and preserved for posterity one of the ancient world's masterpieces.

# 13

# Acting out a Role

OUR arrival in Aden early as a married couple in mid-February 1963 seemed an auspicious reminder that when I had been first introduced to South Arabia, I had known nothing. Now I had acquired a self assurance of someone who had 'been there, done that,' partly explained of course by the experience acquired in the EAP. Perhaps it would have been more appropriate for me to have acknowledged that life may have been pretty easy to date. I was now embarking on something entirely new, in an environment about which I knew very little and, because I had come out to Aden just ahead of my generation in the WAP service, I was the most senior of them and called upon to act in the next position above mine in the hierarchy. My callow ignorance was perhaps balanced by fluency in Arabic, but a conversational version learnt hundreds of miles away. My only other attribute that could be regarded as an asset was a determination not to become a casualty statistic. I remembered Johnny Johnson briefing me for Northern Deserts (it seemed an age ago) and talking casually about a dead political officer being a nuisance. I had certainly learnt to be a professional coward.

It said something about the cavalier attitude, not to say desperation, of the WAP Office that they were prepared to take such a risk in using me, someone as unprepared as I was, as they did. It was pure expediency that I was so used; it had nothing to do with any sort of career path planning for me. To employ me in so many jobs was to mean that I acquired a shallow experience of both Protectorates. As the demands grew for someone with a degree of first-hand experience and, concurrently, the numbers of such officers shrank, so I was to be catapulted up the tree. It resulted in my being the officer who had served in most

122

places in both Protectorates by the time the whole framework had come crashing down.

We had been invited to stay at Government House for our first few nights in Aden, a nice token of Sir Charles and Lady Johnston's appreciation of the hospitality they had 'enjoyed' (Lady J had been so frightfully ill) in Maifaah. Now I was to succeed the debonair John Harding as adviser to HH the Sultan of Lahej, premier Ruler of the WAP states and minister of defence in the Federation government: it seemed a plumb appointment. Our base was to be at Lahej itself, an oasis-type centre, out across the barren 40 miles or so that separated Lahej from the Aden township of Sheikh Othman. Our residence was a former 40-roomed sultanic palace, which included a cinema gallery we converted into a badminton court. I wrote enthusiastically:

> The house and surrounds are quite the best thing I've been put into yet (possibly the Hadhrami quarters are as good) but it far outshines my quaint existence in Maifaah. To start with, it is quite vast: four floors with countless little roofs on top of each other. We occupy only one floor. Push-and-pull on each floor and our main room is a big 'L' shaped one. Furniture not bad at all but, as there is so much space, we could do with some more ... Although there are masses of mosquitoes most of it is netted and there are fans. L is busy making cushion covers on a new Japanese sewing machine (electric!) and the sitting room will look very nice in the end. I forgot to mention we have a large garden round the house, enclosed by a wall and plenty of water (I hope). What rather adds an exotic touch is the collection of peacocks pacing round the house, three cocks and a hen. They go down well with visitors.

Actually, the WAP Office only intended to allow us to spend a couple of weeks out there, before temporarily installing us in a modern flat with all conveniences (in Al Ittihad) to take over as acting Senior Adviser (West). This was the first of many acting senior positions I was to occupy over the next five years. But I managed to persuade the WAP Office that I could do the job equally well from Lahej and, with some reluctance, we were allowed to stay put, and still relieve the Senior Adviser (West), to go on leave. This was Robin Young, one of the most significant personalities in that period of my life; yet, in the context of the total picture of what was to happen in the Middle East, an intrinsically trivial and rather pathetic figure on the Aden scene. I am still equivocal about the man, years later. I liked him, yet distrusted him; I never knew what he really thought about what I was meant to be doing.

As with Ralph Daly, Robin was a late product of the Sudan Political Service. He was immensely personable and (like a number of others in our service) remained a bachelor; he was large, avuncular and hospitable. He was most welcoming and kind to us on arrival. He lent us his personal motorcar, to which he had given the unlikely name of 'Esmeralda'.

Driving down from Government House on the day after we arrived, with Lynette at the wheel, we gently ran into the back of a car stopped in front of us. The embarrassment I experienced in telling Robin of the mishap was much worse than confronting the owners of the car we had run into (we bought the damaged vehicle). I expected Robin to be understandably annoyed, but he barely showed it. His strangely husky voice, no doubt damaged by his incessant pipe smoking, might have thickened a bit at the news, but he remained polite, making some joke about, 'Poor old Esmeralda.' I should have preferred more of an over-reaction. It was not a good start to a relationship with Robin, but somehow I doubt if our association would ever have been more than cordial, Esmeralda or no. I would have had to have started in the Political Service at Robin's knee, as it were (as did some of my colleagues who were deeply fond of him), for it to have been closer. I was always rather in awe of him.

There was plainly never between us that particular affinity that often develops between those doing a similar job. Perhaps that was it: we were not doing anything similar, except in the vaguest sense. I stumbled on, reacting to daily crises, making do the best I could. Robin, on the other hand, was so deeply engaged in machinations, I suspect mainly of his own making, so up to his neck in scheming and skulduggery (much of which undoubtedly passed for policy in the Western Protectorate) that I honestly believe he would have been incapable of viewing life from my perspective.

Robin Young was playing his scenario of 'The Great Game' (that Imperial Indian version of countering the Russian threat to Britain 100 years before). It was a year or so later, when I happened to be relaxing with Robin over an evening drink, that he started to tell me something about what he had been up to; he seemed to think he would have my sympathy for the mental torment he might have been feeling. It involved arranging for anti-tank mines to be placed on the other side of the border, where passenger trucks passing in and out of the Yemen would run over them. The resulting carnage would be blamed on the Egyptians.

Robin himself, like most of the stranger of his contemporaries, is dead now. His diaries (which he kept faithfully) would make interesting reading. I do not think that I have been too hard on him: from my viewpoint he was a strange man. How much he would have shared in outlook with our common boss, others can judge: I never got properly acquainted with Kennedy Trevaskis, the British Agent, except in the most cursory circumstances; until he was appointed to that substantive role, he always seemed to be away, or acting High Commissioner.

During those early days of 1963 in the Western Aden Protectorate, all was new and invigorating, and the (acting) Senior Adviser (West) was also new (and green); he had to learn something about his new bailiwick, running from the furthermost western tip of the WAP (opposite the Straits of Hormuz) to include Dhala, Lower Yafai, the Fadhli sultanate, and east to encompass Dathina and the Audhali state. I trotted out these strange names and areas, just to delimit the extent of my total ignorance. I started with my 'home' state.

The sultanate of Lahej straddled the territory surrounding the colony of Aden, which was why it was the first mainland state with which the British signed a treaty. It included a minor state, that of Haushabi, which was subservient to Lahej and, after we had presented ourselves to the Sultan's brother for luncheon in Lahej (a sumptuous palace with marble pillars and white-uniformed staff in attendance), it was on the Haushabi Sultan, Faisal, that Lynette and I called, once Ramadhan, the Muslim period of fasting, had elapsed. We had a great welcome in a modern little palace; it was Lynette's second visit to a Sultan's harem. Faisal seemed, at first acquaintance, to be an unassuming, pleasant person.

Lynette was usually able to travel with me round the western area on most of those early visits, to get to meet the local notables and for me to assess what each area was about. The relaxed security situation was to seem like a dream only a few months later when, following the overthrow of the latest Imam of the Yemen by republicans in September the previous year, the Egyptian presence in the Yemen increased its backing of the dissidents operating into the Protectorate and into Aden itself.

I took Lynette up to the Yemen border, through some rugged country but over tracks that were luxuriously smooth, by normal WAP standards. Most of our travel was on the coastal plain, except when we ventured into the foothills rising near the border. We travelled just in the one Land Rover, with a driver and a small gnome-like orderly who wore the uniform of the Lahej police, a sort of Wolseley helmet with a flap down the back.

The forts I was to inspect wherever I was to tour throughout the Federation were manned by Federal Guards, smart in their black and green. They had been originally an HMG-paid British agency force and the rulers' local gendarmerie; on federation they were amalgamated into a state force, with a part of the Federal Guard that served anywhere in the Federation, and a locally-based gendarmerie that was used solely by the state authorities. The Federal Guard was a practical balance to the Federal Regular Army; the former was controlled by the minister of internal security, Sultan Saleh of Audhali, and the Sultan of Lahej, as minister of defence, was responsible for the army, most of whose officers were recruited from the powerful Aulaqis, the neighbours of the Wahidis at the other end of the Federation. It was designed as a careful balance between competing influences; I was gradually to learn the politics.

We next travelled to Dhala, on the Yemen border, and stayed with Godfrey and Honor Meynell. I had been briefed about the remarkable Godfrey; he was the political officer there, and I was warned to expect a mixture of 'Sir Nigel' in Conan Doyle's *The White Company*, and Father Huddleston. Godfrey was to be awarded an MBE (at the same time as the Beatles got theirs for music) for apparently grappling with a fanatic who had stabbed Colonel Roy Watson, commanding the Federal Regular Army battalion in Dhala. I was told Godfrey had actually seized the bare blade. He plainly did not fit my chosen status of professional coward, nor did his father who had won a posthumous Victoria Cross. Godfrey longed to encourage agricultural development of the mainly barren and anarchical amirate of Dhala; he should have been an EAP officer, instead of being based in a fort on the borders of the barbarous Yemen.

Godfrey rolled towards us, his normal gait halfway between that of a sailor and a prize fighter; his welcome a mixture of hospitable charm and urgency to enlist my support to obtain resources for whatever scheme he was pressing at Dhala. He was constantly frustrated and depressed by what he saw as lack of practical help from those such as myself based on Al Ittihad. Some time later I was to find on my desk some notes written by Godfrey, which I took to be for me. They were in fact about me (he had left them out in error); they expressed his frustration at not getting immediate action from me. I did try, but it was very hard.

On that first visit we were to take Sunday morning breakfast up the Jebel Jehaf, the massif that loomed 7000 feet up above Dhala, via a rough vehicle track that lurched over rocks, with a sheer drop of a few thousand feet just a yard from the wheels. It was beautiful and forbidding country. To the left was the Yemen; on the slopes below us were a few thin terraces of cultivation clinging to the sides of the cliff. A neat cantonment of military tents was stretched out, away from the Dhala township. That was a company of 45 Royal Marine Commando, based somewhat incongruously 80 miles from the nearest sea. There was also a battalion of the Federal Regular Army, commanded at that time by a British officer but with most other officers of WAP origin, and there was the Amir of Dhala's contingent of locally-based Federal Guards. There was an expatriate intelligence officer and his wife. That was it.

A short while after, I was at another part of the border, at Mukeiras, where over a three-day period I met all the locals. Driving back was down the most terrifying pass I had ever descended — six miles of hairpin bends and a drop of nearly 2000 feet. This time there were two more of my political officers along with me, Peter Hinchcliffe and Stephen Day (who later married Lynette's middle sister, Angela, who had come to Aden, as did my own sister Sabrina, to make their personal contribution to 'the Fishing Fleet'). Peter and Stephen were on their second or third tours; their daily work was one enormous adventure in a larger-than-life game of cops-and-robbers, with the locals to be kept on one side and the baddies over the border to be kept at bay. There was always a strong rivalry between the two; their local knowledge, like Godfrey's, was profound and their humour infectious. I liked them both. Stephen entertained us and Angela at his base in Abyan: we rode the Sultan's well-schooled little Arab stallions.

I found it hard to relate these cursory tours in the Protectorate to my other life based in Lahej. The two seemed so disconnected. This feeling of unreality was not helped by a hectic social lifestyle, mainly in Aden itself. We also made the best of our palace in Lahej by entertaining visitors from the colony, who were intrigued to sit in our garden with the lion cages (dating from a previous sultanic owner's predilection for such pets) eating Lynette's chocolate cake, while feeding bits to the peacocks. Senior officers and their wives from HQ Middle East Command found this fringe of the Protectorate glamorous after the enclosed existence of being cooped up in Aden itself.

Even the High Commissioner, Sir Charles Johnston, made the trip one day, in company with the British Ambassador to Ethiopia (John Russell, son of the famous Russell Pasha, the Commandant of the Cairo Police who had taken a camel over the point-to-point there). The Johnstons were shortly to leave after their tour expired; Lady Johnston's health had deteriorated in the Aden climate. We missed them. Sir Charles was later High Commissioner in Australia.

We went to dine with the current head of the Besse family, Tony, whose father had been responsible for hiring and then firing my Uncle Archie in the early 1930s. It was strange to think that years later his nephew, as a guest, was able to enjoy a drink on the Besse's magnificent balcony, in company with Lord and Lady Shawcross (Hartley Shawcross was a previous British attorney general). There were also dinners at Government House, on one occasion for all the Federal and Aden Colony ministers to meet the important Mr Eastwood from the Colonial Office, and other visiting British VIPs. My Bedouin Arabic was stretched as I struggled to translate such passages as, 'Her Majesty's Government welcomes the opportunity of Aden having joined the Federation of South Arabia, and of encouraging closer links with the Federation.'

The political pressure was increasing on Britain, through the United Nations, where it was proposed in May that year to send a delegation to Aden to find out for itself whether the British were really preparing to hand over to the locals and to press for the removal of the British base. There was strong opposition, I had noted, in the WAP Office to such a visit, and the British government refused to extend an invitation.

Towards the middle of 1963 it was apparent that the customary peace enjoyed in Aden as a major duty-free port was about to be replaced by an increasing turmoil of strikes, demonstrations and, eventually, assassinations. The revolution in the Yemen was the main cause of the anti-British forces in Aden gaining renewed impetus; the National Front for the Liberation of 'South Yemen' (as Aden and the Protectorates were styled by the opposition) and known more familiarly later as the NLF, was formed in Sanaa: the Egyptians sent their forces close to the border with the WAP. Looking back, while all that transpired may have been inevitable, it was the United Nations' indirect intervention that was to signal a change from all that had gone before, putting intolerable pressures on the traditional rulers and making nonsense of the plans for a stable state to be forged out of the uneasy union between the Western Protectorate and Aden.

Seldom can there have been such disastrously mismatched partners in a marriage of convenience. Aden was essentially urban, reasonably sophisticated with a cosmopolitan trading class, and with a large pool of unskilled labour from the Yemen to undertake all the menial jobs. The Protectorate was a polyglot of tribal fiefdoms all vying with each other, controlled by influence and intrigue. Overseeing and attempting to control this mishmash was Kennedy Trevaskis (the High Commissioner-designate), Robin Young and one George Henderson, a gallant but boisterous ex-military man who had won a George Medal for his actions in the Protectorate some years previously. There was also Ralph Daly, the Senior Adviser East, who represented sense, in my book, along with Bill Heber Percy, the political officer at Baihan, and in my judgement the one presence that could exert some influence on my superiors. Ralph's administrative skills in particular were to be used later when, as Permanent Secretary to the Federal Minister of the Interior, the Audhali Sultan Salih, he (and a few others at the end, such as John Weakley) attempted to be the Federal Government's mainstays, when all about them there was increasing chaos.

As the political strikes in Aden increased, there was still no particular sign in Lahej, at least, that there was to be trouble. Lynette and I had made friends with the Sultan's nephew, Ali bin Ahmed, who bore a striking resemblance to Colonel Nasser, but who was a strong supporter of the *ancien régime* and a colonel in the Federal Guard. Ali drove a blue Jaguar, which he lent to us for a function in Aden that June (I drove all the way to Government House, Lynette at my side, with the heater jammed full on, by mistake. It was the hottest time of the year: I did wonder at the air-conditioning functioning so badly).

My Junior Assistant Adviser in Lahej was the nicest of men, Hussein al Wazir. He was small and precise; he was also of the cadet branch of the deposed Imam of the Yemen's royal house. He had no love for the Imam but he also had no illusions about his republican successors, whose habits were as barbaric as those they overthrew. Hussein liked to talk about his one visit to Britain; he brought us his photo album, to show us pictures of his charming wife in Trafalgar Square.

Turning the page, there was a large ceremonial arch, the 'Bab al Yemen' (Gateway of the Yemen). It appeared to have spikes with pumpkins sticking all over it. 'The heads of the male members of my family,' said Hussein, briefly. He explained that in an earlier attempted coup against Imam Yahya, his family had been rounded up (he was exiled in Aden) and the men beheaded, all except for his father who, because of his status, was allowed to be garrotted with a silken cord after saying his prayers. Hussein we liked very much. He was to be assassinated a couple of years later. He was the bravest (and most foolhardy) of men and was too proud to take precautions.

I concentrated, with Lynette, on the tranquil pleasures of living at Lahej: we were concerned that the summer heat was wrecking our zinnias, while the peacocks destroyed what else was left of the garden; one of them brooded on five eggs; and we tried to rear a baby hyena one of the guards had brought in. Lynette had started nursing again and drove every day to the clinic in Sheikh Othman, where she helped treat women and children for women's complaints and the usual range of childhood diseases, including measles and those other potential killers in Third World countries. There was only one female doctor and many of the patients had left their visits to the clinic almost too late.

Our existence was strangely suburban, leaving for work at regular times, Lynette to Sheikh Othman and I to Al Ittihad. Then life in Lahej suddenly changed. And it was never to be the same again.

# 14
# A Fiery Pace

GEORGE Henderson had departed on leave and Robin was back, acting as head of the WAP Office; I was the acting Senior Adviser West again, and I came to a meeting in Robin's office, to discuss the incidents reported of armed dissidents in the Lahej State, apparently stirring up the Subeihi tribesmen living over in the western section. Now there were reports of disaffected tribesmen disobeying court orders, and the like. I had met a few Subeihi myself; they were small in stature, with pointed ears showing either side of the little pointed hats they wore. The report had been received via HH the Sultan himself and if Fadhl bin Ali was worried, then it was time for the WAP Office to take note.

'I think you should accompany the military, Michael. Show the flag. Stay around there for a period and then back you come.' It seemed straightforward, if a bit pointless, given the other demands on me which mainly focused on providing what Godfrey needed in Dhala. My job would really be to stop the military overreacting. The last time I had done that was in Wahidi, when there had been one tribesman with a guilty conscience, letting off one round at us. He would be very foolish to do the same on this occasion, I had thought.

We were moving in considerable strength. We had a couple of companies of Federal Army infantry, a detachment of armoured cars and a troop of the Royal Horse Artillery (RHA) towing 75 mm. guns.

I told Lynette that I would be away for a couple of days; she did not like being left on her own in Lahej and so I arranged for her to stay in Khormaksar, the suburb of Aden that housed many of the service families. Given the amount of hospitality I had lavished on countless military visitors, I was slightly surprised that one particular colleague was not all that helpful, but anyway Lynette found a temporary berth.

I joined the convoy early the following day in company with a major from the Lahej Federal Guard and a local Laheji official; their job was to explain to the locals why we were making war-like noises through their territory, all in the name of peace. A long line of trucks, armoured cars, guns and light vehicles moved westwards into Subeihi territory. The actual travelling time was only a few hours, but it was necessary to stop frequently, to talk with village headmen and to ensure that any high ground ahead was investigated before the convoy proceeded.

The terrain was generally flat, but the track took us near several stretches of high ground, which merged into the foothills rising to the mountainous backdrop of the Yemen to our north. Reports coming back from the vanguard suggested that there was no need to secure the high ground, since there appeared to be no one around. Otherwise there would have been further delay, while pickets were posted to cover the slow progress of the vehicles past the spot. We ground on interminably, the dust settling everywhere and the heat making the slow passage almost unbearable. We stopped in the late morning, outside a depressed looking settlement of dwellings, most of which appeared to have been constructed in a hurry out of pieces of old sacking and grass. The Subeihis were very poor; apart from a touch of brigandage they fished and grew subsistence crops.

The baked fields were bare and the irrigation ditches were dry. The convoy had drawn up on a flat space near the village, which was set in a low basin of hills not far from us. I was trying to understand the village headman who had emerged furtively; the Laheji officials were firing questions at him. There was much waving of his hands in the air and shrugging of shoulders. It transpired that yes, he knew the men we were after but no, he had not seen them for a long time. Perhaps they were in the Yemen? It was decided that he would send one of his men with a message to them to come and talk. No harm would come to anyone who did; we just wanted to talk.

This meant that we would at least be there overnight. I explained the situation to the British officers with us; there was one with the Federal Army contingent and the Royal Horse Artillery had three. Their captain was a bespectacled, rather intense, fair-haired man. He could have been mistaken for a schoolmaster rather than an artillery officer. He nodded and called over his various non-commissioned officers, to

132

explain what was happening and how they should prepare for the next 24 hours. The Federal Army soldiers were starting to unload their trucks in a desultory way; some of them were making fires preparatory to brewing up a cup of tea. Then, without any warning, there was a slight whistle and a clunk, immediately followed by the crack of a rifle as a bullet smacked into the side of the dwelling near where we had been standing. It was followed by a ragged chorus of more shots.

Suddenly the somnolent atmosphere had changed: the men of the RHA had not yet unlimbered their guns and they quickly moved off, to take up position behind a ruined mud wall. Most of the FRA ran forward to stretch out in the nearest irrigation ditch, where I joined them, along with the Laheji officials. The headman very sensibly was nowhere to be seen. The military vehicles were streaming away from where they had been parked to a flat space the other side of the village. They were still not out of range, but at least, spread out, they presented a smaller target.

The two 'Ferret' armoured cars took off towards the source of the shooting; they had only proceeded a couple of hundred yards when they halted; a dried water course with steep sides and soft sand further on made it unsafe for them. They returned and parked. The soldiers on either side of me were returning the fire with enthusiasm, though I doubt if they could see the target. Shots hummed overhead or thwacked into the dried soil near the top of the dyke. I kept my head well down; the dust and sweat trickled down my face and into my eyes. There were flies starting to settle irritatingly. I looked out over the edge of the ditch towards the hill crest from which the shots were coming. I could see nothing in the shimmering heat haze. Another shot hummed over me. I buried my head below the parapet.

The RHA captain threw himself down next to me. We discussed with him and the others what to do next. It seemed we were bailed up by only a handful of tribesmen, but the danger was that as darkness fell they would be joined by probably hundreds more, only a few miles away over the Yemen border. We could doubtless protect ourselves, but it would be a long night and it was really not worth it. We discussed calling for air support, but thought better of it: we should return to Aden forthwith, while we still had daylight. The artillery captain suggested that he put down a couple of shells to interrupt the opposition's fire while we were regrouping. I doubted it would achieve much, but I agreed.

Hastily we passed the word to the drivers who swung their vehicles back into line, facing the direction from which we had come. We ran to them and as we did so, there was a satisfactory roar as two shells straddled the hill top. There was dust that swirled away and then silence. Then there was another crack of a shot and the opposition were at it again. The RHA immediately limbered up and the convoy groaned its way back along that interminable track.

We were lucky to get out before nightfall: we were coming up to the stretch of high ground we had passed without incident on the way in. Suddenly, the convoy halted; soldiers left their vehicles and took up positions behind whatever cover there was either side of the trucks. There was a crackle of shots from ahead, and back came the word that once again we were under attack. This was potentially even more serious; if we were pinned down until dark we would be unlikely to extricate ourselves the next day without sustaining casualties. It was far too close to the border and, because darkness would soon be upon us, we could not rely on the RAF to lift the blockade. A quick decision was needed.

We would bunch the vehicles nose to tail and they could move through as a concentrated block. All passengers would trot alongside, keeping the trucks as cover between them and the attackers who appeared to be grouped just on the one flank. The armoured cars could provide covering fire, if needed. We had about a mile to cover. With my .375 held loosely at 'the trail', I jogged along, into the area where the track wound along a defile with steep ground on either side. The firing sounded close, the noise sharp against the growl of engines in low gear.

We were through, with only the odd hole in the canvas and splash of paint removed from the truck bodies. We regrouped in a hollow hundreds of yards away from the danger area. It was still very hot; we had had nothing to eat all day and only a limited amount to quench our thirst. Now we were past the tiresome stretch we would 'brew up' and enjoy a cup of tea before we tracked that last stretch into Aden. I was just relaxing against a truck wheel, my hot mug of tea propped against a stone, when there was a phut! I could barely hear the rifle crack: a shot had hit the ground next to the tin mug, showering my tea with small stones. It was a fluke, fired from maximum range, and it reminded me that we should be moving. Disgustedly, I threw out my tea, accepted another (not nearly so delicious) and we departed, metaphorically tails between our legs.

With the Subeihi operation having been put on hold, I returned to Al Ittihad expecting to resume my more routine duties. At home we were preparing for our first grand Sunday lunch party, to which we had invited a number of local luminaries, including the Senior Air Staff Officer, Air Commodore Peter Cribb and his wife Vivienne, and Ali bin Ahmed. The cook, Mohamed, was looking forward to presenting some choice Hadhrami cuisine. It was early Sunday morning and, as usual, I pitched up for a half day's work at my desk at Al Ittihad. I had promised to be back in Lahej in good time to welcome the guests. I was already dressed in suitably informal shirt and slacks, ready to greet them at the gateway. The Lahej State Band was going to play for us. It would be an occasion.

Quite suddenly two things happened to ensure that the lunch party never took place. There was an urgent phone call from across the bay and, just a moment later, an enormous racket as an RAF 'Belvedere' twin-rotored helicopter settled down outside my office, with dust being hurled everywhere. It was for me, and the call was from Government House to summon me to an emergency meeting. All would be explained there. I grabbed a clipboard and scrambled in. There was the most fearful vibration and smell of kerosene. There were no seats, just struts to hang onto. We cut across the bay, over the lines of moored ships and above Government House, where we put down on the flat ground nearby.

I hurried into the main complex and into the conference room. It was an incongruous sight. Robin Young was there; he was apparently acting High Commissioner and our would-be luncheon guest, Peter Cribb, was acting commander in chief. Peter too had been dressed informally for lunch and so were all the other service chiefs. A major emergency had taken place with many of the top brass away.

The previous day a group of 45 service men and women had gone out on a weekend's 'adventure training', the euphemism for a camp under the stars round a campfire, and a barbecue, that sort of thing. It was to take place in the flat sandy area just out of Aden and a long way away from the troubled Yemen frontier. The party travelled under strict orders, which included stopping every hour to make contact with Aden and to report its position, by radio. If it were unable to get through for any reason it was to return.

The group was commanded by Major Walter Ormerod, OC Aden Garrison and a professional soldier. His second-in-command was also a major, but a lawyer, the deputy judge-advocate-general in Aden. The rest of the party was mainly RAF office staff (clerks, signallers and drivers, with just a small number of actual fighting men including a couple of Royal Marines) all of whom had been attached to head-quarters (HQ) and were aching to have a spell away. All male members of the expedition carried arms but, with the exception of the trained frontline men, there was no ammunition: that was packed in boxes in one of the lorries to the rear.

At first everything had gone to plan: one hour out and they reported to HQ that everything was OK, and on they went. The next time they did not get through and Major Ormerod decided to push on a bit before trying again. He and his Number Two had had words; the lawyer remonstrated at the non-adherence to orders, and Ormerod reminded him that he was in charge. By then it was getting dark and the terrain had changed: the group found itself groaning up a steep track that wound between hills and along soft wadi beds. It was lost and was heading straight into the Yemen.

The Yemeni tribesmen just the other side of the frontier could hear the sound of heavy engines and see the lights of the approaching convoy. They thought it was some sort of invasion and they determined to protect themselves. They ambushed the forward vehicles, just across the border. The front vehicle stalled, with its headlights full on. Behind it the other trucks stopped suddenly and put out their lights. The firing, coming from a mixture of shotguns and rifles, had continued spasmodically.

Inside the first truck next to the driver was a large captain of the Women's Royal Army Corps, who clambered out unhurt. A number of the passengers travelling behind, including some female clerks, had been wounded, mostly by shotgun pellets. The captain moved into the light of the stalled truck's headlights and spread her skirt to show she was a woman. The firing died away.

Further back along the convoy there was total confusion in the darkness; the groups huddled together for the rest of the night. The men who had their loaded rifles with them conferred; they decided to creep up at first light to assess the situation. This they did and the Yemeni tribesmen, observing their movements, shot them as they crawled. They lay in the wadi bed just across the frontier, calling for help, as the sun rose. Nineteen of the party in the vehicles behind escaped into the high ground and were eventually rescued from that side of the border.

C Company of 45 Royal Marine Commando was on its way to the nearest Federal Guard position at Tor al Baha. I was to see what could be done to recover the party and to keep in touch with Government House. The British government had no diplomatic relations with the Yemen and had to rely on the US government for help in any negotiations that would be necessary. I climbed into my horrible smelly, noisy and vibrating helicopter and we flew to Tor al Baha, where Lynette and I had visited only a few weeks previously.

I was landed near the Federal Guard fort and was told that all had been quiet since dawn. The Royal Marine major took me to where his men had taken up position overlooking the wadi and into the Yemen. It was a shocking sight: there were the bodies of the four men shot down as they crawled forward. Three were motionless and the fourth moved and called out. We could not hear what he said. There was nothing we could do to help him. We were expressly forbidden to cross the border. The Yemenis had apparently ordered the men and women from the vehicles to move away and they had been shepherded into a Yemeni fort out of sight. The 19 who had escaped from the trucks to the rear were already on their way back to Aden.

Ali bin Ahmed joined me from Lahej later that day and, with the fort commander's help, we contacted the Yemenis. I asked him to allow us to rescue the wounded men lying in full view in front of us and to release all the prisoners, particularly the women. There was only a limited response: we kept trying. I signalled Aden urgently to request the Americans to use their good offices with the Yemeni government and the latter's Egyptian overlords to allow us likewise. The answers were slow in coming but, just as it was getting dark, Aden replied. We should tell the Yemenis across the border that we had been informed by their government that they could let us retrieve the wounded men and that they should await instructions from their government about the prisoners they held.

About one hour later it was agreed that the Yemenis would let my driver and Federal Guard orderly move into the Yemen and retrieve the bodies in the wadi. They were all dead by that time; the one that had been twitching had been motionless for some hours. I was touched that my orderly, a tribesman, would agree to handle a corpse. He and the driver, one by one, gently lifted the bodies onto a stretcher. They were strapped into the back of my Land Rover. It was not easy fitting them in. Rigor mortis has set the out-sprawled arms at angles that blocked the access over the side of the Land Rover. The faces were very young (unseeing dust-coated eyes, open mouthed) and around the Land Rover hung that unforgettable sweetish aroma of human corruption. One of them had died early that day; the last had expired quite late on. He had only been wounded in an elbow but had bled to death, there, just in front of us. (The Commander-in-Chief presented a personal rifle to each of my men, later on. That was one occasion when a present of a rifle was fully merited.)

By then word had arrived at the Yemeni fort from the interior that they could release the wounded and the other four women. I got them away by 11.00 p.m. that night — young frightened faces, one with glasses, fair bedraggled hair in the headlights. I returned by helicopter, changed and slept. I was relieved that Lynette had been told that I had had to move out for the duration; the lunch party was postponed indefinitely (poor Mohamed) and she was keeping in touch via the BBC, where it was the top news story. I was back in Tor al Baha the next morning early, this time with the American consul from Aden.

It seemed that the Yemenis were sending an Egyptian colonel of intelligence to negotiate the future of the 18 prisoners, led by a defiant Major Ormerod who was refusing to let the Yemenis remove them. Ali bin Ahmed and I faced a press conference and gave the world's media that news. Ormerod was built up into something of a hero in the British tabloids. In Hampstead my mother was getting ready for an evening's bridge; Sabrina, who was watching the news called out, 'Mummy. It's Michael, Quick!' My mother cancelled her bridge and sat in front of the TV all night. I never appeared again.

The Egyptian arrived a day or so later. He was in uniform with a couple of rows of those bakelite-looking medal ribbons and the ubiquitous dark glasses. He was pleasant enough: Ali bin Ahmed and I conferred with him for some time. The Colonel was quite definite; the prisoners were to be taken back to Taiz where they would probably be put on trial. It might be easier for them if they were allowed to pass over a bit of Protectorate territory to get to Taiz by an easier route. Nothing came of that but it was the end of the negotiations. Major Ormerod was ordered to cooperate with his captors, to avoid any chance of their being maltreated, and they apparently had to undertake a very hard walk to Taiz, where they duly arrived.

Intensive negotiations resulted in the party being freed: the Yemenis seized the six vehicles and their contents, and were 'compensated' for the indignities they suffered from the 'invasion'. Major Ormerod was court-martialled and, probably because he had been featured in the British press as a hero, got off very lightly given the deaths caused and the loss of face we suffered, to say nothing of the propaganda used against the British government. He received a severe reprimand, two years' loss of seniority and was fined £200. At about the same time a young British subaltern had had his service pistol stolen while he was taking a bath somewhere in the Audhali sultanate. He was court martialled, received a severe reprimand, a loss of one year's seniority and a fine of £100. Major Ormerod was transferred to Germany where, I learnt, he was subsequently promoted to lieutenant colonel.

Perhaps the only nice postscript to the whole affair was the action of the General Officer Commanding the Middle East land forces, Major General John Cubbon; he had only been appointed a short time before, so I did not really know him. He wrote to me, in his own hand, as follows:

> Headquarters Middle East Command
> 28 June 1963
>
> Dear Michael,
>
> On behalf of the Army who started the whole unhappy affair, and for my own part, thank you very much indeed for your untiring efforts on our behalf at Tor al Baha from 8.00 a.m. 23 June until final negotiations on 27 June. We are most grateful for your help and guidance and I am indeed sorry that you were put to such inconvenience resulting from a clear-cut error in map reading by a recreational party.
>
> All good wishes.
>
> Yours sincerely,
>
> John Cubbon

There was a three months lull but it passed in a flash. Life at Lahej had become almost inconsequential while we busily occupied ourselves, I at Al Ittihad and Lynette at Sheikh Othman. The political news, especially from Aden itself, was unsettling. There were more strikes and protests from the large Yemeni part of the local population, who saw that the Federal rulers with British backing were determined to enforce the Aden merger into the Federation, if necessary by deporting the more vociferous of the Yemeni opponents. In the WAP itself the leaders among the sultans talked darkly of subversive elements inciting local dissidence. Sultan Faisal al Haushabi called at the WAP Office; Robin handed him over to me with an instruction to see what he wanted, and needed, in the way of material support. It was quite simple: Sultan Faisal required rifles and ammunition, he said, to keep his people on side, to keep them from being subverted with better offers from across the border, especially while he was overseas. He also asked that the Federal Army patrol near the Yemen border, to 'show the flag'. It seemed an awful lot of rifles and ammunition and more than I was authorized or prepared to release. Robin signed the 'two and two' book, without demur.

I returned to Lahej that day, worried that I was heading even deeper into problems that I could not begin to imagine. I told Lynette that I was to accompany yet another military force for a few days. We made arrangements for her to be moved out of our house, again ('like a parcel,' she had remarked). The force, this time with hundreds of troops, headed for the trouble spot, I hoped, without the hassles on that Subeihi venture. It was to turn out to be just as tiresome.

# 15

## Frontier Rites of Passage

W E were almost battalion strength with the infantry (about 700 men) plus the guns and armoured vehicles, which this time included 'Saladins' and 'Saracens', big armoured cars and what amounted to self-propelled guns. It was all very impressive and, even if it was a slight case of overkill when I considered our potential opposition was 100 or so tribesmen, I also had to remember that Headquarters Middle East Command needed to exercise the considerable forces stationed in and around Aden. (On a later occasion the then Commander-in-Chief, Admiral Sir Michael Le Fanu, offered me a Royal Naval aircraft carrier and supporting vessels to steam to Mukalla, just on the unconfirmed news of disturbances there.)

It was to be 11 days sitting in the open, the sort of operation Robin had expected of me on the earlier Subeihi venture, and from which I had fled with my military colleagues on the same day we had arrived there. This smart about turn would not be possible with the latest foray. On our arrival at a particularly uninviting piece of Haushabi real estate (all flat rock and sand) the army colonel in charge had methodically selected a suitable site for the force to, in effect, dig in. There were large tents to be erected, messes, proper field latrines and, of course, sleeping accommodation. Each tent had a small stone wall (*sangar*) built at least knee-height around it, providing protection while one slept. Luckily we had not had far to move that day; the soldiers were busy establishing the camp until just before dusk.

There were of course sentry positions set up, wherever there was judged a need to hold high ground; there were plenty of outcrops overlooking our camp. The guns were sighted on fixed lines of fire, which meant that anyone silly enough to open up from a point covered by a field gun or Saracen could expect to receive a direct response.

There seemed to be no local tribesmen anywhere on our side of the border; just over there was the Yemen lowering over us. The Colonel and I strolled round the perimeter while it was still light; the officers' mess glowed cheerfully. The Colonel asked if I played bridge. I said I was afraid I did not; he thought he had a four already. We dined well, seeing that we were living in the wilderness; it seemed very peaceful outside. The Colonel suggested a rubber of bridge.

The first shot was fired straight down the length of the tent, past the four bridge players on one side of the tent, and me on the other side, seated near the light, reading. The light was knocked over, there were a few more individual shots and then I could not tell whether the opposition fire continued or not, as all the guns on fixed lines opened up. I had crawled to the tent entrance: it was a pretty sight, if very noisy. There were shells lobbing in lazy trajectories, bright red tracer and then a couple of star shells to the edge of our camp, to try to identify from where the firing was coming. Our fire died down, and there was relative silence, broken only by the shouts of soldiers coordinating the response.

The opposition's few shots was more or less the pattern every night, except that we no longer dined in artificial light; we ate before dark. There was no more bridge and once it was dark we sat with no lights, a drink in our hands, talking quietly. Following on the evening's customary shots from the tribesmen out there, there was no longer that massive response of fire power, just a selective reply, based on whether the military thought they could identify from where the firing came. As a mere civilian, I was content to lie on my camp bed, knowing that I had that small wall of rocks protecting me. The danger, though slight, was there; the army had suffered some light casualties, but the whole operation was proving rather frustrating.

The days were tedious; I concocted various letters, which were sent off to the local tribal heads via a couple of locals I had brought with me. I was encouraged by a response: I thought we would soon receive a few visitors. They may, however, have been put off by the military, passing the time by mounting small vehicle patrols within the vicinity of our camp. Even so, there was little local movement. I wondered why this was so; after all, the locals were used to army movements round and about and it was not as though the sight of heavily-armed individuals was a rare one in those parts. Then I found the answer.

I was scrambling round one or two of the outcrops from which it had appeared firing had been coming during the night. Sure enough there appeared to be in one location a prepared position, a crudely-built *sangar*: discarded there were some instantly recognizable pieces of cardboard, the yellow and red packaging of 'Kynoch' .303 ammunition. It was new, and the serial numbers were on both discarded boxes.

Back in my tent I compared the numbers to the counterfoil of the chitty in my 'two and two' book: there was absolutely no doubt. These were two numbers from the list of boxes of ammunition issued to the Haushabi Sultan, before he left for overseas. I was extremely angry. We were coming to the end of a week of a tedious and expensive operation, mounted specifically to support Sultan Faisal's control of this benighted area. We had two soldiers slightly wounded already and we had tied up hundreds of men, not forgetting myself, prevented from doing anything meaningful. I sent an urgent signal to the WAP Office, reporting what I had found.

Plainly my message had some effect; the Federal Government contacted the Haushabi Sultan in London, requiring his immediate presence to explain why he had stirred up the tribes the day before he had departed. Three days later a military aircraft landed on our temporary airstrip. Sultan Faisal stepped down holding out his hand effusively, for me to shake. I ignored it and, in front of everyone, accused him to his face of trying to have me shot, producing the boxes and empty cartridge cases issued to his tribesmen. He had no answer but returned to the aircraft in high dudgeon. The military packed up and we returned to Aden. I was still resentful, perhaps rather naively, but I wondered how people in my position could be expected to subject themselves to every sort of discomfort, not to say some danger, if those whom we supported were snakes in the grass, and so blatantly at that?

It was a pointless line of reasoning and perhaps once again demonstrated a temperament unsuited for the role I had been given. The army withdrew to Aden, I to Lahej: Lynette had rather a miserable time staying with people in Aden during the 11 days' absence, never knowing when to expect me. It had been a rotten time for both of us. Then came the final shock: three days later, when I went to the WAP Office as usual, I was informed by Robin that we had nine days to pack up at Lahej and move to Dhala.

It was explained that Godfrey Meynell desperately needed a relief so he could go on leave and there had been difficulty about a replacement. That weasel of a Haushabi would have complained, with reason, that I had blackened his face in front of others (I had certainly done a good job of that, which was the only satisfaction I derived from the affair). Accordingly I was to provide the political presence at Dhala until we went on leave in March 1964, about four months hence. The sudden posting, however much I had brought it on myself, made me think hard about future service in the WAP; the 'plan' was for me to come back to Lahej after leave but it was by now clear to me that it was just a staging post for any vacancy elsewhere, or to go rushing into the blue at short notice. I decided to apply for a transfer back to the EAP on our return from leave.

We travelled up the stony road to Dhala, with a strong escort of Federal Guard. In the past it had been the most important route from Aden to the Yemen and it passed through territory of the Qataibi tribe, renowned for its defiance of authority and love of brigandage. It was to feature prominently in the operations conducted by the British Army, in the following year, but Lynette and I passed through without incident; our convoy toiled up the Khoreiba Pass, heavily picketed for our assent. It had been a trouble spot for ambushes ever since Indian troops in 1904 had constructed a track for mules. Dhala itself had been a security preoccupation with whomever was nominally in control, ever since the Turks tried to run the Yemen; there was a Turkish castle there.

Godfrey and Honor (she had already departed the scene ahead of him) lived in a house that was part fort, part residence. On the bottom storey there was a large empty room and an office; the large room had been used as a sitting room until a predecessor had been attacked and killed after dinner there one night. The sitting room was now located further up the edifice; so of course were the bedrooms. Godfrey had moved into the spare room preparatory to going on leave. On the roof was the usual flat parapet and a clothes lines. It was also used for informal entertainment, provided one could sit, with a drink in one's hand; there were sandbags around the low walls. The other rooms had ammunition boxes, filled with sand, sitting in the window embrasures; it made for that extra element of security, even if it did not add to the feeling of a home from home.

144

1959: From the sublime ...

... to the ridiculous

The Naid of Hora and his 'adviser'.

Al Abr friends – Shaikh Mohamed Said al Kharusi BEM, and his multifarious family.

RIGHT Chasing the Dahm

BELOW LEFT A Hadrami Bedouin
Legion 'Naib' (sergeant).

BELOW RIGHT And a
parishioner'.

fter lunch with the Muflahi
haikh and sundry followers.

Aden 1967: Lynette relaxing.
The Tarshyne Club. Charles
exchanging a joke with his
sister.

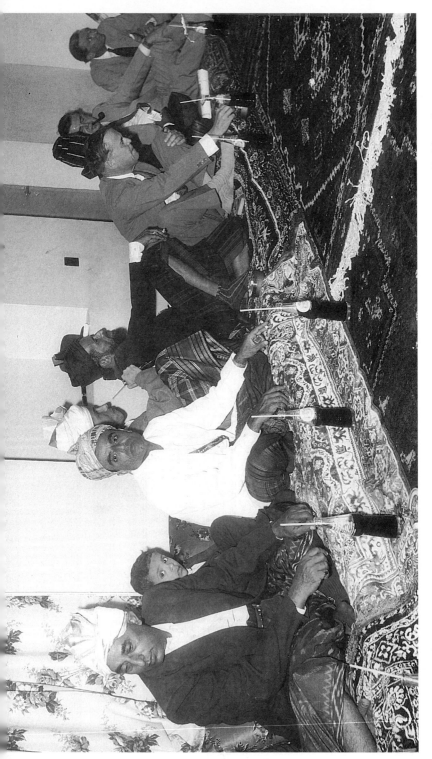

Government in the Federation of South Arabia, 1963. The High Commissioner, Sir Charles Johnston (third from the right), being farewelled by Federal Rulers. Kennedy Trevaskis is next to HE. Ralph Daly looking typically quizzical is

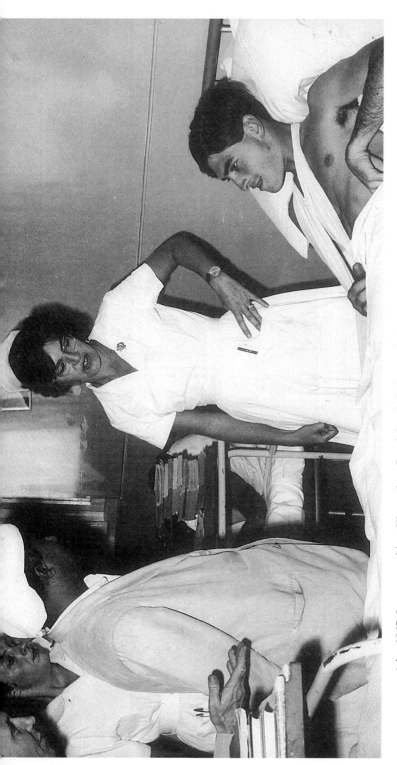

Aden 1967: Lynette working. Khormaksar Beach hospital. A wounded service man chatting with Sultan Salih, Minister for Internal Security. Ralph Daly looks on.

The last of the traditional rulers and the ultimate recipient of my 'advice': HH Sultan Ghalib bin Awadh bin Salih al Quaiti. He gave me this portrait just before I was ordered to flee Mukalla and desert our friends.

I wrote to my mother in London:

This is a cantonment of the North West Frontier kind; we go armed to the teeth, sleep behind sandbags and have barbed wire and sentries round the house the entire time and a two soldier escort round the clock. White women here permanently are taboo, except for Lynette and the intelligence officer's wife ... we have had a nasty shock. The second night here in our bedroom upstairs we were shot up by enemy tribesmen in bright moonlight, with one of the bullets hitting the wall in our room, about a foot above L's head. Another bullet hit the passage. Anyway, we kept our heads down and there were no casualties, though the room was showered with plaster. Lynette stood up to it with great fortitude but it was a shock for both of us. There has been nothing close like that since, thank God, but you can see what I mean about the EAP being a better place for wives.

Godfrey Meynell was certainly getting very nervy when he left here but he never spared himself and was a real fanatic to work with.

I continued that we had got the house looking very nice, but we were both suffering from the local water, or just the local germs. We had no piped water supply and what we used was transported in four-gallon tins or jerry cans by donkey, to the house, where it was manhandled to whatever floor it was to be used. Hot water for the bath was heated on the stove and then trundled to the bath. Once washed in, it was poured into the lavatory, to provide the essential flush, not available otherwise.

I was settling into the routine of political life, which consisted mainly at that stage of keeping in touch with the Amir and of trying to analyse the flood of misleading information being passed across the border when news came of a momentous incident in Aden. Duncan Sandys, the British Secretary of State for the Colonies, had summoned the Federal and Aden ministers to London, to confer. The High Commissioner, Sir Kennedy Trevaskis, Robin Young and George Henderson were standing at the airport waiting to see the party off. A grenade was thrown into the crowd, presumably aimed at HE: George apparently hurled himself in front of Trevaskis and copped the blast, as did a wretched Indian woman awaiting a Jibouti flight. Both died,

George after lingering for a period. (He was awarded a posthumous bar to his George Medal.)

We gritted our teeth: Christmas was coming up and we strove for a degree of normality in an increasingly worrying environment. We invited our respective sisters to join us (they would have to fly up and back because, in the few days since we had moved in, the road to Dhala was increasingly under attack). We had made friends with the Marines, where there would be a carol service, and we had obtained a turkey. There was nearly an official embargo on the women being allowed to fly, but they managed it, on Christmas Eve.

'It was a lovely day,' I reported,

and we collected a couple of young officers from the Marines and Federal Army and took a picnic lunch up Jebel Jehaf. We sat about 2000 feet up drinking Pimms made by Ł and it really was fun. Then we had a little rock scramble and got back before it got too cold. That evening the field intelligence officer and his wife gave a barbecue next to the house, in a spot surrounded by a six-foot wall which was comforting both from the point of view of security and of the cold! We roasted meat and drank warm wine until after 11.00 p.m., and then some enterprising types went off to a midnight mass at the Marines' camp, taken by a bearded naval parson who had flown up for Christmas. We didn't go because we couldn't face the drive in an open Land Rover.

The next day after presents the Amir called officially with his little boys and we filled them up with chocolates, as we were still having breakfast. We went to a short carol service with the Marines and then had very strong Marine drinks and the girls were all given cushion covers by the hosts. After a cold lunch we drove off to the frontier to clear our heads by gazing into the Yemen. The Marines, by the way, were presented with a bullock by the Amir, which slightly surprised them as they have most of their food out of tins. It arrived on Xmas Eve and was made a pet of so they had to butcher it quickly before the Marines decided they were too fond of it. Someone had thought it might be too cold during the night so they took it into a tent; they then thought they didn't want to lose it so they painted their name on its side.

The Christmas dinner that night was a great success: it was to be our last touch of family domesticity until we went on leave. In Aden George Henderson had lingered on until he expired, just when we had heard that he was out of danger. I flew down to help interrogate his alleged assassin, one Khalifa Abdullah Hassan al Khalifa (a prelude, had I known, to my future involvement at this disagreeable pursuit). In Dhala itself life continued 'normally': one evening Lynette and I were sitting on our roof watching the Marines and military responding with that bright red tracer to about 70 rounds having been fired at their camps, from Jebel Jehaf, behind. The Marines provided a touch of light relief with their mess nights. We sat in the open, well rugged up, watching the latest film on a huge white screen. There would be the whizz and crack of shots, and all the lights would go out. We would quickly get down behind the *sangars* round the camp. There was the rapid response of machine guns opening up on fixed lines, the deafening roar of a big gun. Quiet. The film resumed.

Away from Dhala itself there was a big Federal Army operation taking place, in Radfan. We could hear the guns booming on a still night. Then the dense mists and drizzle closed in and we went through a bad psychological patch, just for a few days, feeling hemmed in. Lynette was unwell, too: her back had been giving her trouble and to add to her miseries, one day I had poured a steaming four-gallon tin of kerosene into her bath, having heated it up on the stove under the impression it was water. In her hurry to luxuriate in hot water, Lynette had stepped into the hot kerosene, before realizing what was wrong. She developed a severe allergy that made a swelling start at her feet and gradually move up her body until at one stage her face was so swollen she had trouble seeing. The Marines' medic gave me something to inject into her behind but that was not a success. She seemed to be able to tense her muscles when I took aim and she ended up injecting herself, much to my relief.

Then the mists cleared and Lynette came into her own. A message arrived from a remote village saying there was a woman in desperate need of medical attention. There was no way of getting there overland, even if the increasingly poor security situation allowed it. I consulted the Marines; as it happened there was a pair of 'Wessex' Royal Naval helicopters temporarily based with them, presumably as part of the 'Operation Nutcracker' going on below, in Radfan. Lynette and I took off in a Wessex, with a Marine escort and a health assistant from Dhala, over the spectacular landscape of ridge after ridge of sharp peaks and meticulously terraced strips of whatever soil there was.

Lynette had never been in a 'chopper' before and she was transfixed by the open door and the way the naval pilot seemed to fly just above the hill tops. It was at some speed, so we would have been unlikely to have attracted accurate fire, but even so, we were glad to put down next to the village. The Marines took up positions round the helicopter. No one stirred for a moment and then, there was a slight movement and a small number of wizened-looking tribesmen came hesitantly forward. It was the first time they had seen any sort of flying machine on the ground and also the first occasion that the women and children had even seen Europeans.

There was some disputation while the health assistant tried to persuade the family of the sick woman to allow her to go by helicopter for treatment in Dhala. Lynette went to see the patient for herself; she was grossly swollen (she was later relieved of 24 pints of fluid from her abdomen; she was suffering from ascites, a condition brought about by untreated bilharzia). Suddenly, permission was given and everyone wanted to come aboard, There was another argument to make the point that there was only room for a couple to accompany the patient, at most. This was brought to an end by the patient being put on board and most of her relatives being forcibly ejected, and we took off swiftly, to make it back before an incident developed.

I was very proud of Lynette on that occasion and so apparently were the Marines. It is rare for a civilian woman to be allowed aboard a machine under active service. The Marines presented Lynette with a specially made pair of cardboard 'wings' with a crest attached, with the inscription, 'Dhala — flying doctor 1964.' It was useful to have a wife with nursing qualifications.

The end of Ramadhan in Dhala was celebrated, as elsewhere in the Arab world, with the Eid al Kabir (Big Feast Day), but in Dhala it was particularly memorable. Every house along every ridge was illuminated with fires. There were fireworks and the Federal Army fired off Verey lights. Tribesmen gathered to chant in front of the Amir. There were rifles going off all over the place and the faithful were called to prayer at 4.00 a.m. by a mortar; we were in a certain state of fear and trembling by the time the initial celebrations were under way. To remind me that it was not all fun and games, a mine had been laid on the track to Dhala, apparently intended for my assistant returning to his base from Aden: it went off under a loaded Yemeni truck. Strangely no one was killed, but a week later a Land Rover with nine Yemenis travelling the same route was mined. It was particularly horrible, as reported to me. Six of them blown into fragments, a nine-year-old boy among them; the driver and his seat were the only whole items left in the vehicle and it was only ten miles from our house. That meant no more drives up Jebel Jehaf and everywhere I went I was preceded by an armoured car.

It was all getting to be a worry, especially as we were soon to start packing again, prior to our leave and a re-posting (we hoped) to Mukalla. There was the problem of getting all our possessions by road to Aden; the last convoy had been mined twice. The mines incidentally were mainly of British origin at that time (Mark VII anti-tank) via the Egyptians, to whom the British withdrawing from the Suez Canal had left stockpiled in the canal zone. Talk about chickens coming home to roost! It became the habit for them to be laid one on top of the other to ensure damage to armoured vehicles. The best one could expect, I gathered gloomily, if one's armoured Land Rover went over a 'double' was for one's thighs to be shattered. I tried not to think of that possibility and we arranged for the tracks to be swept.

We were to be left with the Federal Army battalion only in those last few weeks in Dhala; there had been a mutiny of the Tanzanian Army and our company of Marines had been suddenly withdrawn and sent to Dar es Salaam to help restore the situation. We missed them: although the active fighting along the Dhala road had temporarily died down and the Federal Army was garrisoning Radfan, it was plainly taxing the military who had suffered 5 killed and 12 wounded, in the recent engagements. They withdrew from the areas they had temporarily subdued, away from the road, and the word was out that the Federal Army had retreated. Dissidents moved in again and Voice of the Arabs triumphed that the 'puppet imperialist forces' were being driven out. The propaganda war of the airwaves was almost as heated as the one on the ground.

## An Element of Luck

Reports received in Dhala were again rife that arms and ammunition were being smuggled through the amirate; I was sure this was so, but I hoped fervently that nothing would occur to prevent Lynette and me taking our leave as planned. It very nearly did.

# 16

## At Disaster's Edge

T HE Marines were still in East Africa; George and Liz Bowden
(the intelligence man and his wife) were away. Lynette and I
were the sole expatriates in Dhala except, as it happened, for a
dejected blue-eyed girl from some Midlands town who had married a
tribesmen who had been serving as a seaman on a merchant ship. He
had wooed this naive creature with stories of his castle in the
mountains. She had married and accompanied him back to Dhala,
where she was one of a number of his women who bore him a child
every year and carried water on her head, from the wells to the edifice
above. She was in effect her husband's property; there was nothing
Lynette or I could do for her except pass on her pleadings to be allowed
to go back to her parents.

Not even the British commanding officer (CO) of the Federal Army
battalion in Dhala was there; he had deliberately flown to Aden for the
weekend, leaving the senior Arab officer, his second-in-command, in
charge of the battalion. This was part of a policy of handing over
eventual control to the Arab officers and this particular senior *Wakil
Qaid* (Major) was destined to be the first Arab CO in his own right. I
have forgotten his name, but he was a thin-lipped Aulaqi with
punctilious manners towards me and the sort of self-righteous look that
made it hard to warm to him much.

The first I knew that something serious had happened was when I
heard a rifle being fired irregularly, as a signal, some way off. The
messenger was a Federal Army soldier on foot who arrived at my door,
out of breath. He had been a member of a major patrol from the
Federal Army battalion based in Dhala, which had been sent to follow
up on a caravan of camels. It was believed to be carrying arms and
ammunition from the Yemen to the Radfan dissidents, who at that time

were regrouping in anticipation of the major British Army thrust that was being prepared: this was to follow up on the Federal Army's 'Operation Nutcracker', designed to show that the government's writ ran where it chose.

The heavily-laden caravan had been sighted by the patrol and it was plainly up to no good. The cameleers were Shairis, well known for their devotion to all things outside the law. The patrol had nearly caught up with the camels; for some reason the acting CO had been leading the patrol. Forgetting his role as the senior officer and all the expensive training he had received, he had relapsed into the good old tribal tradition of throwing caution to the winds. He had dashed ahead of his men, intent on halting the Shairis. Apparently their leader had very deliberately turned round, dropped to one knee, aimed and fired. The *Wakil Qaid* fell over stone dead, and bang went that particular experiment in leaving a local in charge of some 700 men for three days.

The patrol had collected the body and was returning. The messenger had come ahead to alert the battalion back in their base, who, heedless of any wiser advice, were streaming out like angry ants, intent on wreaking revenge on anyone they might find in that particular location. I found out there was no one capable of restraining them. In fact, of course, there were no Europeans around at all. That was when I started feeling quite helpless.

However, matters began to sort themselves out without the need for an immediate decision by me or the army. The Shairis had gone to ground and had even managed to secrete their camels somewhere in the ravine-like country to where they had been pursued. Then, another *Wakil Qaid* came to see me and briefly made it clear they were losing control of their men. The army was still thirsting for revenge and he was fearful that the incident could escalate, with a force dashing off into the sort of country from which they would need to be rescued later, with all the problems that would cause, to say nothing of another propaganda coup for Voice of the Arabs. We discussed some kind of aerial response that would calm local feelings. I got onto the WAP Office. The Federal Army had the map references. The RAF was able to identify the area with the help of a forward observation officer, and was prepared to take the appropriate aerial action, which would be of a nominal response rather than anything particularly meaningful.

A couple of hours later I was sitting at the top of the gorge down which the Federal Army patrol had pursued the caravan. There, to the left, was the village where the Shairis had gone to ground and that bigger building had been identified as the village head's, where it was thought he had been aiding the Shairis. There was no sign of life; earlier I had witnessed a gaggle of black-robed women shepherding a mob of goats out of the village and taking refuge in some caves along the side of the gorge. They did not return for a day or two, still fearing retribution from soldiers or aircraft.

From my right and below me, quite suddenly, screamed in a pair of Hawker Hunter jet fighters, 200 feet below me. They steadied, aimed and neatly put their rockets through the biggest building. Faint sounds of shots reached me. Another couple of sorties and the aircraft climbed steeply and then flew off towards Aden. I took my Arab orderly and we climbed our way down the track already busy with grim-faced soldiers of the Federal Army.

I would arrive at the bottom in time, I hoped, to prevent those before me from killing the two or three wounded reported, who may or may not have been anything to do with the camel caravan. The camels themselves had been located; there were no rifles but they were laden with ammunition. Within the bigger building that had been rocketed lay the body of one man. He was still alive but, to my inexpert eye, it seemed hopeless: he had lost the entire back of one thigh and the floor was awash with his blood. I had taken a field dressing off someone earlier and I strapped this to the raw flesh. My orderly and I lifted him onto a solid wooden door, blown off its hinges, and we staggered with him towards the path.

We came across some soldiers; we put the door down, with its cargo. I told them to take it over: they refused: there were mutters of finishing him off and, perhaps, me. This was one of those times in life when one's immediate destiny is totally controlled by the events that take place, where any semblance of free will seems absent. Even allowing for the customary chaos in the WAP, I was usually at least able to make a decision as to what I might or should do. But on this occasion I quite suddenly recognized that I was helpless to do more than slightly influence events, and then in so peripheral a fashion that it hardly seemed to matter. The man was probably dead, anyway. I felt fatalistic, in a numb sort of fashion.

These tribesmen in uniform just could not be taken for granted, and I had a very uneasy feeling that I had overstepped the mark. What was I doing down there, anyway? Where was my resolve to be a professional coward? And what about Lynette, left alone like some medieval chatelaine awaiting the foolhardy crusader who never returned? I was a complete idiot who had lost his nerve. Standing not far away there was an Arab *naib* (sergeant) who had not so far shown any signs of getting involved, one way or the other. Mustering all the firmness I did not feel, I told him to assume control of the situation and instruct those men to remove the wounded man. He actually complied and, to my utter relief, they did what they were told. He was carried all the way up the pass to the local health unit in Dhala (such as it was). He took two pints of plasma that night in Aden and I was amazed to hear later that after a massive transfusion, not only did he recover, but he was able to hobble away, with just a stick for support.

At that point I was almost weak at the knees with reaction and the climb out of the valley and back to my anxious wife was almost too much. It had been a stiff walk from midday to nightfall, with no lunch. Lynette had been watching the jets wheeling and diving, but was unable to see at what they were aiming.

It was a grim thought that the need to hand over the key military positions to the locals as part of the political moves to establish federal self-sufficiency should, in one minor incident, show itself in effect to be a prelude to all that was to occur, in the rapid disintegration of the Federation of South Arabia. However, in the next three days that incident was forgotten and there were tribal meetings with federal ministers up from Aden, to discuss the future. Lynette and I finished our packing and flew to Aden, leaving our 17 cases to follow (safely, as it happened) by road. We caught a French passenger liner to the Far East, which was the start of a wonderful time away from our strange *Grimms Fairy Tales* world.

On a lighter note a mock military instruction was circulating around Aden military circles (doubtless the product of some bored duty officer) on New Year's Day January 1964, which was a succinct and witty reminder of the grotesque situation then current in the Western Aden Protectorate. It was entitled 'NOTES ON THE EMPLOYMENT OF FIELD ARTILLERY IN SUPPORT OF PICKETING TROOPS — MOUNTAIN WARFARE — ARABIA.' After a preamble that solemnly took off the military practice of stating everything at least twice at the start of such a paper and continuing with some in-house jokes, the paper continued:

> *Enemy* — consists of FRA (Federal Army) and FG (Federal Guard) personnel on leave, armed with rifles on loan from their parent units and supplied with ammunition by the political staff. Occasionally they are reinforced by small numbers of tribesmen and they are normally commanded by an FRA or FG officer on leave of field rank who normally has access to the headquarters controlling the operation.

The mock paper, after other pointed gibes at the uncomfortable relationship between the British and Arab military and the role of political staff, ended:

> *Successful Picketing Ops* — The enemy having fired a few rounds at extreme range, change into civilian clothing and then proceed on foot through the advancing main body to report to the political officer (who retires to the base area when the firing begins). On meeting the political officer, they make loud verbal protestations of loyalty to the government, accompanied by signs (normally the rubbing together of the thumb and index finger) and are given small supplies of rifles and ammunition as a reward for their devotion.

In our absence the pressure on the Federation from the Yemen was to increase dramatically. Aircraft attacked a village in Baihan and there were some other incidents involving their aircraft overflying the border. The Federal rulers demanded a formal response from the British government, in retaliation for the Yemeni provocation, and the RAF attacked a Yemeni fort with rockets (having given the customary warning). This went down badly, not only at the United Nations but also in Britain. It was considered that any further retaliatory action had to take place within the Protectorate itself and this duly eventuated in the Radfan, with the three British fighting services contributing to the occupation of various hitherto virtual no-go areas and having to fight their way into territory that, once cleared of dissidents, could not be held for long. So while the immediate political objective was achieved and the military involved acquitted themselves with distinction, the whole expensive operation eventually led to nowhere. Perhaps the campaign was best remembered for the names given by the British media to the tribal dissidents, the 'Red Wolves of Radfan', and a horrible incident in which two members of the Special Air Service were killed and their heads were displayed in the Yemen.

One of the main problems for Headquarters Middle East Command was that the political direction in Aden for the Radfan campaign had to come from Al Ittihad; as usual the combination of senior WAP Office staff and the Arab leaders they advised was really incapable of providing the sort of brief that could be seen at the time, or subsequently, to justify much of the substantial military and aerial action that took place, other than in terms of 'showing the flag' on behalf of the Federation.

It was also unclear to what extent the military cart had driven the political horse. As I had noted from personal experience in my various forays with the military to flag-wave, the presence of large numbers of British troops needing gainful use in itself generated the potential for military activity, which, in hindsight at least, could probably be seen as having been unjustified. The availability of the SAS in Radfan, while not quoted as a direct example of this, suggested its involvement raised the expectation of the level of conflict. It had been coming out to Aden for an exercise in any event and when the Radfan operation was launched, it was 'for real' that they were involved, in a crucial role, as it happened. All due credit to them for the way they performed, but it was an indication of how military resources could perhaps tempt the Federal and WAP politicos into escalating the scale of things.

The Radfan campaign did result in a Federal presence being maintained in the area for a time, but to what end, it was increasingly unclear. There was a privately expressed feeling at the time that perhaps the statement made in 1962 when Aden was merged with the Federation (that the military base would be retained) might just not come to be. At the time the policy was publicly expressed, the military was having problems with both Cyprus and Kenya as bases, and Aden had seemed the answer. But in July 1964, as if partly to answer the many doubters like me, the British government announced that the base would be retained; the catch was that independence would be granted to South Arabia by 1968. To many of us the two intents were mutually irreconcilable.

Our policy in the Protectorate of first inducing our sultanic friends to stay with us and placing reliance on their stability, then forcing them into unrealistic arrangements, such as their taking over the complete running of their own affairs in a ridiculously short time span (all this against the opposition generated in the United Nations, a strong body of opinion in Britain, the concerted political and subversive opposition of the Egyptians, and the antagonism of the urban classes of Aden) showed that we really were blind to the realities. I can make excuses for those of us on the ground (we were preoccupied in 'just keeping the show on the road') but for Sir Kennedy Trevaskis and his top advisers, with their overview of the true situation in the WAP, I really do wonder at the narrowness of perceptions at the highest levels.

We were all certainly guilty of naivety at best, and arrogance at worst. And the pity of it was that the Western Protectorate was to be no better off when we left than when we had arrived. The area remained insecure, undeveloped and backward in almost every aspect. Two examples: the educational standards throughout the Protectorate (outside areas like Lahej) just did not compare with Aden's. They were pitiful, in fact. Communications were a disgrace (it was no wonder that my road building in Wahidi should have aroused such admiration): there were barely a dozen miles of bitumen outside Aden.

By March 1964, when Lynette and I left for Japan, there was a growing preoccupation with the political problems in Aden, with its urban citizenry anxious to embrace the nationalistic mainstream of anti-imperialistic Arab fervour and throw off the despised status of 'colony'. We in the Protectorate had no real idea of how significant was the threat of industrial unrest and the related machinations, as I read of them in the routine intelligence reports that usually reached me some days after publication. They had seemed to describe another world from that of anarchical Dhala; perhaps their impact on and significance to the Protectorate tribesmen was much greater than I had realized. My early days in Northern Deserts with the most humble of Bedou listening in to Voice of the Arabs was an indication of how everyone listened, and believed in what they wanted to believe.

The politics emanating out of Aden and the Yemen (and to a lesser degree the more sophisticated parts of the Protectorates) was complex, made more so by the acronyms employed for the various factions that emerged. Two main political groupings had emerged in Aden itself, by that fateful year of 1964, that were anti-British and anti-federal in policy; and a number of splinter groups arose, merged and often reformed under different names throughout the latter period of the Aden struggle. The oldest (and in the earlier days probably the most significant) was the South Arabian League (SAL) founded in the early 1950s with the aim of achieving a unified state in South Arabia. Its most interesting feature was that initially it drew support from Lahej, the Hadhramaut and Saudi Arabia, mainly under the leadership of members of the al Jiffri family, prominent Seiyeds originally from the Hadhramaut. Its influence, never great with the general populace, waned with the emergence of the two other principal groups, which were far more radical in their approach and methods of achieving power. The most sinister of these was to be the NLF (National Liberation Front) to which I referred earlier, whose principal leader was Qahtan as Shaabi who had worked in the Protectorate Department of Agriculture. It was violently anti-British and against the Federation, drawing considerable support not only from sections of the Aden population, but from tribesmen who welcomed the chance to be armed with automatic weapons (we usually handed out .303s only). It was not formed until 1963 and it was not taken really seriously until its members showed they were ruthless in liquidating not only the British (civilians and military) but those Arabs who were members of the other principal political grouping, or who just got in the way.

This third political party or grouping was formed in 1965 and was known as FLOSY (Front for the Liberation of South Yemen). Like the NLF it was pro-Egypt and anti-Federation and also supported the Yemen. Unlike the NLF it claimed not to favour violence and its power base was the Aden trade unions, which gave it credence with certain British institutions, notably when the Labour government came to power in the UK in October 1964. Initially the Aden trade union movement had formed a political party, which was known as the People's Socialist Party (PSP), led by a solid sort of individual called Abdullah al Asnaj. It was a combination of the PSP and the SAL that had initially joined together to form FLOSY.

Looking back, Abdullah al Asnaj should perhaps have been cultivated more as the potential leader of South Arabia when Anthony

Greenwood, the new Labour government's secretary of state for the colonies, was visiting Aden (because of al Asnaj's contacts with the British Labour Party, via his own Aden trade union connections). However, he was regarded as anathema by the Federal rulers and as a left-wing trouble maker by other government figures in Aden itself. Al Asnaj himself had been conciliatory to the Greenwood visit and that would not have endeared him to the more extreme of his fellows, nor to the Egyptians who would have liked to have him toe the Egyptian line.

Perhaps, 30 years on, it is an unnecessary truism for me to note that it was the failure of the British, in concert with the Federal rulers, to find any common ground with a moderate like Abdulla al Asnaj: it laid the way open to the bloody period of strife that characterized my remaining years in South Arabia. The NLF had also briefly joined FLOSY in 1966, but soon broke away to further its own policy of bloodshed to control. The NLF was therefore dominant as the solitary organization that could take over when the British left in 1967; its often blood-stained marxist-oriented progress was a pointer to the 'rule of law' under which the state of South Yemen was governed, once the British had pulled out.

The 1964 campaign of violence in Aden was intended to take attention off the Radfan, where the British military had achieved a temporary dominance. It was also probably intended to coincide with the election of the British Labour government and the Greenwood visit in November. There were 36 terrorist incidents recorded (all in the last two months of the year) resulting in a number of military and civilian deaths and nearly 30 people wounded, of whom most were British troops. The atrocities set the pattern of the sort of incidents that were depressingly commonplace over the next three years. A British teenager killed by a grenade; a special branch officer assassinated (the NLF were to wipe out the entire Arab special branch staff in the next year or so).

Three years later there were nearly 3000 terrorist incidents in 12 months: although of these over 700 concerned British troops, there were at least 1200 Arab casualties, with many more uncounted in the ferocious inter-factional fighting that occurred towards the end.

But that is, of course, much later than the context of this narrative. The developments in that crucial year of 1964 provided a background against which I was to pick up the threads of what was ahead of us, once Lynette and I had returned from leave in mid-1964. My request to be posted back to the Eastern Aden Protectorate was granted, to our joy; but until we were to arrive back in Aden from our leave, it was not definite, such were the day-to-day apparent vagaries of political postings in either Protectorate. The WAP Office had the ear of the director of establishments in Aden and appeared to be able to override any appointments to the EAP if the needs of the WAP were unmet. Luckily for me, however, there were three new political officers, all unmarried, arriving in the WAP about the time we returned. The avenue was open for me to introduce Lynette to another way of Protectorate life.

At last we could look forward to settling into a community where there were other wives and a comforting routine that, however tiresome in its petty squabbles and social conflicts, did represent a sort of normality. Above all, Mukalla held out to us at least the prospect of a more secure lifestyle, free from mines and bangs and rifles everywhere. There was that superb beach for Lynette and me to enjoy together, and picnics. It was all going to be wonderful. And so it was — up to a point.

# 17

# The Slide Continues

IT was like coming home: I was welcomed by the Residency staff and we moved into the quarters to the left of the Residency main gate, as you enter from Mukalla's main street. Nothing seemed to have changed outwardly, except the expatriates. There was still David Eales, cordial, charming and always ready to accept an invitation to a drink or meal. There were Pat and Edith Gray, and Tubby Dawson, now married. The Resident Adviser was new to me, one Ted Eyre, a bachelor of exemplary habit. His deputy was the excellent Jim Ellis. There were a couple of others I had known from Aden; otherwise in Mukalla they seemed to be new to me, but a model of what a small community living in some isolation should be like. We dined together, picnicked on the beach, fished and generally lived in each other's pockets. There were the anticipated social cliques but enough wives not to make that unpleasant at all. At a baby clinic Lynette helped to distribute UNICEF milk and vitamins (most of which appeared for sale in the souk. She was puzzled why the babies never seemed to put on weight). The cook Mohamed was content; he had come home at last, with his wife and five daughters, after what he had regarded as the wilderness of Wahidi, the arrogance of Lahej and the sheer barbarity of Dhala. We even acquired some chickens. Lynette was expecting our first baby. Domesticity reigned.

At work, I enjoyed the emphasis on economic development. In Mukalla, sophisticated in comparison with any other urban centre in the Protectorates, there were organizations to overseeing key municipal functions, with the encouragement of us advisers. One such regular gathering is best remembered in verse, though it was composed in 1964:

## An Element of Luck

*Minutes of the 13th Ordinary Meeting of the*
*Quaiti Health Board held at the Residency*

*Present*
Minister to the Sultanate
Chairman Mukalla Municipality
Director of Education
Naib Mukalla Province
Sh. Abubakr Barahim
Senior Medical Officer
Resident Adviser
Assistant Health Adviser (East)
Sh. Abdurrahman Bazergan

At the table sitting round
Mukalla's Health Board to be
found,
Wasting everybody's time
Causing me to write this rhyme.

MSM is in the chair
Foxing everybody there,
Hiding funds beneath his coat
Denying that there is a vote.

RA sits and loudly wails,
Tries to keep them on the rails.
But, alas, his temper frays
As distracting points they raise.

On the flank sits Doctor John
Fuming as the words flow on,
Brings his temper to the boil
When they try to dodge night soil.

Doctor Tayib writes copious notes,
Tries to get the meeting's votes
To raise his status and his pay
And send the Doctors Khan away.

Old Bubakr Ba Rahim
Not so blind as it would seem.
He is expert Number One
At ensuring nothing's done.

Abdurrahman Bazergan
Listens to each mooted plan
But no comment to be heard
'Cos he never says a word.

Ali Baashan sits and smiles
Certain that his cunning wiles
Will ensure, when sinks the sun,
The night soil truck will neve run.

They all sit down at half-past ten
At half-past one they rise again,
Having come with firm decision,
Certainty and great precision,

To the startling conclusion
(Causing Doctor John confusion)
That points about Mukalla city
Have to go to sub-committee.

(Anonymous)

162

This piece of doggerel on the Mukalla Health Board, commemorated by a bored predecessor of mine, aptly recorded the cross currents, the machinations and the characteristics of the local members. While it might be seen as a caricature of local government committees everywhere, it certainly summed up the development stage of the Mukalla administration, at that time. The ongoing attempt of the British to focus influential local merchants and the heads of the various Quaiti administration on matters germane to the local community was always an uphill one, particularly as we were in an advisory role only. The composition of the Health Board itself, a mixture of the Quaiti 'old guard' and the British was not to last the decade and at least one member (Badr al Kassadi, my old friend from Northern Deserts days) was to be publicly executed, years later. However, it was not obvious in Mukalla at the time that violent change was ahead, although there were some worrying events that suggested our traditional peace and quiet might be about to disappear.

It seemed to start with the row over the Egyptian teachers. Traditionally the Quaiti Education Department had relied on a supply of teachers from the Sudan to staff the schools. This was an arrangement that went back to Hugh Boustead's time; he had used his good connections with old Sudan colleagues to obtain trained Sudanese administrators and teachers who generally were sympathetic to the British presence. Not so teachers from Egypt, who were inspired by the rhetoric of Colonel Nasser and would use their influence to whip up anti-British feeling in Mukalla, when we needed it least. That was the unofficial attitude at the Residency and, consequently, Egyptian teachers were barred from the EAP.

The Mukalla populace took it badly; trouble started with a strike and this was followed by small mobs parading down Mukalla's main street past the Residency compound and clouting a couple of HBL guards as they went past. Our house, being one of the two facing onto the road, was pelted with rocks, along with the Residency gates. I was acting Deputy British Agent at that stage and so had a direct hand in the security precautions taken. The main worry was of course that our families might be threatened, and Ted Eyre as a bachelor felt out of his depth, coping with some of the histrionics from the more vocal wives.

As it happened, probably because the Residency community was easier to protect and the HBL was on hand, it was the bank that suffered: windows were broken. The row over the Egyptian teachers simmered on, but its significance was more that it was symptomatic of the poison beginning to infect the hitherto cordial relations enjoyed with the people of the EAP. It was a 'tiresome week', I wrote to my mother, and that about summed it up. It did not seem serious enough to interrupt plans for her to join us for Christmas, which should have gone well but for the fact that Lynette's mother also decided she would like to come too. That was a difficult combination: two mothers-in-law do not necessarily jell harmoniously, however well they get on together elsewhere. One was allowed to take over the Christmas preparations in the kitchen (which caused the cook to sulk) and the other mother sat frostily by herself.

Politically it was surprising we had felt so secure as to have visitors. Only a month after the Egyptian teachers' flare-up I wrote to my mother, 'We still have the border crisis with the Wahidis looming; there are talks in Aden now, which the RA is attending so I am in charge here.' The next reference was to my old acquaintance, Abdullah Hassan Jaffar of the days with PCL. I continued:

Then we had a horrible murder up in the deserts when a chap I knew very well from the time I was with the oil company, was killed by his own guard. He was an Adeni but had been up in the deserts for years. No one knows why it happened but this chap was looking at a road site with an Italian tractor driver and as he returned to the car the Italian saw the man fire three shots deliberately at Abdullah Hassan. He then saw the man turn the rifle onto him so he ran off into the desert. He spent all day wandering around, no water at all and speaking no word of Arabic and little English. He was frightened that the murderer would come after him so he hacked the heels off his boots (in case he could be tracked). Eventually he was found more dead than alive late that night. Then the body, by then stinking, had to be driven 90 miles to be put on a plane. All very sad. We had patrols out all over the place but the murderer being local made for a hideout, probably in Saudi, so we took hostages from the tribe and things are now settling down.

The pressure was on. I concluded, 'I've had a bad time for some days which has contributed to the bad spelling of this letter.' However, up until Christmas, and the interlude of the mothers-in-law (whom we took in a long convoy through the Wadi Hadhramaut, one mother-in-law travelling at the front and the other at the rear) there was a calm that coincided with the cool weather. I applied to the High Commission office to do an Arabic course at the Middle East Centre for Arabic Studies (known widely by its acronym of MECAS) in the Lebanon, and to our joy I was accepted. It really seemed that HMG was still able to spare political staff to encourage advanced language skills.

In late February 1965 there was a move to encourage the reclusive Sultan of Mahra and Socotra to visit the mainland and, in particular, to consult with the High Commissioner in Aden. This was to do with future plans for the Federation of South Arabia (in which the British government and the Federal rulers were keen to include the states of the EAP). It also concerned the Sultan's nominal suzerainty over the large mainland mass of Mahra territory, where the oil company was intending to prospect but where the government writ extended barely south of Sanau.

I flew to the large island of Socotra for three days in a lumbering RAF Beverley aircraft that was to collect a party of British servicemen completing an exercise there. Socotra is large enough (about 90 miles long) to be identified on world maps as a spot off the 'horn' of Africa and it was part of the EAP.

We landed, apparently down wind, on a frighteningly short strip, pulling up just before a large massif. It was splendidly isolated. There was little to do apart from convince the Sultan he needed to make this visit (which he did, subsequently, but to no apparent result: there had been a British expedition into Mahra and there was a British political officer stationed on the coast, but with little thanks to the Sultan). I explored the area near where I was camped, admired a stunted cow (a special breed of dwarf Socotri cattle) and bought a pearl for Lynette, a rug and some honey.

On the second day the HBL radio operator brought me a disheartening message from Mukalla: MECAS had been cancelled, 'owing to the acute shortage of administrative officers.' We were dreadfully disappointed, the passages having been booked. But it was the good old WAP Office in a rage, in its state of chronic shortage of staff, that had brought the pressure for the arrangements to be nullified. If I was free to go on a course I was free to work in the WAP. That was to be it: I was appointed acting (always 'acting' but I was, I suppose, young for a substantive role, not yet 30 in mid-March 1965) Senior Adviser East, this time, in charge of Baihan, the Aulaqi states and Wahidi. Heigh ho. We had had no posting in our married life longer than nine months and our 17 packing cases might just as well, we felt, be left half packed. This time our faithful cook, Mohamed, would not leave Mukalla again, and I could not blame him.

After my return to help Lynette finish the packing we suffered a mood of listlessness, once I was surplus to establishment in the EAP. Our last function, which served as a farewell to Mukalla, was a cocktail party given for the new High Commissioner, Sir Richard Turnbull, who had been drafted by the new Labour government to replace Sir Kennedy Trevaskis. Dick Turnbull had been a highly successful senior administrator in East Africa and I had known of him there — first as a provincial commissioner in the northern frontier district of Kenya and later the Governor of Tanganyika at independence there. He was to wonder why he had come to Aden, I thought later.

We were based at Al Ittihad before the end of that month; we would have to get ourselves another car; we had not even finished paying off the government loan for the first one. We could have done with at least a short holiday together, before tackling the rigours of the Wild West. However, our abode made up for a lot: it looked well built, it was modern with lots of glass and a view across the bay. Our new home was situated at the end of a line of new houses constructed for senior expatriate staff at Al Ittihad.

Security had been thought of: there were arc lights shining on a space surrounding the houses and a watch tower, just out of sight at night, but manned continuously by Federal Guards. The main road from Little Aden round to Khormaksar ran just 100 yards or so across our front, but we were not worried by the traffic. It seemed peaceful and comfortable.

We have been extremely busy getting into the house, [I wrote to my mother,] and are beginning to feel settled. There are lot of advantages of living in a modern house, but we both miss the charm of the Protectorate houses where you can just knock in a nail as you feel like. A lot of our stuff there is just no room for. However, we feel better about things now — and the chickens appear to have adapted well ... Lynette got an Aden licence after passing her test easily so she is independent of me when I am tied up, which is a relief. The baby grows apace and she finds it very heavy and has difficulty moving around. I hope there will be no loud bangs to start things moving before they should.

Our small Yemeni boy is proving reasonably hard-working but came to us knowing nearly nothing. L is doing all the cooking which is a mixed pleasure for her. Lots of work in a hot kitchen but with modern aids, unlike the dreadful places in the Protectorate.

Domesticity apart, I had been extremely busy at work. Shortly after my arrival I had been up to Baihan for a couple of days and was much relieved to see for myself that all was calm. I was pleased too soon: Egyptian jets strafed where I had visited and the Yemenis shelled border positions, though with small loss of life in both incidents. I drove the whole length of the border; one of the routes was pocketed with mine craters — the result of the efficient system of local guards inspecting the track each morning to pick up the mines.

Back in the office it was as though I had never been away from the WAP Office — screaming Bedouin demanding assistance. There was some light relief, though. My opposite number for the West, and in my old job, also acting as Senior Adviser, was Peter Hinchcliffe, who exercised his keen wit wherever and whenever the opportunity arose. The first memorable event was that of the self-important Brigadier (he was not a bad chap, actually, who went on to greater things, I believe, in Kenya and then the Far East).

Peter's and my office were adjacent: seated on a bench in the corridor outside were our Federal Guard office orderlies. They were smartly turned out, but they were small and they did look like leprechauns. One day they had been sitting on their bench, laughing and chatting as was their wont, when the Brigadier strode by. They apparently paid him no attention and he thrust his head round the door of Peter's office where I was talking with him. 'How about teaching those two gnomes of yours the compliments due a senior officer?' he had said irritably. 'Sorry, Brigadier,' Peter had responded smoothly.

The next time the Brigadier strode by, there was a transformation. Both figures snapped to attention and saluted, as one. The first then said crisply, 'Good morning Sah! I am *G*nome!' The second then said just as crisply, 'Good morning Sah! I am *G*nother *G*nome!' And then together, 'we eat human meat!' They relaxed, secure in the knowledge that in their newly found powers of English (they spoke not a word) they had greeted a British Army Brigadier according to army regulations.

The other occasion on which I particularly remember Peter's wit was when Robin Young was about to go on leave. Robin was travelling by sea and he was escorted to the ship in Aden harbour where his colleagues sat on the deck enjoying a farewell drink. There was a stir: a smartly dressed government messenger arrived on board, asked for Robin, saluted and handed him a sealed letter from Government House. He tore it open: his face whitened (Robin was of ruddy hue, normally). It read (in part):

My dear Robin,

I am very sorry that I did not see you before I departed to London but forces of circumstance and lack of time militated against me.

I feel, and this may be a grievous disappointment to you, that with so many of the First Eleven, so to speak, away in London, I have to ask you to postpone your leave. I am very sorry to spring this on you at the last moment, but as Horace so wisely put it — '*dimidium facti qui coepit habeti sapere audet.*'

I hope this letter will reach you in time to postpone your travel arrangements and I really must apologize for any inconvenience caused by this last minute change of plans, but we are all worshipping at the same altar named 'Exigencies of the Service' and all that sort of cock.

Yours very sincerely,

R.G. Turnbull
(the familiar signature of the High Commissioner in his red ink)

Robin looked up when he read the last phrase which was the deliberate give-away; up to that point he had been totally taken in. He glared at Peter Hinchcliffe who looked innocently away — he had perfected the High Commissioner's signature after much practice and the Government House letterhead had been filched by an accomplice.

Our first-born, Charles, arrived feet first in the Aden Clinic, in the early hours of the morning. That was the only place for expatriate civilian mothers to give birth, in the depths of Crater, which was by then an unhealthy area for any Britisher to go, especially after dark. The forces' wives were well catered for: they had the new gleaming RAF Hospital with all modern conveniences, but I took Lynette down to the clinic and was forced to leave her as she took her place 'in the queue'. It sounded terrible, what she went through, having to crawl at one stage to the delivery room, through a vestibule area where there were babies recently delivered and not expected to live.

At 1.00 a.m. I returned to the clinic, my Arab orderly/bodyguard Salim keeping an eye on my back. At last Lynette was safely delivered of our strapping son. The room in which she spent some time was smelly and antequated and there was a problem with the bird life; big black crows used to fly into the rooms and, on one occasion, had come to grief in a ceiling fan, landing in a mess of feathers on Lynette's bed. A colleague of ours, a doctor in the Protectorate Medical Service, had taken his very pregnant wife to see the Hitchcock film, 'The Birds'; shortly afterwards the birth started and she was taken to the Aden Clinic. The next day she was lying in her bed, her newly born next to her, when she opened her eyes and saw a large black bird sitting on the end of her bed. She screamed and insisted on her husband taking her home. The Aden Clinic was not an experience to be tried more than once.

Lynette settled back into life at Al Ittihad, which seemed a haven of peace compared with what was happening elsewhere in Aden and in the Protectorate. An Arab superintendent of police had been murdered leaving the mosque. The increasing number of such atrocities was by now attracting much attention, little of it favourable, from the world's press. There was a certain amount of the British military forces at that time 'playing to the gallery', with mock operations taking place in Aden, which suggested that while the services had control, movement was impossible without armed guards. It was, however, somewhat prescient; in mid-1965 we could in fact still go to the beach and enjoy similar excursions, provided we took precautions.

We had some really shattering news in mid-June: David Eales had been murdered by his own men while travelling through Mahra country. We only learnt some days later what had happened; it took an age to evacuate his body, under much the same disagreeable conditions as with Abdulla Hassan Jaffar's. David had been sharing his soldiers' rations and, if I knew him as I thought I did, this would have been a deliberate attempt to sponge off them, just as David had tended to live off his colleagues. Apparently, it was all very quick and we hoped he would not have felt anything: his assailant shot him dead while he slept. So much for travelling unarmed, anyway. It was well known to everyone that David Eales spurned carrying a weapon.

By contrast the next two months passed pleasantly enough for us: Charles flourished and Lynette was occupied sufficiently with him not to worry about what I was doing, although once I had had to be evacuated by an RAF 'Twin Pioneer', having gone down with acute gastro-enteritis after an Aulaqi feast.

When back in Al Itttihad between trips I was able to escort Lynette and the baby out to Abyan, to stay with Lynette's sister Angela who had married Stephen Day. They were apparently surviving in the wilds on a diet of operatic music. Stephen had also acquired himself a Kalashnikov rifle — doubtless lifted from a dead Egyptian in the Yemen, where the Egyptian troops were encountering some stiff resistance from the royalists backed by the Saudis and by the British out of Aden, via the intelligence services. Our baby Charles was also presented with a Kalashnikov as a christening present from Mubarak Assaham, the *éminence grise* of the WAP Office. He was an elderly tribesman who had been adviser to countless British politicos since Belhaven's time (one of the first political officers, who wrote of him in his wonderful account of those earlier days, *The Uneven Road*).

To make our household complete (we already had a small cat) I was given a very nice young Saluki bitch by a tribal leader who remembered when I had said casually that I would like one. Life was really much better for our little family than I had ever dared expect after being forced from Mukalla. Even the transcript of a Voice of the Arabs broadcast by one Ahmed Said, calling on the oppressed to rise up and exterminate those wicked political officers, 'Karoosh' being named as one of them, failed to affect our morale. We were thinking Lynette and Charles might go to Kenya in September to avoid the humidity. Those plans suddenly changed.

# 18
# A Day of Reckoning

I provisionally booked Lynette's and Charles's passages to Kenya, for a month from 7 September. July in fact was not too bad for that torrid climate, with only one memorable sand storm; as at Mukalla the sea temperature dropped in summer, and swimming was a joy. In the meantime our social life continued apace: Ali bin Ahmed came to lunch with us at Al Ittihad. He had returned from Britain where he had been a guest at sister Sabrina's wedding. She had married her Royal Anglian officer and he had returned to an unaccompanied posting in the Oman, and Sabrina was back in Aden, continuing to work as an air hostess for Aden Airways. Ali had brought them a packaged dinner coffee set which he presented at the wedding and they had casually tossed it aside until after the festivities. On opening it later they were thrilled to find it was the most expensive bone china and luckily unbroken after the casual handling. Ali bin Ahmed asked us back to lunch in Lahej, in early August.

In the meantime we looked after Anthony Verrier who was writing for *The Economist*. He had a rather worrying reputation, up to which he lived in his first article on Aden, in which he described the Commander-in-Chief (while staying with him) as being keener on building roads than fighting a war against dissidents. He had also hinted at a possible mutiny in the Federal Army: I took him up to Baihan and kept a close eye on him while he interviewed the Amir, who said just what he thought of Mr Secretary Greenwood's policies.

Jamila, the Saluki, was gradually settling in, though at one point she slipped her lead and was off across the sand desert that surrounded Al Ittihad. I went out in a vehicle at 5.00 a.m. the next morning and by pure luck found her ten miles away. I had got into a habit of walking her last thing in the evening, around the security light pylons, to ensure she went comfortably to bed.

The first week of August was steamy and the evenings were heavy. On 6 August we had given Salim, my personal orderly, the day off and had spent that day at Lahej, lunching with Ali bin Ahmed. Poor little Charles had felt the heat during the drive to and from Lahej; that evening in our upstairs bedroom Lynette put him down in the wicker-work crib in which he slept, on the verandah close by the double glass doors, open to catch any breeze that might be around. She was standing in the same area, ironing, with the lights full on, so as to see what she was doing. The curtains were tightly pulled back, so as not to interrupt the breeze.

I was waiting for the end of the TV news at 8.30 p.m., so that I could put Jamila on her lead and promenade her round the security light standards, as had been my wont. At 8.30, before I could go out, the phone rang; it was Sabrina, in Maalla across the bay, having just returned from a flight. We had not spoken together for some time and exchanged gossip for about ten minutes. She gave me news of her Bill and I told her of our day at Lahej and how Charles was progressing. Before I had put the phone down there was a loud rattle of a machine gun close outside the house.

Lynette and I reacted quite instinctively to the accustomed sound of gunfire. She turned out the lights near her and crawled on hands and knees to pick Charles out of the crib, hurling herself on top of him. I just had time to snatch at the other light switch, above the telephone, and beat the world standing record for a sideways leap. With Lynette still crawling and holding the baby I landed on top of them both and, as I did so, there was the most petrifying BANG. The wall above the telephone disintegrated as a bazooka anti-tank missile penetrated the stone, having exploded on impact.

Bits of white-hot metal and phosphorus shredded all the furniture and shattered the glass doors, windows and mirrors into jagged fragments that also whistled round, just a foot above my head. There was then a sudden silence in the room: we were both partly deafened by the blast, and choking in the dust and fumes, unable to see clearly. I heard Lynette, 'Oh my baby! My baby!' and then — the best sound of all we could have hoped for — the wail of a badly frightened baby, having been wakened from a deep sleep and hurled into a corner,

Charles and Lynette were alive, and I was fine. Charles had collected a bruise and a few tiny burns on his back, but that was all.

There was chaos outside as I staggered to the phone. It was working. The operator came on the line and I bellowed, *'Towari! Towari!'* (Emergency! Emergency!) and gave him my location. Meanwhile the Federal Guard had opened up with enthusiasm, firing in all directions, but not at anything in particular. They had been caught completely by surprise, as had we all. There was a pounding on the stairs and a mob of Arab soldiers burst into the room. Someone helped Lynette and Charles towards the door; there was a smell of burning, of cloth and a sound of crackling wood. We pulled open the built-in cupboards to find that bits of shrapnel had penetrated the doors and set light to the contents. Soldiers reached inside to grab at smouldering cotton towels and ran round the ruined bedroom, trying to extinguish them. The scene did have its comical side.

As we were being helped away the phone rang. It was for me and it was the BBC correspondent across the bay in Aden. 'I hear there's been a bit of a to-do over your way,' he said laconically. I told him what had happened but was too shocked to be able to give him the whole picture. That was clear, once it was daylight. The next day the British papers carried front-page reports, based mainly on my brief interview. Lynette was very brave throughout the whole ordeal and I was proud of her — it was her second close encounter. My mother cabled her congratulations on our close escape.

I was unable to claim a direct link between Voice of the Arabs and the attack, but it had been organized carefully to take advantage of the house being positioned at the end of the row, of Salim being away for the day and of my stupidity in walking the dog every night at the same time. It had been a small gang: the plan was for the getaway car to be parked on the main road, only a few hundred yards away. The gang was able to take up a position behind a sand drift just a few yards from one of the security light standards, around which I walked nightly. The scheme was to gun me down as I stood (they could hardly have missed), create whatever diversion they could with the missiles and withdraw in the confusion to the car, which would take them to the border crossing. They had to be there by 10.00 p.m. before a certain customs officer went off duty.

Sabrina's call threw the whole plan out — the timing was so tight. Accordingly they opened up with the machine gun and managed to fire three missiles, two of which exploded harmlessly off the garden walls. The postscript to the story was how I got to learn the details at all; the gang was later captured and interned. I met them a year after and one of them, quite cheerfully, told me the story. He seemed to bear me no personal ill will. As for my emotions: he meant nothing to me by then.

We had to spend some time away while the house was rebuilt and, since Kenya did not seem to be an option (Lynette's mother could not have us to stay), we booked a short expensive holiday in Ethiopia, spending a few days in Addis Ababa and then a week in Asmara, where I left Lynette to relax with Charles for a bit longer. We were due to take proper leave at Christmas and visit Kenya, South Africa, Australia and New Zealand — all part of the quest for where to settle after Aden. Ethiopia was interesting but hardly relaxation. Addis was a contrast of modern hotels right next to squalor; great eucalyptuses towered above bare red eroded slopes. Asmara was like staying in a pleasant, rather boring, Italian provincial town.

Strangely enough, after the incident it was possible to throw ourselves once more into the swing of life, without dwelling on what might have been. I had learnt a valuable lesson, and at the right time. The murder gangs were now in full swing, although they were often as inept as they had been with us. In Aden the increase to 237 casualties, from 36 the previous year, was an indication of the serious deterioration in the security situation. There were also strikes and demonstrations, as though to show that if not all the murder attempts were successful, the local Aden population was in general thoroughly subverted and controlled.

The High Commissioner had attempted to react with vigour to the decline in the Aden government's ability to carry out normal administrative tasks. A state of emergency was declared which, though it made it easier for the security forces to undertake what needed to be done, was a setback to those who had hoped that the new Federation would progress smoothly towards running its own affairs. It was also a propaganda victory for the terrorists and their fellow travellers whose aim was ultimately to make Aden ungovernable, and force withdrawal of the British. On 4 October 1965 *The Daily Express* described the worsening situation just as we, on the spot, would have put it:

'Demands for independence. Demonstrations by students who do more demonstrating than studying. Strikes. Riots, buildings fired, cars smashed, Britons stoned. And then the bomb throwers, the terrorists whose target is the British serviceman, his wife, his children ... This was Aden yesterday. This is where we came in, so many yesterdays ago.'

Sir Richard Turnbull, rather later on, circulated a pamphlet to British residents that in matter-of-fact terms clearly identified the almost daily deterioration from the perspective of the residents of Aden, rather than from that of a visiting newspaper reporter. I reproduce it here because it was at this stage of the escalation in urban violence that everyone should have known what was happening, although it was only much later that it was thought necessary to state what was by then self-evident — and not leave publicity just to the press.

It must be obvious to everybody that we have a far more dangerous situation on our hands than before. Here are a few points that require your urgent and careful attention.

1.    The mine in the Maalla flat that killed two European women on 28 February was planted by a servant! The NLF are now claiming responsibility for this. You should search your premises often, especially if the flat or house is unattended during working hours. Take this seriously and do not think, 'This could not happen to me.'
2.    Do not leave your appointment diary open so that others can see it. Only you need to know that you have an invitation but this information may be of vital interest to someone else.

The *Dhow*, the forces' newspaper, had a special column headed 'DHOW Security News.' This was a typical entry:

*24 December 16.45 hrs.* explosion in baggage shed in civil airport Khormaksar. Two members of security forces slightly injured. One local national was also injured.

*19.10 hrs.* Grenade thrown into yard of Police Station Tawahi. No casualties or damage.

*23.40 and 23.55 hrs.* Two explosions in FRA workshop compound, Seedeseer Lines. Two vehicles damaged no casualties.

*25 December 18.40 hrs.* Two grenades exploded in area of Aden supply depot, Maalla. No casualties.

*19.13 hrs.* Grenade exploded in area of Tawahi bus depot. No casualties.

*19.55 hrs.* Rocket launcher fired in Mansurah area of Shaikh Othman. Some damage and one soldier injured.

*21.53 hrs.* Grenade explodes in Dukes Way, Little Aden. No casualties.

*23.59 hrs.* Grenade explodes near Bank of India, Crater. No casualties or damage.

*26 December 20.15 hrs.* Grenade thrown in Dolphin Square, Maalla. No casualties, civilian car damaged.

*21.55 hrs.* Grenade thrown at mobile patrol outside armed police barracks, Crater. Four local nationals injured, one subsequently died. Four members of security forces injured.

*28 December 19.50 hrs.* Grenade thrown at mobile patrol in Shaikh Othman. Two members of security forces wounded, one local national killed and six injured, four seriously.

*20.30 hrs.* Two grenades thrown at mobile patrol in Shaikh Othman. Two members of security forces injured.

*1 January 20.40 hrs.* Two grenades thrown into compound of Aden supply depot, Maalla. Slight damage no casualties.

I wrote to my mother in October 1965:

The last week has been quiet enough apart from the nightly grenades which do practically no damage, but that natural Middle Eastern weapon of mobs has been in full cry — the schoolboys. Schoolmasters have organized strikes of all boys up and down the Federation and practically all schools have been closed. In Aden it has been the same but of course with the added attraction of British troops to stone. I must say they have behaved awfully well under fearful provocation.

I continued my account with what now seems a thoroughly over-stated diatribe against the mobs, but which was understandable in the context of the time.

As for turning cars over it was mostly poor wretches who were quite unable to defend themselves. I go everywhere with my guard armed with a Sterling sub-machine gun, and I think I would have no hesitation at all in shooting on a mob. I hope it doesn't arise but we take no risks and life is quite dull.

In spite of all the woes of Aden and our personal experience it was possible to note there were some progressive happenings in the WAP, especially after the British forces' efforts in Radfan. My political colleagues, who included Godfrey Meynell, laboured long and earnestly to introduce some measure of development into those areas isolated by warfare and poor communications. *The Aden Chronicle* of 30 December 1965 contained a typically hopeful (yet hopeless) press release: 'MORE LOANS FOR UPCOUNTRY [*sic*] FARMERS — The Federal Ministry of Agriculture has, in an attempt to step up agricultural development in Shaib Shaikhdom, provided the sum of SA £7500 to be issued as agricultural loans to individual farmers in the State.'

At vast expense a road was built up the Wadi Rabwa; medical teams provided some basic assistance to remote communities, but it was just too late in the political scenario. Mines continued to be laid and convoys on the Dhala road were frequently attacked. However, the political staff must have felt encouraged; at least we were spending some money that was not just on arms and ammunition. I too felt a touch of euphoria brought about, I suppose, by the simple notion that we had survived so much. We were also nearly off on leave and it was to be a good one, intended to be enjoyed with nary a thought of what we had left behind. I wrote:

## A Day of Reckoning

All sorts of moves behind the scenes we are told regarding new
appointments, promotions, etc. I suppose there is a faint chance
of my being 'upped' permanently, but I think I am really too
young. In any case, if I do come back at my substantive rank
(Assistant Adviser) I should like one more tour up-country and
have asked to be considered for Baihan. Unfortunately [*sic*] Bill
Heber Percy has done very well there and has taken over from
me in this job; he is angling to get back to Baihan on my return.
We shall see. I shall be fed up though, if I come back and find I
am expected to act again. I've been doing that for three years
now!

All things considered, this has been a good tour, bazookas etc.
aside, with interesting work. What has been lacking has been
leadership from the top, added to which the government in the
UK and UNO have done their best to disturb our friends and
encourage our enemies by vacillating and by oozing bonhomie
at the wrong moments. It will be interesting to see the set-up
here when we get back because we are leaving at a time when
there is a political vacuum. Sorry — I've rambled a bit.

(I certainly had: looking back, I must have been suffering from a touch
of *cafard* — desert madness — but they say you seldom recognize it
when you get it — Figgis obviously did not.)

However, I was able to indulge this nostalgia (for that is all it was)
for a last posting in the blue by taking Lynette and Charles on a tour of
part of the eastern sector of the Western Aden Protectorate. This would
have been the last tour of that type undertaken by a political officer, his
wife and small boy, before conditions had deteriorated irrevocably to
the stage that even officers travelling alone did so with extreme care.
We too had taken precautions.

My trip was primarily to 'show the flag' and specifically to call on
my ex-orderly Salim, whose son was the same age as Charles, so that
the wives could coo over each other's offspring. The other call was on
Ali Misaed Babakri MC, he who had been my assistant political officer
in earlier, less troubled times. We travelled in some style. Our huge
armour-plated Land Rover had Charles and Lynette firmly buckled in;
ahead and behind us there were trucks of troops and two armoured
cars.

179

As we bumped our way down the picturesque but traditionally treacherous Wadi Yeshbum, with its huge castle-like houses looming on each crag, we received a great welcome at every point, the tribesmen lined up to deliver their traditional fusillade of greeting shots whistling over our heads. Charles in particular was a great success — a little fair-haired youngster, he was adored in the various harems that Lynette visited. In Wahidi he received the ultimate honour of being presented with a two-thirds size *jambiya* (dagger) customarily given to the son of the head of the tribe.

We flew off to Kenya for Christmas and then via South Africa to Australia. I had known South Africa from my early days, but I wanted Lynette to be able to see for herself that that was no country in which to bring up a young family, despite it being intrinsically a wonderful part of the world. We were lucky that Charles was such an equable traveller who accepted being bundled on and off aircraft with equanimity. Lynette was by then also expecting our second child and she too bore the constant travel patiently.

At that stage I at least had determined to live where we could bring up a family, without the constant worries of being shot at or of being moved around the world at the whim of a government service; so that ensured there would be no future prospects in a transfer to, say, the British diplomatic service, even if my language skills and my temperament were judged as suitable for it. I knew they were not.

I had also developed a deal of personal antagonism to the policies of Mr Wilson's Labour government, and an impatience with what I saw as the British politicians' hypocritical and expedient policies, proclaimed under the banner of outdated socialist dogma — the emergence of indigent people from the colonial yoke, that sort of attitude. Not that I held anything for the right wingers' approach to South Arabia's problems, either: they were just as unrealistic in their approach to how to deal with the mess before us, which had been to push for a situation of self government in a Federation run by local institutions that were plainly unready in most instances to control anything more sophisticated than a village council. This was not a criticism of that handful of excellent Federal leaders, such as Sultan Salih the Audhali, the Sharif Hussein of Baihan and Shaikh Mohamed Farid of Aulaqi — just the medieval institutions they represented. Essentially it was a small number of British keeping it together.

Whatever the 'right' course of events I could see there would be no future in staying on: I was keen to make a fresh start, well away from the Middle East.

New Zealand looked about as far as we could get (at one stage we had quite fancied Arizona as a base, but the expense would have been unrealistic). However, it was in Western Australia that we came across the site of our future home, in the hills of the Darling scarp to the east of Perth. Like so often in life, it was chance: we had had an introduction to friends of friends from Kenya; we went to visit them and there we saw where we would like to live. Rejoicing, we bought our acre and a bit of sloping countryside looking north over miles of rolling forest. Later we were to purchase the 'block' (as they call it, in Australia) immediately below, and the site of our future home became the focus of our dreams from then on.

We continued across Australia before spending a few weeks in New Zealand, just for a 'look-see' now that we had found our future base in Western Australia. Awaiting me at the poste restante in Sydney was a formal looking, bulky envelope. It contained not a notice that I had been promoted, recommended for this or that, but a formal offer to be prematurely retired from the service on being superseded, as part of the Arabization policy. This was the procedure to draw indigenous officers into the senior part of the administration, by accelerating their promotion over the head of the most senior on the list. That happened to be me at that juncture; and the Arab officer so recognized was my old colleague from whom I had taken over in Wahidi, Mohamed Said Nagi (poor fellow — he was assassinated within the year).

We had mixed feelings. On the one hand there was that lovely piece of land awaiting us: on the other, we had already arranged to return to Aden. If we accepted the offer we would be leaving in rather messy circumstances: we (or I at least) would probably have to return to pack up bits and pieces, in any event. We had not made our farewells to anyone; and the final convincing argument to return was that we could not afford just to pull out at that stage. How like government, we thought, to face us with this quandary half way through a leave, when we had committed funds to travel.

I notified Aden we would be back; we flew on to New Zealand for a wonderful three weeks' exploration (beautiful but provincial — rather like a mixture of Walthamstow and the Yorkshire Moors, I thought).

We weathered one fairly strong earthquake in Wellington and caught the P & O *Orcades* back to Aden. We stopped at Fremantle, hired a car so we could drive up to the hills and gaze at our land — and very nearly missed the ship's sailing. We were back in Aden, as planned. Life was very different from when we had departed, five months before.

# 19

# Calamity and Challenge

THERE were two press reports in *The Aden Chronicle* that jolted us on our return and that perhaps reminded us that the situation was continuing to deteriorate: the first, dated 13 January 1966, upset us a lot: It was headlined: 'FEDERAL OFFICER SHOT AT DOORSTEP' and it continued:

> An Arab assistant political officer working in the Federal Government was assassinated Tuesday morning as he was leaving his house to go to his place of work. Hussein Alwazeer was shot in the head and neck at 7.30 a.m. at Al Mansoora by a masked gunman. Sanaa Radio broadcast that the National Liberation Front had executed Sayed Alwazeer after he had failed to heed several warnings sent to him to desist from the kind of work he was engaged in.

I can still see Hussein — meticulous, impeccable in his precision as he spoke about his contempt for thugs and the bullies of gunmen, the sort who would have been sent to murder him. Now there was a true patriot and gentleman. The second newspaper report was dated 13 January and it was much more dramatically composed to catch the eye of the war-weary Aden reader — 'THIRTY BULLETS TWO GRENADES RIP COMMANDER'S CAR BUT HE ESCAPES DEATH, CHASES ASSAILANT.' It was our old friend Ali bin Ahmed who had been travelling from Shaikh Othman to Lahej with his children and an escort. The newspaper account continued:

As the car slowed down near a road junction he heard two shots in the air then more shots hit the car causing it to crash. By then he had an inkling of what was coming on [*sic*] and as he pulled out a pistol, he was hit in the chest by a man standing very close to the car while two others covered him. The commander [*sic*] pushed out the door and shot the man who disappeared, apparently wounded. He chased them for 200 yards, bleeding all the time, then heard shots behind him from another trio of assailants. By then he was too weak to continue the fight and was carried to Queen Elizabeth Hospital.

This wonderful piece of the best Aden journalese was unusual. Generally the local journalists were careful not to express any sort of praise for the Establishment. There was an understandable fear of the NLF's reprisals, but this report did not disguise the writer's admiration for Ali bin Ahmed's personal courage, to which he plainly owed his life: he has since survived through to middle age.

This was all history by the time we arrived, but the two incidents were typical of that year's events: Aden was in effect on a war footing, or at least fast heading that way. The catalyst to chaos was the announcement in February by the British Labour government that the Aden base would be withdrawn no later than independence. The timing of this announcement could not have been worse: Colonel Nasser had been on the verge of pulling his forces out of the Yemen and, far from convincing the world that the British withdrawal should be welcomed as a genuine gesture of goodwill, it was seen as the weak climax to a series of disastrous political posturings on the part of our British masters. It gave quite the wrong signal to those who were all too ready to believe the worst of a faded imperial power. It was at the least embarrassing to Britain's supporters and, at worst, death to those friends of ours who were caught in South Arabia.

Not that this sentiment would have impressed the clever men at the top then, any more than it would convince today's diplomats and politicians. After all, it is part of the human condition that the individual psyche is protected from the effects of news of great disaster by a shield of indifference, beyond, of course, an initial reaction of, 'Oh dear, how sad!' when one reads such newspaper headlines as, for instance, 'Two hundred lost in cyclone.' The cynical disinterest of politicians to anything that does not affect them personally illustrates this maxim. That supreme egoist and Labour ideologue, Richard Crossman, was reported in the Grenada TV series *End of Empire* to have recorded in his diary: 'Really, we have been miraculously lucky in Aden — cancelling all our obligations and getting out.' What a way to view such a record of political mismanagement and human loss. But that was at least a year ahead.

I was posted to the High Commission in Tawahi which I found to be increasingly under the direct influence of the Foreign Office. The new Deputy High Commissioner, John Wilton, was a diplomat and was excellent; he was perhaps an exception to what seemed to me to be the norm of Foreign Office appointees at that time. My new colleague, a non-Arabic-speaking stranger, greeted me with reserve. I was appointed as (acting, once again) Senior Adviser, Political Division, succeeding a colleague from the old days in the EAP, John Weakley. The irony was that John was being promoted to a senior position in the Federal Government — promoted over my head because I had been superseded in the Arabization scheme. It was a bitter anomaly: because my name had been at the top of the list I had lost my promotional prospects, but the (thoroughly deserving) officer junior to me on the list had been favoured. It hurt: I had served in more areas of the Aden Protectorate than any other officer of my seniority, had acted more or less continuously in senior positions — and been subjected to more physical attacks than most. Of course, initially at least, I had no option but to accept the status quo — after all, I had no quarrel with my friend John Weakley — but the injustice was to rankle, especially when I had been hurled into the variety of duties expected of me. I held my peace.

Lynette, Charles and I moved into an old-fashioned but comfortable house in Khormaksar which had been incorporated into the wired-in compound of the RAF families. There were sentries on the gates; Arab staff were searched as they entered and left. Our first concern was where Lynette could give birth. The authorities had apparently given no thought to the position of civilian expatriate mothers-to-be. ('Well, they wouldn't, would they?' commented my practical wife, 'No one else was so silly as to want to give birth in Aden then.') The RAF Hospital was not available to civilians and Crater was a no-go area, certainly for me — and I would not contemplate my wife being sent down there, on her own. I pleaded with my superiors that Lynette be

185

accepted at the RAF Hospital. This was flatly refused, initially; if we did not like Crater then special arrangements could be made for the delivery to take place at the local Queen Elizabeth II Hospital, where there were no maternity facilities, no gas unless it was laid on specially. Then a week before the birth was due, permission was given for Lynette to be admitted as a private patient to the RAF Hospital, provided I would pay fees upward of £100. Catherine was to be born there — and the High Commissioner 'found' the necessary funds to ensure I was not out of pocket. The stress was quite unnecessary, in the end. I wrote to my mother.

Aden, 29 July 1966

Another Friday and I was all set to take it easy with a letter to you and then a day on the beach, but last night I was up from 12.45 a.m. after hearing the shocking news that poor old Pat Gray, OC HBL, was shot and killed outside his house in Mukalla by the HBL sentry (a Wahidi). Edith, his wife, was also hit in the chest and is also dangerously ill. They were off to UK next month, she for good and he possibly also. The poor British community in Mukalla will be quaking and I shouldn't be surprised if this means the end of Mukalla as we know it. Anyway, as the phone was ringing all night neither L nor I slept and I was in the office anyway.

Pat and Edith had been to the cinema, in the HBL lines, round the back of Mukalla. They were driving to their house which was not far from the HBL and, as they reached their house, the sentry on duty outside very deliberately shot them both, from practically a point-blank range. Old Pat, near death from a horrendous wound, realized that Edith was badly hurt. He managed to turn the Land Rover round and drive the considerable distance round to the Residency compound, to the assistant Health Adviser's house. He brought the vehicle to a halt outside and slumped at the wheel. Edith was rushed inside and tended to (she was evacuated to Aden) and by the time the helpers had come out to look for Pat, he was dead. On the horrendous drive in he had apparently been exhorted to pull himself together, by someone who had

186

heard what had happened and thought Pat was just dazed, swaying all over the place.

I made all the funeral arrangements for Pat: Edith was flown to England, where she was months under treatment. I laid on an RAF 'Argosy' aircraft at a cost of £4000 and flew down the entire expatriate community from Mukalla (this without authority but I knew they needed a morale boost).I had a major from HQ Middle East Command working under me. Attended by the High Commissioner and the Commander-in-Chief, the Royal Horse Artillery did the honours in the, 'bleak but rather beautiful setting of Silent Valley.' I wrote to my mother.

> Pat would have loved it — gun carriage, rows of RHA in flash-
> ing dress, a squad which stood with arms reversed and which
> later fired three volleys over the grave ... and the lone Union
> Jack fluttering at half-mast against those moon-like peaks. Pat's
> medals were carried by a young captain of the RHA on a velvet
> cushion behind the coffin ... the graveyard is filling up a lot
> these days — almost one burial every three days — no wonder
> the RHA are perfect at the ceremonial.

I felt Pat Gray should be remembered for his great courage in saving his wife: the post mortem revealed that the injuries were so severe and so extensive (including lungs punctured) that Pat must have been technically dead by the time his vehicle had stopped outside the doctor's. I researched whether there was a posthumous award that would fit the circumstances. The 'Albert Medal' seemed just right and I was encouraged to draft a citation. It was eventually turned down in London, on the grounds that no more would be expected of a man than that he saved his wife. Maybe so, though I doubted it, and the Mukalla community could have done with that extra boost to morale.

Running simultaneously with the funeral I coordinated the military operation to capture the two persons involved with the murder (we managed to catch one) and made a concerted effort to provide efficient backing to the Resident Adviser in Mukalla, for whatever support he needed from Aden. Much of the latter was either supplied by the military or involved its services and I maintained a close liaison with HQ Middle East Command, mainly via their General Staff Officer (2), who was a charming swash-buckling sort of man, John Slim. John (the son of *the* Bill Slim and with good Australian connections) and his wife Buffy became good friends over the next 12 months. He was a restless soul who yearned for the challenge of his own command and bored quickly of whatever desk duties confronted him.

Apparently he had access to the C-in-C's 'Andover' aircraft when its rightful user had no use for it and, on two occasions, he arranged for us both to be flown to RAF Riyan and round the Hadhramaut, on whatever mission was required at the time. The flights were reminiscent of the best flying boat journeys — a uniformed steward served us canapés both ways and we were treated as if it were our own private conveyance, John apparently accepting this as his natural right.

In August I received the most charming letter in Arabic from an old friend of Wahidi days, the head of a tribe living near where my famous road was being constructed. Translated it read:

To my friend Mr Michael Crouch

[After compliments] We are pleased to welcome your arrival from New Zealand, the country that is loved by every visitor, and is inhabited by people of comfort and honour. I have the honour to submit to you these sincere words, hoping that you are in good health. Similarly, I am well. We have learnt of your arrival in the beginning of June, and have become sure that you are now stationed at the High Commissioner's office at Tawahi.

I am very grateful for your assistance in planning the way concerning the scheme of water for Amaqin. We have obtained assistance from Her Majesty's Government and the 'bold men' [*sic* — I never did discover to whom Shaikh Ali was referring] and we have started extending the pipelines on Thursday 16 August 1966. But I think that the assistance is not sufficient. You will do your best to make representation until the water is extended into Amaqin. We hope that you will visit.

Some time ago I have sent to you a letter to New Zealand, but received no reply from you. Perhaps you were too busy to send a reply. We are faithful to you and never forget the friendship.

Remember me to Charles and to your wife. I look forward with pleasure to the day when I will meet you.

With my sincere compliments.

Yours faithfully,

Shaikh Ali bin Mohamed al Aaqel bin Faheid

The EAP continued to concern us. The High Commissioner had visited Mukalla and Saiun and this presaged some demonstrations in the souk — what was particularly sinister was a grenade thrown in Mukalla, which killed one person and wounded 45. We were all a bit edgy about the British presence in Mukalla and a company of paratroops was ordered up to RAF Riyan. It was accompanied by helicopters, a minesweeper offshore and jet fighters overhead. I flew up with the paratroops and was helicoptered into the Residency. All was quiet: the HBL and other local troops seemed in control. Ted Eyre, the RA, looked at the end of his tether, white and tired. I heard he would not be coming back to Mukalla from leave but, there again, he was not a particularly good choice to head a community that included wives and children. That particular scare subsided; I returned to Aden to my High Commission desk.

It was October. I had been involved with helping organize the visit for Mr Roderic Bowen QC, 'out here now looking into interrogation methods etc. — he seems, I gather, a decent sort of chap but much political capital is being made out of his arrival. Terrorists are being very cocky on being caught and the interrogation teams are having trouble.' So I reported: and that 'difficulty' to which I referred was to draw me later into an area of work that was to distress me. Bowen had been appointed by Her Majesty's Government to try to forestall an international investigation into the many allegations of torture put about by the NLF. Bowen found little to complain of, but the suspicion was there. Suddenly I was swept up in quite a different enterprise.

Further down from Mukalla on the wild Mahra coast, almost on the border with Dhofar, a guerilla training camp had been established, to keep the supply of terrorists slipping into the Oman and to Aden. Egypt, with Soviet support and with the help of ex-EOKA terrorists (Greek backers of their fight with Britain to throw the British out of Cyprus) was keeping up the pressure in the Middle East, in an area where the British now considered it possible to do something about it.

Accordingly, under strict security, an amphibious force was sent the 600 miles east from Aden, to clean out the small dissident base of Hauf.

I was appointed as the Aden political link in the civilian advisory presence sent with the Brigadier who commanded the operation. Jim Ellis, by now Resident Adviser in Mukalla, was 'choppered' on board as we passed Mukalla. Our troops were one battalion of Irish Guards (fresh from public duties in London), a detachment of SAS, and accompanying Marines and RAF. We sailed in *HMS Fearless*, which was the Royal Navy's latest — an amphibious warship that had cost £17 million and had only been completed 12 months before. She and her sister ship, *HMS Intrepid*, were to feature prominently in the Falklands campaign some 16 years later. The Hauf enterprise — Operation 'Fate' — was the first and last active service operation of *Fearless* until then.

George Brown was the British Foreign Secretary in late 1966. He very nearly stopped the whole thing. We understood that he was intent on making close friends with the Egyptians — a relationship he was convinced would not only demonstrate British good faith to the Egyptians, but might convince the world we meant no harm in South Arabia and were just about to move out. Reason prevailed and we embarked. I shared the commodore's cabin suite, with Jim Ellis.

There was meeting after meeting on board to coordinate the very tricky business of getting everyone in the right place at the right time; and there was exercise after exercise to ensure that everyone was moving in the right direction at the right time — two soldiers in full kit each going different ways and meeting in a narrow corridor could block everything. D-Day was two days after embarkation in Aden and we were up by 01.30 hours and were assembled on the 'tank deck' by 02.45 hours. I found it most dramatic.

This vast space to the rear of the ship had 500 men lined up to be given their orders to board the landing craft. These were floating inside the ship. When the order was given, *Fearless* just opened her stern, took in nine feet of sea water, and the landing craft swept out of the ship. In addition to the landing craft we had six helicopters, and the SAS went ashore in its 'rubber duckies'. We got the order over the ship's PA system, 'ASSAULT STATIONS, ASSAULT STATIONS — BOARD!' and we poured into our allotted craft and were immediately out at sea.

190

It was very calm; otherwise I do not think it would have been so pleasant. We could see the mainland about two miles in and we silently drifted, or quietly motored, down the coast until opposite the area we were to invest. At H-Hour, which was 05.05 hours, the helicopters came in very low and put pickets all round the village and we turned towards the shore.

Right overhead there were Hawker Hunter jet fighters. My landing craft got to about 20 yards from shore and then stuck on a sand bar. The front went down and the troops poured into the surf. There was some horrible language as they went into four feet of water, many of the tall guardsmen carrying brand-new cameras they had purchased in Aden, before they had embarked. The SAS had done its work: there was no shooting. There were 25 prisoners to take back to Aden; they had been identified by the hooded informers brought with us from Aden. That afternoon *Fearless* was on the return voyage and I accompanied Jim by helicopter to Mukalla and from there via Aden Airways. I had a date to fly up to Ataq before *Fearless* was due back in Aden: one of the Federal Army battalions with which I had been associated was receiving new colours.

I was offered a lift to and from Ataq by an RAF helicopter, piloted by the air officer commanding in person, Air-Vice-Marshal Humphrey. I gathered that, like Prince Philip, he always liked to keep his hand in and fly himself. Ataq was still a grim outpost on the edge of a stony plain at the other end of which was my old haunt, Al Abr. In those days it had seemed sophisticated, even luxurious — it had been such a different world then. Back to Aden to meet *Fearless* and to participate in the 'debrief', which was attended by the Commander-in-Chief. So ended Operation 'Fate'. Captain Hugh Corbett had Lynette and me to dine on board after *Fearless* had returned from South Africa, to transport a battalion of British troops from Swaziland to Aden. I presented him with an ancient muzzle-loader for the wardroom; he made me an honorary member of the ship's company for the duration and gave me the *Fearless* tie.

One week later there was a 'flash' message on my desk to say that an Aden Airways Dakota was missing on a flight from the EAP (which worried my mother in London). In fact it had been on a flight from Maifaah in Wahidi and it been sabotaged by an explosive device placed in a holdall under someone's seat. On board was old bin Said, the state secretary, and Tim Goschen the Assistant Adviser (Wahidi), who had only been coming to Aden for a break to attend a social gathering. Eye witnesses on the ground described a violent explosion: the tail came off and then the nose, and the remains went into a spin from 6000 feet. It crashed not far from Ahwar (on the Aulaqi coast, which I had visited with Lynette and Charles). Bodies (in bits) and luggage were scattered over a wide area. Robin had the ghastly job of identifying what remained of Tim.

There was another sombre ceremony at Silent Valley. Tim had been a Royal Inniskilling Dragoon Guard, so he had a military funeral with the full ceremonial. He had been the only child of rich and doting parents, so I gathered. I did not know him well, but he had had about as many attempts made on him as had been made on me — once in the Audhali sultanate a bomb had gone off under his bed and in Maifaah a grenade had been rolled there (but it failed to explode).

I missed bin Said a lot. A rogue he might have been, but he certainly deserved anything but that. I turned my attention to the next problem, which was how to fly people and materials to Mukalla for the coronation ceremony for the new Quaiti Sultan, HH Ghalib bin Salih, a pleasant 19-year-old who had succeeded to the sultanate on the death of his unlamented father. Ghalib was a sophisticated British-educated youth who faced every sort of worry for the future. I wished him well — but how to manage the air transport to Mukalla? Understandably, the Aden Airways flight crew were refusing to fly until security had been improved. They had every reason to worry. Not only was the Aden Airways booking office under Abdullah al Asnaj, and therefore a hotbed of FLOSY supporters, but there was nothing to stop another bomb being placed on board any flight — it had, after all, been done once with impunity. I left Aden Airways to sort out when they would fly; the RAF once again turned up trumps.

# 20

# Alarums and Excursions

A L Ittihad, with its violent memories, still represented where I belonged and I continued to feel an outsider, even superfluous, in the High Commission in Tawahi. This was strange considering how busy I was dealing with a stream of correspondence from Mukalla, London and New York, responding to requests for information, drafting telegrams to the Foreign Office, assessing information, preparing briefs and meeting aircraft. I seemed never to stop this routine, from seven in the morning to late in the day.

I did, though. There were some other more time-consuming and unusual duties I had been required to assume at this time, which tended to occupy my thoughts and actions round the clock. They had resulted directly from the increase in political pressures on the authorities in Aden from the outside world, and from a deteriorating security situation within. And they centred on how we dealt with the grenade throwers, the assassins and those we had good reason to confront as NLF supporters. Our principal problem was that, even when we caught or rounded up the villains, we could not put them on trial (no jury would have had the courage to convict, for a start). So we detained them in a large camp. Prior to their being held in the camp, however, most of them were interrogated and there were persistent reports of torture at the hands of the British authorities.

Those of us on the fringe of what was happening would have certainly assumed that such interrogation was harsh, but torture? Whatever the situation, however, from the international perspective it mattered little: the understanding was that the British had something to hide. As usual, on those frequent occasions when the British government found itself again on the defensive, the response was first to deny everything, and second to forestall international demands for an investigation by appointing a special investigator — who in my time had been Mr Bowen QC. His report was, however, greeted with some derision by the United Nations anti-colonialism lobby and, having originally been refused permission to investigate claims of British atrocities, a delegate from the International Red Cross was reluctantly invited to Aden.

This happened while we were still in Australia and I had returned to take over the role of liaising with Monsieur Rochat, the delegate appointed by the International Red Cross in Geneva. Contrary to various reports subsequently stating that M Rochat held a doctorate and was a senior diplomat, I discovered he had been trained as a pastry cook. His main qualification was that he was Swiss: he was pale, sandy haired and unassuming in appearance, but obsequiously determined to seek out '*la verité*'.

His obsession with being recognized as an international figure locally took the form of having large red crosses attached to his cloth hat, his lightweight suit, his briefcase and the little white car he had hired, which was not only emblazoned with the St George's symbol back, front and on both side doors, but on a flag standard. I could well understand this obsession with the display: M Rochat was petrified of being gunned down, under the delusion he was one of 'us'. I cannot remember in all my Aden days meeting someone who was so obviously terrified. Perhaps he need not have worried: I was the one who felt conspicuous being seen with him.

M Rochat and I got on well enough. My job was to be with him whenever he called on detainees, or toured the various establishments in which tortures were alleged to have taken place. I was as helpful as I possibly could be, even translating for him on occasion (though never officially — that would have been the last thing the Red Cross would have condoned; just imagine the wicked comments I might have inserted into M Rochat's text). But there was one area of the work we shared on which I was not prepared to venture an opinion, make a suggestion or be drawn in any way: that was the interrogation centre.

In the heart of the defence establishment in Aden was the complex of Fort Morbut, a collection of nondescript buildings containing bare bleak rooms and a number of cells: it was there that the interrogation teams worked. I knew a part of it well, for I too had been asked to work as part of a two-man (amateur) team — by Jock Snell of all people.

Jock must have proved himself invaluable to the Aden Police. After leaving the EAP, he was in Aden when the last of the non-Arab Arabic-speaking special branch was assassinated. There was practically no expatriate free at that time to whom the security forces could turn and on whom they could rely to extract the essential information they needed to take the initiative in the fight against terrorism. Ironically, the High Commission seemed to be filling up with ex-colonial police who spoke not a word of Arabic.

Jock had asked if I would help him interrogate a Wahidi tribesman, who had been picked up after a trip to the Yemen. Jock briefed me: all he wanted me to do was to question the man quite casually about what he had done over there, whom he had seen, and so on. Jock would then take over where I left off, in a much more hectoring tone than mine. It was the classic 'soft-hard' approach, but I found there was more to it.

We sat behind a plain table, on the only two chairs in the small bare room, with its one barred window looking out over the rocky fall to the harbour. The prisoner was brought in, clad only in a cloth round his waist. He was middle aged, the usual tribal tousled-haired type. He looked frankly scared and I could not blame him. He was brought to stand in front of the table by two thoroughly hard-looking British staff sergeants, in slacks and loose shirts. They were in their late twenties and had cold, contemptuous eyes: they said nothing but stood back against the wall.

Jock lit one of his many cigarettes and, using all his excellent colloquial Arabic, really got stuck into the man. He bawled at him; he threatened him with terrible retribution; he scowled; he cursed and generally looked like Jock Snell in a rage, ginger hair awash with sweat, blue eyes bulging and bright red face showing every sign of a seizure. The prisoner by now was looking terrified, but he said nothing except to swear by Allah that it was all a mistake. Jock made a disgusted gesture and motioned to me to take over. I asked the man about his village, how long he had been away and what he had been doing in the Yemen. His replies were quite innocuous. I gave up.

Then the staff sergeants moved in. One of them roughly seized the man's arms and forced him to hold them above his head, jerking them upwards when they started to sag. Jock questioned him again; at the first response, there was a gesture from Jock and one of the staff sergeants quite suddenly hit the man above his kidneys, hard, and again, and again. More questions — the hitting started again, this time from the other staff sergeant — and so it went on. I was beginning to feel sick and excused myself, leaving the room. That prisoner was eventually released and some weeks later I heard from Wahidi that he had returned to his village and had died there. 'Whatever happened to him in Fort Morbut?' an Arab friend from Wahidi had asked me (without evident sympathy, I may add). I was not pressed for an answer. I was not required again to participate in interrogations, but day and night the teams were working away in Fort Morbut. Even with this form of 'third degree' available, I am personally convinced, in the vast majority of cases, that there was no need to resort to that sort of strong-armed stuff. Those unpleasant staff sergeants, who so plainly enjoyed their work, were not always necessary. In terrorist circles in Aden the very mention of Fort Morbut had a ring of horror to it, a reputation that fed upon rumour and exaggeration. I learnt that questions from a skilled interrogator were often enough to bring the truth stumbling out just in time, quite often, to alert the intended victim of an assassination or to brief a military patrol.

This then was what M Rochat was tasked to uncover and what I was unwilling to tell him. Had he stuck to documenting the more prosaic, albeit just as revolting, accounts of 'third degree' he might have been better believed. There were also psychological experiments, which I had heard discussed though never personally come across, of sight and sound deprivation, of disorientation. But so often in my presence M Rochat was given the most esoteric accounts of detainees being wired up to electric torture machines, of being stripped and hung from the ceiling, that sort of thing. I believe that these lurid stories were probably invented by detainees who had told all under the threat of the dread 'Fort Morbut', although, there again, they may have been true. Who knows?

Some of the interviews conducted by Mr Rochat were in his hotel room at the Crescent and only the 'watchers and listeners' of the intelligence services would have been privy to those; they were incidental to the main meetings between M Rochat and individual detainees; I was present at those, so I knew exactly of what the interrogators were being accused.

Leaving the Crescent Hotel at speed in his conspicuous lttle white car festooned with red crosses, he would be driven by his hired Arab driver to the entrance of al Mansoura Detention Centre. I met him there. The camp was guarded by British troops who waved us through to Desmond's office (he happened to be my neighbour in Khormaksar, but we did not let on in front of M Rochat). Then there was the 'stroll' through the camp; M Rochat, briefcase in hand, ready to note the complaints. That was where I met some of the men who had tried to kill us on that evening in August the previous year. There was never direct animosity displayed towards me, just sometimes the odd comment, accompanied by a knowing half-grin, '*Karoash, naam, dhabit assiyasi.*' (Crouch, yes, the political officer.) I was apparently quite well known and it gave me no joy.

The camps were comfortable. They were a mixture of semi-permanent and tented areas, neatly laid out. The food was good and, apart from the lack of liberty, the detainees were well looked after. Radios throbbed and wailed; there was television and visitors were allowed. It was like a huge holiday camp without the beach. Murderers, grenade throwers, trade unionists with NLF connections, dissident tribesmen from up-country, Yemenis — many of them came to see M Rochat in the interview room, later, where (with the help of one of them who spoke excellent English and many of the Adenis did) they recounted their horror stories.

These accounts told to the Red Cross delegate were neatly typed up on the thinnest of Swiss paper and a copy, signed by its author next to the imprinted red cross (from the red-inked stamp pad carried and earnestly applied by M Rochat wherever there was an opportunity) was presented to the High Commissioner, to be translated from the original French. On each of his Aden visits M Rochat would seek an appointment with the Deputy High Commissioner, John Wilton, who would have had an opportunity to go through the report prepared on the previous visit. Politely John (in a fascinating exercise of true diplomacy) would tell Rochat that most of his conclusions were based on lies and half-truths.

Luckily we had records of each detainee's interrogation and it never seemed to be those who had really suffered physically who had complained; if they had, they gave an account of much more than being hit above the kidneys. Later, poor M Rochat was to be thoroughly discomfited when, in front of an Arab witness (we did have a few), one of the tellers of lurid tales humbly confessed that he had lied and begged us all not to tell his fellows.

My role in all this was to have noted everyone with whom Rochat had met and what had transpired; then, as soon as we had parted, I would put it all down in a report that was circulated to those who needed to know, from the High Commissioner to the Commander-in-Chief, downwards. It gave me a strange feeling once to attend a meeting with others, in the office of Admiral Sir Michael Le Fanu. There, on his desk, was a copy of my report: required reading, it seemed. Poor M Rochat. Much later I was to read of his complete failure, following the hijack to Jordan of those three airliners that were subsequently destroyed on the ground.

'Lots of bangs in Aden but we live very quietly,' I wrote to my mother in an attempt at normalcy. Then,

> I have been allotted a bodyguard, you will be interested to hear. My duties with the Red Cross brought me into close contact with Aden terrorists in prison and I feel happier to have a full-time chap keeping an eye on us when we go out in the car and so on. He's a soldier from the Royal Anglians and we find him a nice and useful chap. Don't worry about us. We live behind wire in a secure area and we don't take risks. Unlike Roy Somerset, who went shopping in the Crescent at dusk and was hit on the shoulder by a grenade, which [then] exploded; he was peppered and uncomfortable as a result. Jolly lucky not have been killed. But we just don't do that sort of thing.

Indeed, I was very conscious of the need to avoid becoming an easy target. Apart from varying my daily routine and attempting to go to the office by different routes (which was hard because there was really only one way from Khormaksar to Tawahi and that was via Maalla) I used to check my car each day for 'nasties' left underneath, and the engine for signs of trailing wires or strange shapes attached. I learnt to glance constantly in the rear-view mirror (not a bad thing to do in any case, Aden drivers being a class apart), and to keep all doors locked and windows up when travelling, and particularly when stationary at traffic lights.

Doug, my bodyguard, became a permanent part of our household until we left Aden; he was cheerful and tactful; he had received a crash course in personnel protection and he took his duties seriously. Now, on the way to the office, it was Doug who used the vanity mirror in the front passenger seat to eye the road behind us, as he sat with a Stirling sub-machine-gun firmly grasped in his lap. Lynette always travelled with the children in the back seat of our Australian Holden vehicle in Aden; she never sat in the front, at least not until we had arrived in Australia and our car had caught up with us.

It was a sign of the times that I learnt how one civilian-owned supermarket generated some revenue to compensate for its loss of expatriate custom: its cold storage facilities were being used for the storage of human corpses, for the Aden mortuary was unable to cope. By late 1966, apart from the 13 British civilians and military killed, there were 38 dead locals, a figure that was to swell to at least 245 Arabs killed during 1967. In the British ranks there was to be a corresponding upsurge in the numbers killed — 44 military and 9 civilians.

Many of the casualties were a result of street patrols coming under attack, retaliating and then both attacker and attacked coming in together. Aware of the increasing pressures on the medics, Lynette decided to contribute to the nursing workforce; she donned her uniform, left our babies to the attention of our excellent Somali ayah and went to work part time at the RAF Hospital at Khormaksar Beach. It was to there that the wounded and dead were brought. Initially it was hard to tell who was soldier and who was grenade thrower, such was the disguise of blackened bleeding humanity.

Some casualties were a result of 'drain-pipe' mortars; these were pipes with a simple firing device aimed roughly in the direction of British targets and timed to fire long after the assailants had crept away. Although they were noisy rather than a major threat, it was not unusual to hear loud bangs outside the compound and to hope the bombs had missed. Then there were booby traps: I was nearly 'in' at the explosion of one. The scheme was almost faultless. It consisted of neatly wrapped photograph albums (the kind with plastic overlays to protect the pictures) being mailed to certain key figures in the High Commission, suitably wrapped in festive paper (it was prior to Christmas).

The insides of the albums had been hollowed out and replaced with plastic explosive. The detonator was a simple clothes peg, tipped in metal. When the album was opened it pulled the one photo-leaf aside, allowing the two peg tips to make contact. The Assistant High Commissioner's secretary in Tawahi opened the parcel addressed to her boss; the explosion damaged her face and she lost part of one hand. I was nearby and was able to help spread the word to other likely targets. Four other neatly wrapped parcels in various in-trays were awaiting the bomb squad.

Another booby trap was particularly nasty because it was used near where children played or went to school. It was an official looking large envelope, left flat on a ledge or a bench. It contained enough explosive in the form of a flat sheet to maim anyone nearby. The detonator was a ball bearing in a glass tube, which would roll to either end of the tube as soon as someone tilted the envelope by picking it up.

Then there were anti-tank mines, suitably adapted for anti-personnel use, and 'jumping jacks'. The latter relied on being trodden upon; they had three spikes just showing above the ground. Once activated the mine sprang to about groin level where it exploded, often to emasculate or similar, without necessarily killing the victim. It was designed to be an effective morale-lowerer. The anti-tanks were usually exploded in Aden by a timing device, rather than by a vehicle's pressure. Poor old Tom Oates, the other Deputy High Commissioner, was a hard-working bachelor who had a penchant for Jaguar motorcars. Apparently he had driven his latest cream-coloured convertible carefully and proudly from the docks, with just 27 miles on the clock. Just before he got to his house high on the cliffs above Steamer Point, a mine hidden at the side of the road was detonated. Luckily for him it missed the front of the car completely, but the rear was all pitted and torn by small chunks of jagged metal. Tom was desolated by what had happened to his new car. My colleague from early Mukalla days, Cen Jones, now the Permanent Secretary of the Federal Health Ministry was also lucky. He was shot at twice while driving, but was unhurt.

We had to live with these bangs while we tried to maintain normalcy. Throughout the strange pattern of my official existence Lynette and I spent as much time together as the job and the worsening security cum political situation allowed. We went to the closely guarded beach; we enjoyed dining at friends' houses. Gone of course for a long time was the relaxation of shopping in Crater, of casually walking through the markets after dark to one's favourite little shop, to be greeted with friendly smiles. Now it was shopping in 'safe' areas, where British patrols maintained constant watch, or even, with special dispensation, of using the British forces' NAAFI. It was there that we had purchased our huge frozen Christmas goose (far too big for our little family to consume on our own) and we determined we must do our best for the soldiery, far from loved ones. We asked via the commanding officer of the Royal Anglian Regiment, whom we had met, for a couple of volunteers (and we stressed 'volunteers') preferably married men serving away from their families who would like to spend Christmas Day with us. We heard the invitation had been passed on. Shortly before luncheon, with all the formal table setting and colourful streamers curving in the breeze from the fans, we awaited our guests.

Just when we were beginning to think they were not coming, a military vehicle drove up. My impression was that our guests were literally dumped at our doorstep. We looked at each other with a mutual lack of enthusiasm. One was completely silent throughout and ate nothing at all. The other never stopped talking and ate and drank everything put in front of him, with a complete lack of discrimination. It could have been platefuls of bran mash for all the appreciation he showed. The one thing our guests had in common was that neither had wanted to come: they had been detailed to do so by the sergeant-major. As the meal progressed, the eating-drinking-talking one suddenly gasped, 'Where's the toilet, then?' He staggered to the hall where he threw up noisily and copiously. Soon after, our guests departed.

Other social gatherings were remembered with as little affection and with much sadness: 'SIX BRITONS HURT AT ADEN DINNER PARTY — GRENADE IN GARDEN,' announced *The Daily Telegraph* and, further down, 'Last Tuesday a time bomb exploded at a cocktail party killing two women.' We knew guests at both parties and the latter incident was the worst, partly because the NLF in claiming responsibility was reported saying, 'This is not a cowardly act but a noble, legitimate and just act.' Actually, it was horrible. It had been an anti-tank mine placed by the Yemeni servant behind the bookcase in the living room. It was timed to go off when the party was in full swing. The hostess had done some last minute straightening of the furniture and in so doing had shifted the bookcase slightly, so the mine tilted upwards.

When it exploded the room was full. Seven people were either killed or wounded, among them the wife of the resident MI5 man at the High Commission. The force being directed slightly upwards spared the rest of those not hurt by that same effect, as had nearly destroyed us at Al Ittihad — chunks of wood, metal and glass hurtling into flesh. The blast went across the ceiling and out through the door, to wreck a room across the way.

From then on such social gatherings of any size were officially discouraged. In a way, that marked the start of the wind-down of the British presence in Aden; once it was officially put about that socializing was restricted, so was 'normal' life, as people had come to expect it. There was talk of a move to restrict further women and children being based in Aden (at long last) and we too started to think that it might be time to move out, to start a new life on that delectable hillside, in faraway Western Australia.

# 21
## Omega

I<small>T</small> seemed quite suddenly that Australia was likely to be our destination rather earlier than anyone had been prepared to suggest hitherto. In December (1966) Sir Richard Turnbull had called a number of us to the heavily guarded Government House. I do not know when I had thought Lynette and I would be released to start our new life, but I had supposed rather vaguely that it might coincide with that promise of independence to the locals, in 1968. After that meeting with HE I wrote:

> Without going into details it appears that we would be extremely foolish to consider staying on here until [the] middle [of] 1968. Not only might there be turmoil, no British troops after 1 January 1968, but whatever the High Commission turned into, I shall not be wanted. There will be a few miserable fellows held onto to clear up pensions, etc. This means we must now consider leaving here for good by the end of 1967 at the latest. Alas, there is little or no hope of government sending us on home leave before that. I am on the wrong side of the water, in Tawahi rather than Ittihad, for anyone to speak up for me. So I fear we will not be coming to the UK before we sail south.

In the meantime we slogged on: in January (to welcome a new year of trouble) there had been a general strike. I wrote:

> [It was] the excuse for lots of terrorism. I spent 12 hours as an observer in Mansoura Detention Centre watching British troops search cells and persons of terrorists detained. The troops had a lot of provocation but behaved impeccably [and] if you please,

had to be searched by their officers before they left the place so that the Red Cross would not have the excuse of accusing them of pilfering from the detainees. One memorable exchange between a detainee and an army doctor.

Detainee (standing stark naked for medical examination, done after being searched so there could be no allegation of having been beaten up): 'You British pirate, you bloody ... bastard. When we have independence we will not allow you to have an embassy here!' Weary army doctor (with slight north-country accent): 'Now pick up your rubbish and get back in your cage.'

In June the previous year I had been introduced to a giant of a man by the name of John Prendergast. He had been brought out to become chief of intelligence, to replace his pleasant but ineffectual predecessor, an army Brigadier. Not that I personally found Prendergast an improvement on his predecessor, but he apparently had a reputation 'for getting things done,' presumably by being a bully. He had one major disadvantage: he spoke no Arabic and, what was more, he was very short of people around him who did. It was inevitable therefore that I should be drafted into yet another area of which I had never heard until I became involved, the tapping of telephones.

This was a nightly ritual, or at least a few times each week, which, coming after all the things I had been required to do during the day, was a tremendous burden. It was very boring, most of the time. Leaving Lynette and the babies (it was hard on her because she never knew when I would be back) Doug and I would be driven in an unmarked car through the deserted streets of Aden (deserted, that is, except for the foot patrols and the hum of indigenous life around the cafes) to somewhere up in the complex of HQ Middle East Command. There I would be placed in a sound-proof room in front of huge discs of tapes, containing recordings (all in Arabic) of the conversations of Aden's best known trade union leaders, teachers and merchants. Initially it had seemed a waste of time. The recordings were made earlier in the day so they were already 'old hat' by the time I listened, but on one occasion I struck it rich.

I had been idly listening (and chuckling, I must admit; people can be so indiscrete on the telephone) to the woebegone conversation of two shrill Adeni wives; it was black comedy. One of their husbands had been used to carrying a small pistol tucked into his corpulent waist-band; bending down one day to open his safe, the pistol had gone off and shot the end off a certain member. The shrill lamentations did not reveal that the unfortunate man had already fathered a dozen children by his various wives. Then, I suddenly tensed. On another phone line there were heavy and guttural, but explicit, instructions from one speaker to the other to collect a weapon from a particular point and to kill someone with it. I played it back a couple of times, but it was unmistakable — only the speakers were anonymous to me and I was not sure of the intended victim's name, although I had an idea (he was a prominent Adeni not unsympathetic to the British). There might just be time to save him.

I found out that John Prendergast was dining at Government House that night. I hurried there and had him called out. The heavy features of the Director of Intelligence displayed very little emotion and I got no thanks, but I had got to him on time. The intended victim was alerted, not that anyone seemed to mind very much. At that point I suddenly felt revolted and wanted to be shot of the whole wretched business, which was so far removed from the constructive things I used to do in a saner world. Perhaps I was just over-tired and reacting to being surrounded by strangers who knew little about the Protectorate and cared even less.

The next day Lynette and I discussed the future. It seemed there would be more of the same. Why should we linger on, increasingly hassled and taken for granted, by a bunch of non-Arabic speaking careerist diplomats and superannuated colonial policemen? What good was all this 'hush hush' nonsense doing in the long run? I apparently had nothing to gain by lingering in this interminable acting role and I wondered if I would even be missed. The following morning I placed my carefully composed letter requesting permission to retire prema-turely from the service in the Deputy High Commissioner's in-tray: I thought that it would hardly come as a surprise. After all, I had previously been granted a personal interview with the High Commissioner and had asked him to examine my case, for I had been acting in an apparent key role with at least one other expatriate being promoted over my head — all because I was at the top of the list of officers at my grade. I was useful enough to be sought after but apparently barred from being appropriately remunerated. HE had agreed it looked unfair but had been unable to promise any action on my behalf.

To hell with them all, then: Lynette and I looked at the various sailing schedules to Australia. We had better hurry, we thought; soon there would be no ships to travel on. Aden was becoming a place for passenger liners to avoid.

The British forces had already taken over control of security in Aden; in February Sir Richard Turnbull had nearly been landed in his helicopter onto an anti-tank mine at Al Ittihad; the NLF was in open conflict with FLOSY (one result of which was the killing of members of the Aden chief minister's family, Mackawee, himself no friend of the British). Then, in March, we were inflicted with a visit to Aden by a Mission from the United Nations. That was not a success for any of the parties involved.

The Mission consisted of a Venezuelean, an Afghan and a Malian and they came to Aden via Cairo. Both the NLF and FLOSY were against the Mission because they claimed it was a 'tool of British imperialism'. Just before the Mission arrived to take up residence in a hotel, which was heavily guarded against it being attacked by the NLF or FLOSY, it rained. This was no ordinary rainstorm, in fact it hardly ever rained in Aden, but we had over 150 millimetres in under a day. It was unheard of: as there were no drains in Aden, the place was turned into an insanitary lake of about one metre deep; and that meant that everyone got so wet they had no time to throw grenades or to fire bazookas. It was a blessed relief for a day or so, but by the time the Mission arrived the powder was dry once again (so to speak) and we had a period of those interminable strikes and demonstrations, with accompanying bangs.

Unfortunately for the UN Mission, no one wanted to talk to them (and they refused to talk to the Federal Government) and the only way they could get about was by helicopter. They flew to Government House; they visited Mansoura Detention Centre and they tried to make a broadcast, but as that was over the Federal Government's radio and the content was anti-federal, the latter refused to allow it, and the Mission left Aden in a huff. I had rather enjoyed it all, not being responsible for any aspect of the visit.

I was soon to become involved in the next stage. Lord Shackleton was sent out from London to assess what needed to be done. I was appointed his liaison man and together we travelled the Protectorate. He was a nice man with an impossible brief. He displayed much the same sort of stamina as had a previous visitor, Julian Amery, whom I had accompanied a couple of years earlier from the Hadhramaut to Mukalla. Amery had drunk plenty, day and night, and had smoked enormous cigars (rather in the mode of his famous father-in-law), whereas Shackleton had slept when he was not in conference. I could see that public life required reserves of strength that I for one could never hope to draw upon.

May was a mixture of surprises. Following on Lord Shackleton's visit Sir Richard Turnbull was recalled. *The Daily Express* ran what seemed to us, on the ground, a rather good piece that summed up our feelings amid the continuing chaos. 'On the brutally hot morning that a helicopter lifted him from Aden's Government House into the obscurity of dismissal, that craggy, unlovable, realistic, taciturn man Sir Richard Turnbull turned aside from the official parade to speak five prophetic words. "Look after the army, Jack." [Brigadier Jack Dye, commander of the Federal Army]' Sir Richard's reference was to the deepening anarchy within the Federal forces; the reporter then commented on Foreign Secretary George Brown's attempt to placate the Egyptians and the lack of policy that had been the norm for the previous three years. 'We had coerced the sheikhs and sultans into forming a federation and then abandoned it as an unreal feudal government.'

For once, in my opinion, this reporter had it absolutely right. The comment was made at a time just prior to the sound trouncing that Egypt's forces received (in early June), which resulted in the closure of the Suez Canal and with the abrupt and final collapse of Aden as a normal port of call. Nasser had survived and his survival was helped by the supine British cynical and pro-Egyptian policy of the time. The appointment of Sir Humphrey Trevelyan (a previous British Ambassador to Egypt) to succeed Sir Richard made our political capitulation clear: the writing was on the wall. The British really were leaving. So were Lynette, the babies and I — we had nearly started packing.

I was summoned to Tom Oates's office. The Deputy High Commissioner had two pieces of paper on his desk. One was my letter requesting my release. I could recognize it. Tom looked at me in a troubled way; he was a nice man. 'Michael, I was sorry to receive this,' he gestured towards my letter. I thought, 'Now he's going to try and persuade me to withdraw it. Well, I won't!' He passed me the other bit of paper. It said, 'Mr M.A. Crouch (3127) is promoted to Superscale Group 7 as a Senior Adviser, in the High Commissioner's Office.' I withdrew my letter.

The Turnbulls departed, to the sadness of those of us who were not diplomats. 'Many of us,' I wrote,

> [well those of us left] had hoped to have a boss of our service until we left and now there is an overpowering feeling of being swamped by 'Dips'. I have only met Sir Humphrey once; he is short, tough and with immense ears which he can waggle while he talks. There are doubtless other attributes more relevant as to why he has been sent here which I shall discover anon. Otherwise, the picture is that of us keeping going until independence, trying to avoid grenades and averting our eyes from the more disgraceful excesses forced upon our new masters by HMG.

My birthday (15 May) was marred by the Residency in Mukalla coming under machine-gun and bazooka attack. An immediate decision was made to evacuate the women and children (what a relief — I met them off the RAF Argosy). Less constructive news was that the colleague who had been promoted to Senior Adviser with me, and made Deputy British Agent in Mukalla, also decided to throw it in. He resigned precipitously and left immediately. The evacuation of the Mukalla contingent coincided, as it happened, with the thousands of armed forces dependants also being evacuated from Aden itself. This did not noticeably interfere with the building programme for the new British base — never to be occupied as intended and the complex ready just before the last British troops were out.

I was summoned once again to the Deputy High Commissioner's office (this time, John Wilton's) and was given the news that I was required to assume the position of Deputy British Agent in Mukalla, as second-in-command to Jim Ellis. I was taken aback and then momentarily bitter. Why me? After all we had been through, and to think my predecessor and his wife had had a fraction of the pressures we had suffered and had just abandoned us, but I was the obvious choice. I had the experience and I could be replaced in Tawahi. An anonymous diplomat would move into my chair and be as useless at providing backup for the Residency's needs as the one or two others I had met had been. At least the excellent John Wilton was there. I asked for some brief leave to fly with my family to Kenya, where I could deposit them and return to Mukalla.

Lynette was relieved to stop her nursing job which had become a strain and she was losing weight. I wrote:

> The Middle East war has at times made us feel in the thick of it. There has been a lot of Jew-baiting by the Arabs and, at the beginning, tremendous music over the various Arab stations, exhortations and so on. Cairo's allegations that the US and ourselves joined in was believed by nearly everyone here [Arabs] because they *wanted* to believe it. Accordingly, Lynette had bitter remarks made to her at the hospital, but there was violence against the Brits in both Saiun and Mukalla (no one hurt but useful vehicles burnt) and poor old John Shebbeare nastily stoned in Maifaah. He doesn't seem very well. Aden itself just closed up and there have been many runs on petrol, mobs everywhere and a sharp increase in the price of many foodstuffs. We have come through it alright. Of course, getting our stuff to Australia may not be possible for months, so we can only leave the stuff in store and hope we can insure it against being burnt.

We would depart for Kenya: there I would leave them with Lynette's mother and I would return to Mukalla. Our 17 packing cases were filled and deposited in a government depot; we really wondered if we would ever see them again. Our shiny Holden was left in the compound of the High Commission, together with a puny motorbike that I had some idea might be useful as a supplementary conveyance in Australia. (Luckily the only loss was in fact the motorbike, which was stolen from the High Commission compound and for which, with some reluctance on the part of the British authorities, I was compensated. They were meant to have been looking after it.)

Our departure from Aden airport was protracted and even sordid in the manner we had sat like refugees, which, I suppose, we were in a way. The aircraft was interminably delayed and the dirty run-down waiting room depressed us. Charles was no problem, he was happily mobile, rushing around in his usual manner. Baby Catherine was anxious to be allowed to crawl, arching her back, to be put on the grimy floor. She won her way and it nearly killed her. She was to suffer grievously from a virulent germ, obviously picked up from that wait at the airport. In Kenya she was treated by the doctor with a course of the new wonder drug, Chloromycetin. It killed all the bugs in her digestive system. She was in and out of hospital: her tummy swelled to resemble that of a famine child and Lynette was desperately worried. But this was after I had returned from those few blissful days in the greenery of peaceful Kenya, always with the thought in my mind that maybe, just maybe, the savagery to which I was returning might interfere with those blissful plans, our dream to bring up our children in the serenity of Western Australia, far from the muddle and the horrors of a part of the world seemingly always condemned to mayhem and murder. I hated returning on my own.

I had a couple of days in Aden before Mukalla, staying with Desmond, our erstwhile neighbour in Khormaksar. I had returned to an Aden that was plunged even further into its closing scenario of chaos and despair. A series of dramatic events, against the background of the Israelis' defeat of the Egyptians, had precipitated a terminal drop in morale amongst those who had clung to a prospect of a Federation of South Arabia surviving Britain's departure. The Federal Army had mutinied: the rift between the Aulaqi officers and those from other tribes was probably the main cause. The senior Arab officer was one unctuous and stout Nasser Breik, of dubious soldierly quality but with political connections. Strong opposition to his appointment as the first head of the Federal Army after Brigadier Jack Dye stood down led to four Arab colonels being suspended and that led to disturbances that had been put down by other Arab officers, thankfully without British intervention. However, the rumour got about that it was British troops that had fired on Arab troops and that led to an unsuspecting body of British soldiers being fired on by South Arabian police stationed nearby the Federal Army.

Eight British soldiers died and another eight were wounded, with a young British officer later being killed. The mutiny then spread, with further injuries and deaths to British troops as they restored the situation to an uneasy calm. However, the rot had spread. Al Ittihad was seized by mutineers, which was very serious because there were still many British families living out there, protected (as Lynette and I had been) only by South Arabian forces. Some order was restored there, but then another rumour was current in Arab circles that British troops were about to attack the Arab Armed Police barracks in Crater.

Aden prison was overwhelmed and the inmates freed, but the focus was again on the wretched British troops who were responsible for security in Crater itself. There were a number of unpleasant incidents involving (often unsuspecting) groups of British soldiers being attacked by the Armed Police and the net result was that Crater was temporarily lost to British control, with the bodies of 13 British officers and men out of reach. There was hesitation at that point about what should be done. On the face of it, British forces, with their superior fire power, could have stormed back in and retaken nominal control, certainly of the main buildings and security points. But what about the role of the Federation, with its armed forces? Surely it should be left up to them to assert the authority that was being devolved to them, as part of the deliberate policy of leaving the Federation of South Arabia in charge?

Naturally, nothing, for the moment was done. I can visualize in my mind's eye now the setting at Government House and at Al Ittihad, the endless meetings, with my British colleagues representing the Federal rulers, facing the security forces' representatives on the other side of the table, the tortuous reasoning and anguished going over and over the arguments for and against taking one course of action or another. One crucial factor was that British people were still living in some isolation all over the Federation and EAP, to say nothing of those at Al Ittihad, who could well be captured and summarily dealt with, in reprisal. The British armed forces grimly awaited the directives of their political masters, while the murderers of their slain comrades in Crater howled their jubilation. The stalemate continued for nearly a fortnight after I had returned to Aden.

The night of 3 July was unusually quiet, I had thought, sipping a cold whisky and soda outside Desmond's residence in Khormaksar. Then quite distinctly, but so unlikely that we wondered if it were a record player, we heard faraway bagpipes. It was the Argyll and Sutherland Highlanders advancing back into Crater. There was a Verey light or two, a burst of fire, then silence. By early next day

British troops were back in Crater and that darling of the British press at that time (understandably anxious for a hero) Lieutenant-Colonel Colin Campbell Mitchell commanding the Argyll and Sutherlands, was able to strut his piece for the benefit of the world's media.

He was not particularly popular with his superiors, particularly with the General Officer Commanding, Major-General Tower. Colonel Mitchell abominated the likes of me (political staff who knew enough of the likely consequences to see decision making in several shades of grey) but he was plainly the man for the occasion. It was a short-term respite, and the fact that it had had to be the British who restored order and a degree of control in Crater did nothing for the reputation of the Federal leaders, nor of their forces.

My couple of days in Aden were gloomy ones but I was very busy. All round me in the guarded ghetto of Khormaksar were families packing up. 'Aden I found depressing,' I wrote later:

> empty streets, garbage blowing everywhere — nearly a ghost town ... [my] mass of junk to take to Mukalla in the oldest tin trunks will have to be abandoned when I leave here. All had to be searched and the RAF raised some eyebrows at a collection of luggage which would have been spurned by even the meanest Pakistani pilgrim. I brought some cheese and avocados from Kenya and grabbed what vege[table]s there were in Aden to take up with me. Some items are frightfully short in Aden.
>
> On the day of my flight I reported early, took off in the Argosy transport aircraft, only to do one circuit and land again hurriedly. They found half the dials u[n]/s[erviceable]. So I sat at the airport from 8.30 a.m. to 4.30 p.m. and eventually came up by Dakota. The cheese was practically walking, but you can imagine how it is appreciated. Mukalla is very short of all commodities, milk, etc. I shall be living on the bare essentials eventually.

And so it was I returned to the location of what had been my first posting, only nine years before. Nine years — it had been a lifetime.

# 22

## Precarious Proconsul

I had arrived in Mukalla in early July and there was a great welcome from Jim and Joanna Ellis. I moved into the Residency itself, preparatory to taking over from Jim as acting Resident Adviser, while he and Joanna took some leave. They had been through troublesome times: Mukalla was virtually in a state of siege, although on the surface most days passed normally enough. Joanna was the only woman left and fiercely defended her role at Jim's side, but that was not to last long; she would not be back after their leave.

The expatriate community was sharply reduced by the departure of our families. There was the Military Assistant, breezy Major Phil Hillman of the Royal Hampshire Regiment, the pleasant informed presence of young John Shipman (Arabic speaker extraordinary), Tubby Dawson, and one or two others, all living in a somewhat strained and exclusively male environment, not at all what one associated with being in Mukalla. Commanding the HBL, and living in the Commandant's house outside which Pat and Edith Gray had been shot, was the tense Eric Johnson, a man to whom I found it hard to relate on a personal level, although I respected him. Everyone did, he was a super military leader, but he was a recluse (his family had apparently been killed in a flying accident before his eyes, some years previously). Then there was the SAS.

A detachment was based in the Residency to keep an eye on our safety, and to maintain sound communications with its British headquarters at Hereford in the UK and with Aden. It was commanded by a relaxed young captain from the Welsh Guards, one Charles Guthrie. Charles's demeanour reflected that of his men. They tended to appear in public dressed in loose Hawaiian type shirts that might have concealed various pieces of hardware on their persons. Upstairs in the

Residency, where Colonel Hugh had had his personal little office-cum-study, two SAS troopers kept watch on the Sultan's guardhouse opposite. They had a 'Carl Gustav' (a then secret anti-tank weapon) ready to fire if the Mukalla Regular Army showed any sign of emulating the Aden Armed Police. It was reassuring to have the SAS; we could hardly trust the local forces, which had been involved in an earlier fracas in which they fired on the Residency at the start of the Arab–Israeli conflict in June. As for the HBL, it had already disposed of two of its commanders, and I had none of Jim's faith in that lot, though I had been able to put in a good word for the HBL while I was with Lord Shackleton, and a letter arrived from him for me in Mukalla, saying aid would be earmarked for the HBL, to keep it going.

Jim and Joanna left for a holiday in east and southern Africa and it had been with a strange mixture of excitement and trepidation that I saw Hussein, the Residency driver, uncover the flag flying on the vehicle that brought me back into Mukalla. But the euphoria was brief. 'Having been in the saddle for a week or so,' I wrote rather gloomily later, 'I am beginning to settle into the difficulties of senior office. Awfully lonely it is up here.' With memories of previous isolation in more junior posts I settled into a routine that kept me fully occupied. I exercised fiercely with the help of a badminton set that sister Sabrina had thoughtfully sent for my birthday; other means of keeping fit were limited, though we still managed a few cautious expeditions to the beach, Charles as always relaxed in shirt, shorts and canvas shoes without socks, but carrying instead of a tennis racket or fishing rod an Armorlite M16 rifle.

Last Friday I ran an expedition out to that bay to the west of Mukalla ... there was excellent surfing and we took a couple of goats which we had skinned and cooked on hot stones by our Bedouin escort. The British signallers, etc. absolutely revelled in it, as you can imagine. I had a bit of a time getting to and along a monsoon beach which has gone very soft. We do manage to get out quite a bit but always vary our route and timings, just in case some b****** is waiting for us. Even Mukalla is not immune from those infuriating strikes which dogged us in Aden: suddenly everything is closed and we're running out of food. Anyway, the Hadhrami does get cross if he

is asked to strike about something he cares little, for too long.
He loses money and that hurts.

The punishing work schedule made the days fly. I had two main
political roles. The first was to persuade the rulers of EAP (or at least
the Sultans of Quaiti and Kathiri) to agree to joint control of the HBL
for at least two years after the British withdrawal. This was to ensure
that the force would be paid for by the British for that period. The
second priority was to persuade them to join their Western Protectorate
brethren in Geneva, to negotiate a future which would guarantee their
staying on. As it happened, the hours I did spend with both rulers were
a complete waste of time. I got the agreement but it was to mean
nothing; both rulers were to go into exile shortly after I left.

My other priority was to prepare for the British withdrawal from the
EAP. I knew it was coming, but I thought it would be after Jim had
returned to relieve me. 'I enjoyed a night's visit from Burroughs (a
diplomat based in Aden) whom I invited urgently up here to be
acquainted with the various problems of moving out and packing up
the Residency,' I wrote at the end of July.

I found him most helpful at a time when I need all the moral
(and practical) support I can get. Never have I had so many
people and institutions dependent on my cheerfulness and
resolve. I find it difficult at times to summon much of either
but, as long as one lives from day to day, the problems can be
dealt with one by one.

I spent yesterday up in Saiun seeing the Kathiri Sultan and
the two European officers there. Both are twice my age (I am
the fourth youngest in the whole service) and I find this a
handicap at times as they were both rather fed up and suspicious
of change, but after some stiff talking I got what I wanted.
Saiun may well be closed down by the end of August. It depends
how things go here.

It has been a bit cooler with strong winds off the sea. I have
had a helicopter at my disposal for some time and trips after
midday are really bumpy, frightening things, I think. I never
really understood how they stay up! Don't worry about me.

215

There are many people in a worse position. Nevertheless the expanse of Western Australia seems awfully attractive!

The news from Lynette in Kenya was not good. Little Catherine had gone into hospital for 'dietic investigation' and I got a shock to be told this via the British High Commission in Nairobi to Foreign Office London and from thence via the SAS network connected to Mukalla. Lynette had had problems hearing from me; I was posting out my mail via the SAS, so by the time it got to Kenya it was a couple of weeks old. She did hear of us via the BBC, though.

We had a number of 'incidents', one of which might have been much more serious than it was. A mine was buried on the track leading across the dried wadi of the camel park outside Mukalla. Charles Guthrie and John Shipman had gone, on my recommendation, by vehicle to see a chap who had one of those Malabari teak chests for sale. I was not with them, although it was probably intended for me, but Charles reported there had been a big bang and a hole, which cracked the windscreen, appeared just in front of the vehicle (luckily). The SAS man sitting at the back of the vehicle immediately opened up, to provide a kind of enfilade fire, while Charles ran along the line of the detonating wire that led to the device used to fire the mine. There was a small note there which said (in Arabic) that it should only be used against the British. In the meantime the one result of the SAS fire was to scare the wits out of a date picker who had been up his palm and who found himself descending rapidly, in the thick of a burst of fire. 'I stopped writing last night to give the Sultan supper.' I wrote, having briefly described the incident. 'We chatted until just before midnight. I feel awfully sorry for him as there is simply no one of his stature in whom he can confide and his government is full of scheming mediocrities. I honestly don't see him as surviving our departure unless he takes a firm stand now with some of the political characters.'

A grenade was thrown over the Residency wall one night and there were other sundry bangs, most of which seemed to find their way onto the BBC World Service. What we did not see in Mukalla, however, was the rapid deterioration of the Federal Government and the frantic efforts by the Foreign Secretary, George Brown, to develop a meaningful relationship with the Egyptians and later between the British and the nationalist forces, of which the NLF was to show itself to be the

216

most powerful (mainly because it enjoyed support from powerful elements in the Federal forces which helped destroy the NLF's main competitor, FLOSY).

The British Army began its formal withdrawal from Aden towards the end of August, to a timetable for all troops to be out by 9 January 1968. The NLF and FLOSY fought each other with scores killed and hundreds wounded. By early September the NLF was in contact with the British authorities, but made it clear that it was not prepared to stop the fighting. It wanted to be seen as the triumphant conquerors of the British. I was in the picture insofar as the EAP was concerned. In early August I reported that,

> Life has been very tough politically in the past few days, with frantic lobbying of His Nibs and others. HE [Sir Humphrey] suddenly flew up to Riyan the other day and I had to try to get the sultans there. Lots of grumbling and fuss ... and they were most disappointed he hadn't anything to offer them ... I keep well except I've got a blister from playing badminton on concrete. I long for release from here but life is not actively unpleasant. I am very much a family man as you know and every minute away hurts.

Keeping fit was important for one significant reason: if we had to evacuate at short notice under attack from the NLF, it might not be possible to drive out. That would mean having to escape on foot up the steep hillside at the back of the Residency. We practised this, one hot afternoon when (we hoped) Mukalla was slumbering. I even had bare feet and just my .375. Charles and his merry men accompanied me and we made it to the ridge and over the top, to a piece of flat ground onto which a helicopter could land and take us off. It was nice to be able to keep up with the SAS; John Slim tried it with us one day on a brief visit; we left him puffing in the rear but by then his job would have kept him quite close to a desk.

By mid-August I was still trying to ensure that the two principal rulers would attend the conference in Geneva. It was frustrating, not to say hypocritical, by then to suggest that any course of action was worth while, but those were the instructions. I sneaked a quick break in my Beaver aircraft to fly up to Al Abr and, for a last blissful evening, sat

round the fire with my old friends, Abdullah bin Ndail and Al Kaher (a
dear old man with about five bullets embedded in him who enjoyed
squeezing bits of his flesh to make the jagged lumps come to the
surface). I felt quite sentimental. I knew I would not see them again.

Back in Mukalla I was asked to call urgently on the Sultan,

> where there were those discussions going on over the future of
> the HBL. I rushed over wearing just shorts, a shirt (Fred Perry!)
> and flip-flops [thongs]. Out turned an eight-man guard and a
> bugler played the general salute. I was a bit embarrassed at the
> thought of 'Inglizi' eyes looking on to the scene sardonically
> from behind ... ah well, the days of my being entitled to 11 guns
> from a ship entering harbour will soon be over — and soon also
> will be the responsibility, thank God.

Ten days later I was able to write happily to my mother:

> My plans for leaving, as far as I know, [are] to spend a couple
> of days handing over to Jim and then push off to Aden for a
> week or so, getting my final pay and tax, etc. cleared and then, I
> hope, down to Kenya. I got an ecstatic cable from Lynette
> acknowledging the news I am to be released and saying that
> Catherine is at last improving daily ... apparently a virulent 'E
> Coli' bug was found which because it couldn't be found earlier
> had set up a malabsorption of fats ... the relief is tremendous as
> you can imagine.
>
> All our sultans have left for Cairo and Geneva and it has been
> an active week terrorist-wise, though not directed at us. One of
> our friends [has been] killed in the souk (an Arab I mean) and
> two loud bangs [went off] when the NLF blew up an empty
> house to create an impression of seething multitudes. But we
> have been sitting tight in the Residency and keeping ourselves
> alert [for] when we move out ... I am feeling very mentally
> drained and ready to leave.

I had moved into the Resident's living accommodation on the departure of Jim and Joanna, with just the Residency furniture, a couple of
my own cases, some basic utensils and the red metal dispatch box with

its Chubb padlock. Downstairs the fat Residency major-domo, Ahmed al Sameen, still reigned supreme, his team of staff unobtrusively preparing meals and running the Residency as it had always been run. I too kept up what I could of a 'normal' routine. The preparations to withdraw continued: there were files to be destroyed, crates to be filled and items to be salvaged that would otherwise be stolen or vandalized. I agonized over the disposal of the large signed portraits of the monarchs and their consorts. Then John Slim flew in and cheerfully agreed to arrange for the portraits to be taken to the SAS officers' mess at Hereford.

I found the first letter written from the (then) Colonial Office announcing my impending arrival in 1958. It referred in puzzled tones to the fact that I had failed all my Oxford exams, but had reassured Colonel Boustead that I was made of the 'right stuff'. How long ago it all seemed. I had torn my mind back from the reverie of old files, back to the daily ritual of ordering the day's meals, of checking the incidents of the night before, of discussing the overall security situation. It was tempting to respond to the odd grenade being tossed over the Residency wall by contemplating tossing one back; I must have light-heartedly suggested this as a possible course of action to Aden, as I received a very rapid instruction not to respond at all.

A new menacing factor had to be considered. Colonel Eric Johnson, Commandant of the HBL, was living in his house next to the HBL lines. He did not take kindly to jumped-up acting Residents interfering with his way of life by trying to persuade him to move into the Residency compound. However, when a delegation of senior HBL officers came to see me, it became even more imperative that Johnson was accessible. What would their status be after HMG had pulled out? Who would guarantee their pensions? Without firm promises, they regretted that they could not let Colonel Johnson out of his HQ. Cables flew to and fro, Mukalla and Aden, Aden and London. Then came instructions for me from the High Commissioner. 'You may tell HBL that HMG guarantees pensions and all rights,' it said briefly. The HBL restored Eric's freedom of movement. He came to see me. I had an uncomfortable discussion with him about his location and said I thought he needed to have a couple of the SAS with him. He objected to this, but there was some overhaul of how he looked after himself to enhance his chances of freedom. I saw very little of him from then on.

As for my assurance to the HBL — exchanges in the House of Commons over who had actually told the HBL that it had been assured of British pensions continued until well after the British withdrawal. I am not sure if the HBL ever got them. It was both a relief and galling that my word was to be accepted by the recipients of the tidings, and to be as freely discounted by my masters.

I was awakened at 2.00 a.m. by the SAS signaller who handed me a message: 'You should evacuate Mukalla and close down the British presence' (or words to that effect). So here it was at last and Jim Ellis was not even on the scene; I was to be the last one out. The first important thing was that the two expatriate political officers left in Saiun should be safe. Mahra had already been abandoned; the two from Saiun were to be flown to Riyan which had been reinforced with a detachment of the RAF Regiment.

We planned how best to withdraw. There seemed no indications that anyone in Mukalla knew we were off and we would have to keep it that way. If our foes knew we were evacuating they would be sure to make it impossible for us to get out of the town without a scrap, which would show the world that the NLF had chucked us out; and there might be that tiresome scramble up the scree at the back of the Residency. What a way to go, it was not as if we were even under attack (yet), so I decided we should make it look as if some of us were going to Riyan to meet an aircraft and others could pretend they were on the way to the beach (with towels round their necks) and, to add that extra touch of verisimilitude, I summoned Ahmed al Sameen and gave him instructions for an entirely fictitious dinner that night to entertain someone from Aden. I sent two shirts to the dhobi, just to add that extra touch.

In two and threes, equipment and our few belongings surreptitiously taken to vehicles, arms quietly likewise, we waited until that magic hour after the midday meal when the world slumbered. And then, with minimum fuss, we drove out of the compound: the quarter guard of the HBL had turned out earlier for my inspection, for the last time. I caught one last look at the Residency frontage. There flew the Union Jack. The whitewash shone as brightly as it had that afternoon when I had first been driven up as a new cadet, and the world was strangely innocent and uncomplicated. The old gardener raised a hand in salute as I passed by and we turned into Mukalla's main street and right towards the town gate. It was all very normal. There was the camel park and the usual people squabbling over the loads of lucerne and charcoal. I turned again for a last look and caught just a glimpse of that familiar setting, of colour, of the blue sea beyond. It was the last. I was the last. We never went back.

Once safely out of the narrow defile on the outskirts of town we joined the other vehicles. Phil Hillman had collected Eric Johnson *en route* (which was a relief). A helicopter whirred overhead, anxious to ensure we were all accounted for. We confirmed this by radio. It clattered off towards Riyan, to await our arrival. Hussein, my driver, sensed something was different. I told him that we had left for good. He looked shocked and muttered something. I could not say anything more; my heart was too full at that moment.

As Riyan came into sight, I noted the reinforcements of the RAF Regiment troops dug in at the outskirts of the airfield. Jim Ellis was there, looming over those assembled like a Gulliver surrounded by midgets. I briefly told him that the evacuation had been completed and there was little else to say. I felt absolutely shattered. I walked over to the Resident's vehicle and took the flag off its standard, and the spare from within the vehicle. One I gave to Jim, the other I folded and put in my pocket. Taking my revolver out of its strap under my bush jacket, the same one I had brought with me from Britain, the one that had been used to arrest the Vichy mayor of Algiers, I handed it to Hussein and asked him, on his honour, to see that my old cook Mohamed received it. Mohamed had been to see me in the Residency and begged me to leave it with him when I left. He had been very ill. He was worried stiff about what would happen when the British departed. I do not know if he ever got it, nor do I know what happened to that nice man, his jolly wife and his five daughters. I owed him so much and I lost touch with him: he forms part of the guilt always there at the back of my mind.

Then there were others, I forget now who they were, who came out to Riyan and asked what would become of them. Could they come too? Of course they could not and there was nothing I could say to them about the future. I tried to reassure them but I could not convince them or myself. Her Majesty's Government and I as its agent had behaved with a mixture of incompetence and immorality. I longed to be shot of the lot of them.

# 23

# Freedom of a Sort

IT would have been hard not to have felt I was a genuine refugee in Aden, after I flew out of Riyan for the last time, leaving Jim to cope with the doleful delegations of HBL, Mukalla bank staff, our own Residency staff and others who were being left behind. I should have loved to have salvaged some items from the Residency itself, if only to prevent its deterioration under our successors. There was the magnificent carved round dining table, for example, but not even the resources of the SAS could have coped with that sort of souvenir. Instead, I had to be content with the car standard and one other keepsake, which was the Chubb padlock off the red dispatch box. So, with these two items and some of the scruffiest luggage with which an acting soon-to-be superannuated Resident did ever retire, I let the SAS take me over in Aden. It was marvellous. I was treated with the greatest kindness, even deference, which seemed almost inappropriate for a body of highly specialized and effective men who always appeared to know what they were doing, unlike their civilian counterparts. Perhaps I had had a more difficult job. It could hardly have been more pointless.

I found a home for my beloved .375 magnum; a burly SAS captain assured me he would enjoy its use and would cherish it. I handed back my Stirling sub-machine-gun to the armoury and there I was, unarmed for the first time in Aden for years. I was certainly not defenceless: I was given the exclusive use of an SAS stripped-down Land Rover and the full-time services of two SAS troopers, both named Taffy. With these formidable guardians in tow I sped about Aden, making my farewells, checking my various entitlements, seeing to my baggage and undertaking some last minute shopping.

222

In Khormaksar I found the remnants of the WAP Office. Al Ittihad had been abandoned and there in an ex-RAF quarter was the rump of my service. Peter Hinchcliffe was one of them, still with the odd quip but with much less zest in his usually light-hearted manner. I did not linger, there was no point and already I felt detached from them all. I wished them well and turned my back on what quickly became a vague impression in my flood of memories, a bad dream from which I was about to awaken.

I focused on the banalities of departure: my diary had the following listed (so there were still some shops open which I could visit, in company with my brace of Taffys): coffee percolator, shirts, electric frying pan, steam iron. That was mostly to be included with our baggage, still miraculously safe in store, and our motor vehicle sitting dustily in the High Commission compound.

There was no one at Government House I wanted to see. His legal adviser Hugh Hickling was around, with his untried but beautifully drafted Federal constitution (which was to earn him the award of the CMG) but HE himself was in Geneva or in Cairo, trying to enter into direct negotiations with the NLF, which had refused to form any sort of coalition with FLOSY. The NLF did not need to; it had successfully murdered more of FLOSY than it had lost of its own men, concentrating its attacks on persons rather than on property, which would soon become its own. No matter to UNO if the winners were essentially a band of thugs and assassins, but it might have concerned HMG. How could it give independence to a country if there was no government? The answer was announced by Lord Shackleton himself. 'We still hope for a government there, but if there is no government to hand over to, we can't hand over to a government.' Simple, really. In the meantime, as the NLF successfully controlled the Protectorates, Aden disintegrated under the assaults of the rival NLF and FLOSY gangs and the British continued their military withdrawal.

It seems appropriate at this point to round off the Aden story, as a receding background to my own departure. George Brown as Foreign Secretary announced in early November that the British would be out for good rather earlier than pronounced, by the end of that month, in fact, and this was the signal for the NLF (with the help of the Federal Army) finally to demolish FLOSY. The total tally of those slaughtered has not been recorded, but it was in the hundreds, and bits of the

carnage were witnessed by British troops as they withdrew to prepared
positions, ready for the final evacuation.

The British government was at last able to negotiate with the NLF
and a conference took place in Geneva, Lord Shackleton signing a deal
of sorts with the NLF, only a few hours before the last British forces
pulled out of Khormaksar. The British armed services were really the
only group to emerge with any credit from the mess; and as for what
was left behind, the Peoples' Democratic Republic of South Yemen
was soon to achieve a reputation for being one of the more radical and
murderous (to its own citizens) regimes in the Arab world.

The South Yemenis is what they became and remained until the two
ex-Protectorates and Aden joined with (North) Yemen proper in the
1990s, having previously been under Russian (and earlier, in Mukalla,
Chinese) mentors: they are remembered for their style of government
in a splendidly graphic account by *The Guardian*'s David Hirst,
reporting from Aden on the coup that had overthrown President Ali
Nasser Mohamed a few years before.

> Nothing has been removed so far from the headquarters of the
> ruling Yemeni Socialist Party except the bodies of the victims.
> The blood is still on the carpet around the oval table in the
> upper room where at 10.00 a.m. on Monday 13 January, the
> politburo, the party's supreme executive body was due to meet,
> with the 'conspirator and traitor Ali Nasser' in the chair.
>
> 'This is where Ali Antar was killed,' said one guide, pointing
> to the gigantic black patch on the floral carpet. An all-pervad-
> ing sickly aroma had not yet been entirely removed by layers of
> powder and disinfectant. ... In the adjoining corridor and
> vestibules rival bodyguards slaughtered each other at close
> range. Here the blood still lies so thick, a full three weeks later,
> that one slithers down the staircase.

Poor Aden, poor people — let us hope, years on, that such brutality is a
thing of the past. I think it is, at last.

Right up to the last I had been expecting that there would be a hitch
that would prevent me from catching my flight. It seemed so unlikely
that fate would allow me just to walk out. Jarvis, years earlier and
writing about the Egyptian world, had referred to the 'Last Minute

Delay Society' which he saw, tongue in cheek, as a well-organized conspiracy to prevent one from making that all-important voyage. Leaving fate aside though, it was as if I no longer existed, either in the minds of those Foreign Office 'clean brooms' clustered round Sir Humphrey, or even as a likely target. Would my flight arrive? Scheduled flights were scarce.

I worried unnecessarily. The Air India civilian flight from Bombay to Nairobi did arrive on time, but was to take off late, on Tuesday 5 September 1967. Our delayed departure was due to the aircraft being joined by a number of Indian families, all desperate to leave before they too were ravaged in the final holocaust. The last of Aden's small but thriving Jewish population had already disappeared to Israel. Arab resentment after the June war was enough to shift those who had until then decided to stay on, despite the mounting anti-Semiticism egged on by Voice of the Arabs. That left the British, some Somalis, and those who were too poor or too fatalistic to seek homes elsewhere. It was hard on the Indians, particularly. Some of their forebears had been trading in Aden since shortly after the British secured that barren little fishing village.

The variety of strangely-shaped bundles and small children reminded me of my flight from Aden to Mukalla, when I took up my very first appointment as a brand-new political officer. All that was missing were the goats travelling with the rest of the luggage. I had refined my baggage down to just a couple of cases. I held my breath as the Boeing 707 thundered down the main runway at Khormaksar. My shirt was already clammy in the air-conditioning, after the day's oppressive heat on the ground. There below, strangely serene, lay the scene of a good chunk of my life. The harbour already looked small as we climbed steeply; it also looked empty. There were no big ships lying at anchor, just a couple of grey Royal Fleet auxiliaries moored together, offshore. The last view I had was the familiar shape of the crater and then, cloud, and nothing. I felt drained, just a dead sense of anticlimax.

Not for long: ahead were Lynette and the two children I felt I would hardly know. By the time our aircraft was circling Embakasi airport, Nairobi, my mood had swung to keen anticipation: the green spread of the plains surrounding the airport complex was so different from what I had left a few hours before, that already I was finding it hard to remember details of my departure from the dying shell that was Aden.

After landing though, I might just as well have maintained my sense of anticlimax.

There were four plane loads of German tourists (and others) for the Kenyan customs to work through. Our Air India flight had all those Indian families on board, whose presence was anathema to petty Kenyan officialdom. Did they have visas, entry permits, relatives? All negotiations were conducted in basic English, minimal Swahili and with much hand waving and shouting. I shuffled my way along, Lynette's jewellery in my bag still wrapped in a brown paper parcel from when I had retrieved it from the bank in Aden. It took me two hours to be processed and then I had to catch a flight to Mombasa, where Lynette had taken Charles, leaving Catherine recovering in Gertrude's Garden, the children's hospital in Nairobi.

The East African Airways Fokker Friendship had magnificent porthole windows through which to view the African plains, but that was all you could say for the aircraft, I thought grimly. It was as bad as flying out of Mukalla at midday. We were thrown around the sky, avoiding the great thunderheads of horrendous storms. The message came back from the cockpit — we were diverting to Dar es Salaam, in Tanzania — the weather was too frightful nearer Mombasa. We did a steep turn, the clouds breaking briefly to reveal the great bulk of Mount Kilimanjaro, apparently almost at one wing tip, steadied and bumped our way down to Dar. We did not land. The captain decided we were better off back at Nairobi. We landed without incident at Embakasi again and waited in the lounge there until ten o'clock that night for the weather to lift. I nearly collapsed with fatigue.

We were accommodated at a Nairobi hotel for a few hours while the flight was rescheduled and I tried to make contact with Lynette, but the line was too bad; she would have found out her end that we had returned, in any case. Utterly exhausted, drained by fatigue and anticlimax, I uncoiled on the bed, feeling that nothing mattered any more. I had survived Mukalla: Aden. Now it looked as if I was destined to linger for ever, in a purgatory of flights that never were.

Vague flashes of the past few days seemed to haunt me during what was left of that night — Mohamed's pleading face, grimacing with pain when he came to the Residency; the dust at Riyan; the muzzles of rifles sticking up above the heads of the RAF Regiment dug into the stony coastal plain; the Residency; ordering that last imaginary meal;

226

and the utter squalor of Maalla, with the broken windows swinging in the wind, the newspaper blowing round the dusty corners, the barbed wire and the scrawled slogans of hate on the peeling stucco walls.

I must have slept: the knock on the door at 4.00 a.m. made me jump, and this time there was no problem: once at the airport we took off promptly and landed in the soft tropical freshness of the Kenya coast before the sun was properly up. And there was Lynette, all brown and smiling, and a little blond boy who looked quite changed from when I had last seen him a mere couple of months before. 'Two and a half and he can already read 17 words!' said his mother proudly. I had made it: we were nearly all together again.

After a blissful week strolling along the coral sands we retrieved Charles's smiling chirruping sister, now almost institutionalized from her lengthy stays in hospital (she cried bitterly when separated from the charming ward sister). We organized our flight via Mauritius to Perth. We had been accepted as emigrants to Australia and one morning there was a call from the Australian High Commission in Nairobi. Would I mind calling on the High Commissioner himself, to brief him on what had been happening in Aden? I was only too happy to oblige. I had talked very little, even to Lynette, about those last oppressive days and I suspect the words just came tumbling out. I got a fair hearing that day from a man who seemed himself to have very little to say.

I was lucky. HE the Australian High Commissioner, Walter Crocker was both an experienced diplomat and an academic of distinction. He had also been a district officer in Nigeria, a soldier in the British Army and latterly a farmer, and (at the end of his long years in public life he was to be) Lieutenant Governor of South Australia. He was no apologist for British colonialism; in fact, he had resigned from the British Colonial Service and written a book on it but, as he subsequently remarked:

> The proposition that people should want to govern themselves is unimpeachable in principle ... there remains however what happens in practice; and therefore how, and when, to bring in self-government. The anti-colonialist movement has added to instability and violence in the world ... the new privileged have turned their backs on the old disciplines and morality and too

often have no rules of behaviour, no genuine beliefs, no disinterestedness, except to self-interest — men on the make.

(*Australian Ambassador* by Walter Crocker,
Melbourne University Press, 1971)

What I found so interesting was that later I saw myself relating his words about the 'new privileged' not only to those who followed after the British, but also to certain colleagues of mine who, freed from apparent accountability to anyone, were responsible for developing that terrible policy of pushing our Federal rulers, with all their faults, into the pattern expected of the post-colonial world. This model of expediency is also an image commonly attributed to many politicians.

It was to be my last opportunity to think and talk about the tragedy of Aden. Lynette and I seldom spoke of what we had experienced, except in terms of friends from those days. It fast receded into the irrelevancies of memory, of occasionally glancing through a photo album, of responding to a letter. There was precious little nostalgia for the past: there was no time. The sudden realization that the new life for which we had hankered was nearly upon us made me apprehensive, for the first time, at the thought of having cut myself adrift from the support and background that I had come to take for granted over the past decade, and before that too.

It was opportune to do a quick inventory of our situation, in early October 1967, as we stood shivering in the brisk dawn of a Perth morning, having flown for some 22 hours via Mauritius to Australia. We owed money to no one and we had a few thousand pounds in our London bank, put away against this time. I was officially about to become a pensioner, with the commuted sum of £28.39 to be paid me monthly, until I could expect a rise when I turned 55 years of age (I was 32). We owned some land. On the possible debit side we offered no obvious skills to our new country (Lynette's nursing seemed more useful than my esoteric specialty, but her priority was the children). I had better set to, see about a job. But I did allow myself a few days only, to settle ourselves into temporary accommodation, near to where we would start to build our home. First impressions of our new life-to-be were encouraging. I wrote:

The country here is uniquely Australian and therefore difficult to describe. Altho[ugh] the trees are Australian gums, they are all different shapes and there it is anything but a monotonous scene. We have miles of rolling hills covered in forest to look out onto and are about a mile out of Kalamunda which is a small 'village' with a main street, a library, a few churches and a scruffy old hotel which is straight out of the last century!

All the local traders are very friendly and it's fun to have our favourite shops. Food is excellent as is the milk and we get local eggs from farming friends. Lovely they are after the ones we used to get in Aden. There is a big swimming pool and two local schools which both children will probably go to at some stage. This part of the world is renowned for its wild flowers. They are not like the English flowers.

We had found temporary accommodation in an interesting house, quite near our land, rented to us by the first Australian we met (rather, he was Dutch but he had lived for years in the area). He had made a killing and went bankrupt almost as quickly, gambling on the stock exchange and trading in bogus mining shares. He behaved exactly like all the other 'get-rich-quick' artists who flourished in the late 1960s and early 1970s and, although he looked nothing like the proverbial confidence men (the silvery-haired parsons with Peruvian silver shares and the journalists, of whom I had been warned to steer clear), I quickly recognized the brash bonhomie that was common to their species in Perth.

I had only been unemployed for a few days (once my retirement leave from my post as the Deputy British Agent in Mukalla had ended), when I took my first job in Australia. Before I had left Aden my mother had been busy on my behalf. She had written to a British MP friend of hers who had forwarded my curriculum vitae to the Australian High Commissioner in London. An expensively-presented and lavishly-worded response had assured my mother that such a splendid migrant as myself would have no problem in obtaining a suitable job, provided I looked for it on the eastern seaboard. This was no help.

In Western Australia, still regarded as the Cinderella of the Commonwealth, with only a few companies maintaining sizeable offices in Perth, the choices of employment had to be limited, but I tackled them. On our third day in the country I started trudging round Perth streets, dashing off letters and making contacts. A number of possibilities emerged — a clerical position in the state or Federal Governments; Shell; the university, and a largish rural-based conglomerate called Wesfarmers. They all seemed fearfully dull, but — needs must. Just to cloud the decision-making process, my old boss from Aden days, Sir Charles Johnston, now British High Commissioner in Canberra, wrote unexpectedly and somewhat enigmatically to ask if I would like to work for the Australian government, 'on the security side of the house.' I said I would be living in Kalamunda. That contact withered. It had to be Wesfarmers.

In those days the Wesfarmers group was nothing like the Australian giant that emerged in the late 1980s. It operated from elderly premises on the scruffy side of town, with small subsidiaries and branches all round Perth and the state. I had just walked in off the street, asked for Personnel, and was interviewed by a quizzical man who wondered aloud what my strange experience had to offer to such a firm. I wondered myself; my details were passed round the various departments, to see if anyone thought they could use me. I met a youngish man, the future chief executive, who thought he could recognize raw talent when he saw it; and I was dispatched to the printing works to understudy the printing manager.

It was like being introduced to a bit player from *Pinnochio*: Bernie resembled a nut, perhaps crossed with a gnome, with a touch of tortoise thrown in. His grave bevel of a polished pate was mounted on a wrinkled column of a neck that vanished into an immaculate collar, big enough for two. The rest of him was sufficiently dapper to feature as a male model for *Al Capone*. He wore a fedora hat, when most urban Australians had (foolishly) given up their headgear. He was a very nice man and if I have affectionately dwelt on his appearance it is because his exterior concealed a touching faith in my abilities.

Bernie was a relic of the days when printing machinery operated almost entirely in the letterpress mode. His workforce of about 60 ran a laconic factory that did nearly all the group's printing. It was in this old-fashioned milieu of totally strange machinery that whirred and roared and rattled, tended by taciturn men and strange women who eyed me curiously as I was led round, that Bernie saw in me the answer to his most pressing problem. I, this 'Pommy' visitation, was going to modernize his operations for him, I, who knew nothing about printing, about business or about Australia. I accepted gratefully.

I bought myself a hat like Bernie's and a small white motorcar (the Holden when it arrived was for Lynette). I tried to learn what the various machines did; I studied the factory layout; I followed the various stages that a print job went through and I made some tentative suggestions on how to improve the flow. Bernie was enthusiastic. Emboldened, I ventured the thought that the office staff (some three women) seemed rather slack. Bernie dismissed all of them. Thoroughly alarmed by then, the printers held a union meeting and there were complaints made about me and I was abused by one of them. Bernie wanted to fire him too; I persuaded him not to. I suddenly felt totally out of place, and I had only been there a month or so. I wondered what we were doing so far from the familiarity of British institutions.

I was about to start another increasingly dreary day at the printing works when a familiar looking envelope addressed to me was in our postbox. I opened it after I had arrived at work. It was headed 'Foreign Office, S.W.1' and it said:

Dear Mr Crouch,

On your retirement from public service overseas, the Secretary of State has asked me to let you know of his appreciation of your work for the government and people of Aden and the Protectorate and Federation of South Arabia since your first appointment in 1958.

He wishes to thank you in particular for your work under *the trying circumstances* [my emphases] in Aden during the period immediately prior to your leaving.

He sends you his best wishes for the future.

Yours sincerely,

(Miss E.J. Elliott)
Private Secretary

'Immediately prior': when did Mr Brown mean, I wondered. Who got him to write it, and why could he not have signed it personally? I thrust the letter into my pocket to show Lynette when I got home.

231

# 24

# After Life — What?

THE feeling of frustrated helplessness stayed with me, off and on, for at least the next half dozen years. Not that it lingered with the roar and whistle of antiquated machinery; not at all. My reluctant admission that I knew nothing of use and, moreover, actively disliked my new surrounds, far from condemning me to unemployment, ensured a steady progression upwards. The printing works was just a small part of the industrial and commercial group. I was put into forward planning: my total inability to prepare forecasts for liquid petroleum gas sales over the next decade merely spurred my employer to placing me elsewhere, in the marketing and publicity area. I was bemused, but grateful.

Soon I had a company car. I travelled inter-state to conferences, returning to sit behind a desk that grew in size to match my burgeoning status. Came the day, to my utter incredulity, when as part of a promotion to Assistant Company Secretary, no less, and sitting at the centre of apparent decision-making power in the organization, I was appointed as executive director of that very printing works that had taken me off the streets. It was hard to meet the eye of that nice gnome of a printing manager who had seen his inspiration of my guiding him into the future, under his direction, turn into his being the one who was directed. I did very little of that. I still knew practically nothing about printing and intended to leave it that way.

This progression should have provided exactly what was required for me to establish a new career in a new country. It lacked the one essential element on which I had come to rely during those turbulent Arabian years: responsibility. The further I rose in the organization, the less I was expected, or even formally required, to assume personally any accountability for even part of the performance of the company that employed me.

I had tasks to carry out, true, and they needed doing properly. I had meetings to run; I had places to visit and on which to report, but, in the last analysis, my presence was as important and relevant to the wellbeing of my employers as was the landing on the moon (which, incidentally, I had the time to watch, live, in my office on television). Part of the problem was my reluctance to stick my neck out, into commercial areas where I had no experience, no 'feel'; the other side of the problem was that my employers seemed to have no expectation of me that I should. I felt a fraud.

The consequence was that, lacking a challenge, I had to try to make do with ostensible recognition, of which there was plenty. My company car, large desk, expense account and position descriptions would have satisfied the usual middle-level executive. Such trappings, however, have never been particularly important to me, possibly because I never had to worry about them; the emphasis has always been on deriving keen satisfaction from being seen to do a worthwhile job. During those first five years in Australia it was my almost total inability to contribute in any meaningful way and to any purposeful extent that was so depressing. Plainly it was also a reaction from being responsible for so much when so young that made for an unpalatable contrast. I was going through the 'male middle-aged crisis' well before I was 40.

It was all so depressing. Yet, to counter that, at home Lynette and the children, soon to be increased by the birth of our younger son (a true Australian), revelled with me in the feeling of security, the clarity of clean, dust-free air, of blue horizons, of constructing our large garden from nothing, of planting cherry trees, of the enjoyment of friends' company and of happy family relationships among ourselves.

It was fortunate that my chronic sense of uselessness at work was brought to a head by the new chief executive offering me the position of 'heir apparent' to the company secretary/head of administration. In the 20 years' growth of Wesfarmers to the size it is today, it was clear even then that promotion would have evolved into that of a general managership. It was not a difficult decision for me to make: not only was I unqualified to be the company secretary (and with no practical prospects of working towards such qualifications) it represented a lifetime in an organization where I had never found my feet. I declined. Two months later I had persuaded a reluctant Lynette that the opportunity of relocating 1000 miles north of Perth was essential for me and would be good for the family.

So it proved over the next couple of years. I had accepted the post of a superintendent in charge of the personnel functions of one of the world's biggest iron-ore mining companies, the Mt Newman Mining Company. It was run by Australia's largest conglomerate, BHP, and was financed by a consortium of top international operators. At the top it was run by engineers, whose management style could be best described as autocratic, not unlike some of the feudal characters I had left behind in Arabia. At least one knew exactly where one stood.

We were based in Port Hedland, a township whose glaring ugliness was reminiscent of Aden at its worst in mid-summer: the heat off silver fuel and water pipes running over the flat uninspiring coastal terrain, the flies and the stark shimmer of dusty streets baking in a miasma of unaesthetic squalor — there was a certain surrealist aura about Port Hedland that took me back to Aden in those last days before I had departed. The effect was also not lost on Lynette whose natural longing for her garden back in Kalamunda never left her. However, this phase of my working life was not for ever; we made friends who are still with us, and we had the unique opportunity to enjoy the stretches of perfect wilderness along the great De Grey river, 100 miles out of Port Hedland.

We would camp by one of the tree-lined stretches of permanent creeks that survived the infrequent floods resulting from cyclonic rain. The water was alive with fish; overhead, flocks of budgerigars wheeled as one, in a sheet of glinting green. Pelicans and black swans took off, like squadrons of ponderous flying boats. It seemed a natural extension of those Arabian treks, now made magic by the presence of small brown children, engrossed in the totally mind-absorbing pursuits of the moment.

It was the work, however, that finally brought me the sense of self-fulfilment for which I had been searching ever since Mukalla. From seven in the morning, often until the same time in the evening, on call at weekends, the unremitting demands of heavy industry, the vagaries and accidents caused by a large and rapidly changing workforce, the work process continuing for every hour and day of the year (strikes and cyclones permitting) — mining, transporting, processing and shipping the millions of tons of ore that poured into the blast furnaces of Japan — they all demanded of me (to a greater or lesser extent round the clock) that I was available to make decisions, to consult and occasionally to confront.

With vivid memories of my period in Canadian heavy industry, I was at last able to relate my Arabian experience of consultation and persuasion to the challenges of introducing and maintaining work procedures that might be accepted only reluctantly by my colleagues and even less so by suspicious unionists. My role was to establish the personnel function, almost from scratch. My predecessor had departed abruptly to drive a taxi in South Australia, which I had gathered was more his line. I recruited and led a team of people specialized in the minutiae of hiring, of keeping safe and of training a workforce of thousands. It was heady stuff, that post-pioneering period of the mid-1970s. The big iron ore mines had only come on-stream in the late 1960s: there was virtually full employment and there were frequent industrial stoppages. With the shop stewards and their ilk, I was once again in a situation in which the techniques learnt at tribal gatherings came into their own. The atmosphere was always tense and sometimes the communication was difficult (we had 43 different nationalities on site).

It was, I realized, the area of work for which I was most suited, the integration of people into work situations, from which they would derive the maximum satisfaction and consequently perform to their best endeavour. Again, I could see this as an extension of the political-cum-developmental role that had been mine in South Arabia. At last, I felt, I was 'coming of age'. Port Hedland was a stage, however. We really did want to return south; the children needed schooling away from the north, and there was no way I would consider boarding school. I had a satisfyingly fierce confrontation with a useless senior colleague, resigned with honour and a good reference, and we moved home in great contentment.

I decided I needed the challenge of a year or two at university to complement my recent experiences, preferably in the management training and development area. There was nothing suitable in the tertiary institutions of Perth. The nearest seemed to be a diploma in education. Thus, at the age of 45, I qualified with some distinction as a secondary schoolteacher, though in the interim I had accepted a full-time appointment to select and train social workers in management skills and related disciplines for a large state government department.

This two-year interlude had the one great advantage of forcing me to apply my practical experience, of the highly structured environment of heavy industry management procedures and decision making, to a so-called discipline in which the graduates thereof appear to function almost entirely on some innate ability acquired from a social work degree. The fact that I was not one of them by training and certainly not by philosophical inclination made for constant friction. My jokey nickname for the department, 'The Department of Applied Love', got few smiles. However, the training processes I developed and used over this restless period were the basis for my role as an educational management consultant a decade later.

I eventually gave up on the social workers, to mutual relief. I became a schoolmaster and for eight years taught a variety of subjects, ranging from French and remedial maths to accounting (of which I knew nothing and had to keep one chapter ahead of the brighter boys) and economics, the subject area I headed for the latter part of my brief pedagogic career. The classroom contact was immensely satisfying. The challenge was always there, to induce the self-motivation that is the key to the child (or adult) wanting to seek out knowledge for him/herself. It is seldom easy to meet that challenge, especially in a large independent boys' school, where the combination of the range of sporting and cultural pursuits, together with the insulation of the boys by 'the system', makes for narrowness of outlook and often a disinclination to take on the world constructively.

There was (and still is) the tremendous disadvantage of Western Australia's students being educated in one of the remoter parts of the world — 'remote', that is, in geographical and cultural terms from the rest of the civilized world. I did perhaps accept the Bedouins' indifference to much of what was strange to them; they after all had their own culture and structure. Not so here: a Western Australian youth, imbued with a mixture of chauvinistic self-satisfaction and with a perception of values gleaned from American television, is a different creature. I worked hard to widen perspectives, to enthuse. It was stimulating, for me at least.

Towards the end of my teaching decade I had an opportunity to introduce a system of 'teacher appraisal', which I had developed from my time with foremen in the iron ore days. Foreman are the most junior level of management, though probably the most important in terms of getting the daily jobs done to schedule, and they were the most ignored. Communication was usually from the top down, seldom two-way. Foremen, in my experience, tended to opt out of dicey industrial confrontational situations, from which they expected to collect only blame when the crisis worsened. I had done some work on a format for self-appraisal which I felt the incumbent could use as a basis for the annual interview with the foreman's supervisor. I tested it, it seemed useful and I put it away. My employer at that time was not really interested in such new-fangled ideas. Next we would be asking foremen their opinions on things that were nothing to do with them.

I realized that teachers work in isolated environments (their class-rooms) and with that they are not dissimilar to foremen on shift. They do their best (and worst) work in isolation from their superiors. They too are called to account by their heads, often with the latter having only the most general idea of how well a particular teacher has performed. I proposed my scheme and, hesitatingly, the school agreed to my methods being tried. It was a resounding success and soon I had been invited by a prominent management consultant in Melbourne to become his 'appraisal arm'. Some five years later there are schools in every mainland state of Australia using my scheme. Its acceptance has come from those few heads who actually want to communicate fully on a regular basis with each member of their staffs. The majority of Australian heads, however, still seem content to perform their roles as autocrats, reminiscent of the BHP style of management, however benevolent. The current economic recession has encouraged the perpetuation of the 'director' rather than the 'consulter', although the need to enhance effective communications at all levels is especially apparent, particularly in large schools.

It is easy for me to see a parallel between my work in earlier days of encouraging the local benevolent despot to spend some of his income on good works round the state capital (on roads, water schemes, or councils rather than on a new palace) and of encouraging headmasters to spend time and money on sitting down and talking constructively and regularly with each member of the teaching staff. The heads themselves may not appreciate the comparison being drawn, but I am content myself to see my experiences come full circle.

237

I have another interest that is directly related to my earlier days: I help run a conservation foundation that distributes funds, mostly in small amounts, to self-help community groups that are intent on preserving or restoring some part of the local environment. Western Australia has suffered greatly from the invasion of exotic species and feral fauna, consequent upon white settlement. The parallel with my helping to rescue the Arabian oryx from the invasion of the feral species, man, may be rather far-fetched, but I am sure the experience sowed the seed of my current interest in this area.

I have also recognized a need, especially in the conservation area, to involve the whole community in wanting to cooperate in preserving what is left of our heritage and this, I think, applies more than just to the environment. I am sure I am being wise in retrospect, but the common thread running through my life has been that of a catalyst. I have, however, not always been successful in communicating the message of the time in such a way that the receiver is not only prompted to accept it (and perhaps add to it) but, in essence, to believe that it was he or she who initiated it in the first place. But I believe that only if that takes place does constructive change occur and survive and this is because the initiator actually wants it to.

This working philosophy is my personal epilogue to what this account has been all about: a relatively brief sojourn in South Arabia when, like Richard III 'half made up', I helped influence in a minimal way a part of the world that was itself part-formed, at least in twentieth century social and political terms. That was the vital period in my life when I met the wise men (and some wise women too) who taught me (a somewhat narrow minded and ignorant young man) enough to develop into someone who could learn to respect people and institutions for what they were, at least before some of them were destroyed in front of me.

It then took me a lengthy period to recover my sense of self-respect and to find what I could do best: the restlessness, I (and poor Lynette) suffered through my inability to settle at anything for long, in itself was to prove a strength. The many work encounters from which I learnt something new, combined with the ability to cope with self-inflicted changes of career, have provided me with the satisfaction of experiencing much and of perhaps contributing accordingly.

# After Life — What?

It might have been different even just a few years ago: while in some despair at my inability to relate to social work and its disciples I had penned the following gloomy doggerel:

### On Achieving One's 44th Birthday in a State of Unaccountability*

Flaccid, tired before my time,
Living in each moment, slopping through the day,
Contaminated by the bureaucratic slime,
Yet aiming cheerfully to strive at each 'working' day.
It's all too easy to look back 12 years—
Back to an era where a new life lay ahead,
Coping then with the sweat and tears
Of change from an existence long since dead.
And yes, one lacks the stimulus of fears
Brought on by starting life anew.
'State of Excitement' — 'The Wild Flower State'*—
Slogans exhort us to eschew
All but the banalities of Fate.

It is still apparently the fashion among many politicians and not a few diplomats to regard the British influence as the principal cause of strife in the Middle East. Such an approach, it seems to me, is as misleading (even as irrelevant) as blaming the colonists for settling in North America or in Australia. Such triteness also obscures much of what really took place on a daily basis, between the expatriate Briton and the local people, not in a relationship of colonizer and oppressed, but in the context of a mutual inter-dependence, of service, of living cheek by jowl in solitary isolation, of doing the best one could, according to expected standards of behaviour, with limited resources and a sense of humour.

The particular efforts of the British in South Arabia have been shown to have been fatally flawed on two levels. The first I personally

---

* I must have been exasperated at the state government's efforts to compose slogans to describe Western Australia for the delight of tourists. I never felt so gloomy about my working life again. What is more, I can now look back on my days in South Arabia with more than sombre introspection — and what follows is, of course, my personal opinion.

experienced: the extraordinary political muddling in South Arabia itself, a misguided policy of forcing a system of political development onto a people who were patently not ready for it. Secondly, and worst of all, a blatant disregard of the civilized behaviour expected of certain senior colleagues of mine who saw that the means justified the ends: if you can suborn enough people with rifles and ammunition and encourage them to murder your opponents, then eventually it will all 'come good' (as we Australians say). Well, such an approach did not (and never did) have a hope of succeeding which, deep down, I think they knew.

The withdrawal of British forces from the one significant western presence in the Middle East (that is, in Aden, rather than the relatively insignificant numbers of British units in the Gulf area) was partly justified in the case of South Arabia by the prevailing British government dogma: that support for traditionally based tribal institutions was wrong. The result was a sharp decline in South Arabia's advance into the modern world, a political semi-vacuum, a Russian centre for mischief-making and, by logical extension, the eventual opportunity for a modern robber–baron, Saddam, to build his personal power bases.

The fact that the distaste for traditional forms of Arab rule did not extend to the sultanate of Muscat, the Gulf amirates or to Kuwait, where the rulers exercised control (and apparently still do) by various degrees of absolute control, makes a nonsense of this dogma which, at the very least, smacks of hypocrisy. Perhaps it would have been more honest of British politicians of both main political parties when in power to have made it clear that Britain was going broke in trying to maintain its old imperial commitments, but that was not the idiom of the time.

Another perspective to my indulging in the luxury of looking back, is a reference to someone I consider far more competent than myself in commenting on things South Arabian at the time: that distinguished correspondent to *The Daily Telegraph*, the late R.H.C. Steed. I found a cutting among my letters, before starting this account. He was writing in his usual thoughtful way about the effects of pulling out of Aden. On 2 March 1966, under the heading ADEN: A COSTLY RETREAT, part of what he said was:

The great majority of Adenis want Britain to stay in the base after independence, and thus ensure their safety and livelihood. They are the victims of the Egyptian and Yemeni terrorist campaigns which never would have been effective but for fear, now confirmed, that Britain would leave ... Yet if Britain had said a year ago firmly and clearly that she was staying on, the Adeni public and politicians would have cooperated against the gunmen and defeated them ... Mr Healey made a shocking, and admitted, error in confusing the local (anti-British) Aden government with the government of the South Arabian Federation (which is pro-British and which counted on the promised defence treaty with Britain after independence).

All the same, he cannot have shared the widespread confusion about the true position and role of a base. Yet he certainly appears to be exploiting popular misconceptions about Aden in picking it as the branch to be chopped off. ... All the indications are that, in both the short and long term, a decision which is obviously morally wrong will also prove costly in lives, money, security and reputation.

Maybe: strong stuff and still debatable, but containing enough of an uncomfortable truth to bring it all back. For me, it did just that.

# 25

# Full Circle: 'It Never Should Have Happened'

3 April 1993: the Yemenia 727 touches down at Sanaa airport after an overnight flight from London. The jagged peaks of northern Yemen are interspersed with patches of cultivation. Yellow, ocre, dark brown, streaks of green, we taxi past the military area, where a cannibalized helicopter lolls before rows and rows of its fellows painted in dark camouflage brown, with the rosette of black, red and white to identify the Yemeni Air Force. A jet fighter is in the same livery — then, we halt. Steps are down. It is all quite unreal.

The invitation to visit the Yemen had come via Seiyed Rashid Alkaf, the chairman of the Yemeni Company for Investment in Oil and Minerals. Would a small group of ex-politicos care to visit the areas that they left so precipitously, 27 years before? Why? It was not really clear, other than that it represented a 'hands-across-the-seas' gesture, a sort of 'All is different now. Come and see for yourselves and tell the world how it has changed.' It was an amazing offer and, with prompting from Lynette, I hesitated only momentarily. One really should never go back to the scenes of so much trauma and yet I would kick myself later if I opted out.

I forwarded a brief curriculum vitae, as requested, and thought over what I had heard about the two Yemens over the past few years. There had not been much news in the Australian press. *The Economist* had printed a few pieces on the unification of the two countries and the BBC had carried a recent report by a travel correspondent who complained about the lack of western sanitation facilities between Sanaa and Taiz. It was not much to go on. I turned to John Shipman, our group's coordinator, to beef up my scanty knowledge. John was

242

still working for the British Foreign Office; he is immensely well informed on the Yemen and an Arabic speaker of the first rank.

Before 1990 the attempts to unify the Yemen Arab Republic (the north) and the People's Democratic Republic of South Yemen (what had been the British preserve) had come to nothing in the previous 20 years: there had been a right-wing government in the north confronting a very left-wing government in the south. There had been two border wars and three heads of state assassinated or executed. Whatever efforts had been made towards unification were demolished by that bloody revolution in Aden in 1986, to which I have referred previously. More border clashes and then, following the collapse of the USSR, an accord in 1988 that allowed movement of people between the two countries and a deal of cooperation over oil exploration.

Final negotiations had resulted in the new state being formed in 1990, a remarkable achievement given the disparity between the two political and economic systems. Our visit was to precede by some weeks the first country-wide elections for the inaugural consultative assembly. So much for what had been happening since that day in September 1967, when I had scuttled aboard a crowded Air India flight to Kenya.

Our little group was perhaps typical of a collection of characters who had mostly had to start again from a common and colourful experience. We had done very different things in the intervening years. John Shipman has alfeady been introduced. Bill Heber Percy, foundation president of the Anglo–Yemeni Association, had worked in the Oman during the 1970s, prior to farming in the Welsh hills. John Ducker joined the World Bank. It was the first time I had seen him since 1966, though we had kept in touch each Christmas. He, like me, had only flown into London the previous day, in his case from Kirghizstan.

We collected our visas in a rush. I walked down to the London offices of Air Yemenia to check out the flight. A charming Yemeni greeted me with warmth, in excellent English, and enquired whether it was to be my first visit. I explained my background and how it was in the nature of a pilgrimage. 'It never should have happened and you should not have left like that,' said Khalid Rashid. I was moved.

It was a pleasant temperature on arrival (Sanaa is over 7000 feet above sea level) and our welcome was cordial. Almost instantly we were made aware that this was not to be a low-key tourist affair — our own transport to the VIP lounge, a white Mercedes to the plush hotel and, suddenly, we were whisked into the most unexpected but pleasant role of a top-level delegation. Apparently the Yemeni government was anxious to obtain our recollections of where the border lay between Saudi Arabia and what had been the Eastern Aden Protectorate, so, like most Middle Eastern situations, there was also a hidden agenda. We were no mere sightseers, we were to sing for our supper. It was to be a pleasure.

The next few days in Sanaa maintained their surrealist quality: being whisked in a stretched limousine, formally suited, to meet senior government officials and to pour over frontier maps and record our recollections of past border incidents. Luncheon hosted by the foreign minister, Dr Al-Iriani, being entertained by kind British Embassy hosts, the brief evening gatherings of the four of us to catch up on what had happened to each of us over the years. It was the stuff of dreams.

We played at being tourists, too: walks round the friendly streets of old Sanaa, the magnificent medieval buildings set against a hubbub of amplified calls to prayer and the roar of traffic. Outside the city, there were drives at breakneck speed over remarkable highways constructed through dramatic passes, castles crowning steep slopes cultivated by endless strips of terraces, crowded market places, military checkpoints, numerous lines of Toyotas packed with humanity and goods, sudden shabbiness and squalor, a hubbub of littered alleys, crossroads, chaos.

We were impatient to be off. After much discussion it was agreed we should be driven to Aden, from there to Mukalla (all bitumen now), to the Hadhramaut and back via Marib to Sanaa. We were escorted by a couple of soldiery and two helpful civilians, one of whom was Mohamed ash Shami (grandson of the Governor of Baidha, who had been in charge at the time the British had been across the border), who was to be visiting these places for the first time.

The other 'minder', Mohamed Abdo, hailed originally from Aden. He had earned his credentials as a grenade thrower during the 1960s. He described, with a certain malevolent humour, how, as a small boy, he had been assembled with his school to welcome the queen on her visit to Aden in April 1954. This was at a time when each school day started with a daily commitment to, 'God, the country and the queen.' Her Majesty had apparently directed that each of the poor children should be given, 'A glass of milk with sugar in it, one banana and a pair of trousers,' on the receipt of which he had run to see his mother excitedly, to say he had seen the queen wave, 'And she is so *white*. And why am I not like her?' It made a good story. He summed up his feelings towards the British during the troubles: 'We hated you ... but, later, we feel the British had such good rules.' His feelings, I judged, were still equivocal towards the erstwhile oppressors. Perhaps he pined for his East German mentors?

The next four days were a kaleidoscope of impressions — Lahej, our first married home, the palace frontage submerged in modern decor. The desert between there and Shaikh Othman, a mass of houses, towards Little Aden, more urban sprawl. In Al Ittihad (now Madinat-al-Shaab, the Town of the People), our second house, the bazooka repairs still showing in the stone wall. Silent Valley, the slanting sun casting shadows across the familiar regimental names and ranks — South Wales Borderers, Royal Northumberland Fusiliers and, of course, Pat Gray's headstone.

Tawahi, Maalla, Crater, those ex-services flats, teeming with life, washing hanging, noise, cheerful families gathered in cafés that spilled onto the pavements. Scruffy, yes, very, an extension of Crater, but cheerful, colourful, friendly. All except for the sad old Crescent Hotel. Ancient retainers raised quavering hands to dirty turbans. Perched on sofas crushed by innumerable behinds, we drank an over-priced beer, while the shades of earlier drinkers jeered at us from the shadows.

The road to Mukalla and beyond was a long day of frantic speed, interspersed with abrupt halts, as the bitumen culminated in washaways. By early afternoon we were in Wahidi country and stopping at Habban. With Mohamed Abdo's help I traced the tall building where Lynette, baby Charles and I had lunched over 27 years ago. I had a photograph of Charles being held by Ali Misaed Babakri, in company with Mahdi bin Mohsin. There was a heart warming discussion with a relative of theirs; regretful rejections of their offers of hospitality and a promise to forward the photograph to our old friends in Saudi Arabia.

Amazing — the buildings and plots were marked out all the way to Mukalla, which is now a large metropolis — a dual highway on reclaimed land, overhead street lights. The Sultan's palace (tidier than it had been in my day) is now the museum. Inside, all is as I remembered from those interminable meetings at the end — overstuffed, plastic chairs, portraits of earlier rulers and photographs of British dignitaries. All very strange it felt. Across the road, the old Residency, now sadly unkempt, though still in use by the administration.

The Naib Muhatifa, the 'governor' of the fifth directorate comprising Mukalla and the Hadhramaut, Awadh Abdullah al Murshadi, greeted us with warm courtesy. In strode a stocky figure who, after the usual greetings, enquired (in Arabic, mine was just returning): 'Who was there at the end, in Mukalla?' John Shipman indicated me and himself. 'You remember the grenade over the hospital wall?' We did. 'I threw it,' he said simply. And the explosion in front of my vehicle that nearly took out John Shipman and Charles Guthrie? He also. This was Colonel Abdurahim Atik, *Maamur* (Commissioner) of Saiun and our host for the next two days. His hospitality and charm reached through to me: one more ghost had been laid.

The final stages of this so strange an experience took us from familiar haunts in the Wadi Hadhramaut out to the desert fringes of Al Abr (the original fort now in picturesque ruin) and of Zamakh. We had suggested there would be value in such a visit. We were joined by an old friend from HBL days, Ahmed Nowah Barashaid, and by the Rasputin-looking brother of Abdullah bin Ndail. Interspersed by moments of great emotion as we were embraced by old friends, we experienced once more the contentment and camaraderie of those remote times, when a carefree youngster thought only of the present, and perhaps the next day, as he strove to fulfil the expectations instilled by family, by colleagues and by those cheerful Bedou, each vying with the other to impress and to cajole. Fond memories abounded, bad memories submerged. Perhaps that is what our trip was really about.

Such introspection does nothing to describe the real state of the newly-unified country of Yemen, except to note in passing that even surviving this long as a single state is a plus — there is some suspicion between the north and south. Those border discussions to which we contributed might be vital to future oil expectations. There is a refugee problem, there is poverty. The Yemen probably lost 20 per cent of its gross national product during the Gulf crisis, when it refused to back the US line. One answer to future well-being must rest with the private sector, albeit inhibited in the south by an ex-marxist bureaucracy that stifles initiatives. I wish them well. I really do.

*Full Circle: 'It Never Should Have Happened'*

As for me, I am at last at peace with South Arabia. The shades have departed.

# Appendix
# Handing-over Notes for Northern
# Deserts Area — February 1960

### 1. Introduction and General

I intend merely to provide an account of the different matters that are occupying us at present. It is unnecessary to give notes at length on the various characters, except where important, as very full and amended notes on them have already been provided by ELLIS and KHARUSI, and will be found in the *District Book*. Finally this last has also been brought up to date and should provide any of the background necessary. Therefore I shall touch on subjects quite at random, starting in the Western Area.

*Relations with Quaiti*

In the west one's area overlaps with the territory of the Naib of Western Province, Hora. It is usual to try to bring him in on any tribal matters as he does not like being left out of things. The present Naib, Sh. Ali bin Breik, is very easy to work with, and although not as *shedeed* (Arabic — 'tough') as his predecessor, Naib Badr Kassadi, appears to get on well with the locals. Secondly, matters Manahil technically come under the Naib of Shibam, Sh. Ali Amari. It is necessary at times to drop in on him to give him the news from the north as it affects the Manahil, but I should say that this Naib is quite content to leave the Manahil in the north, to one. Finally, there are certain sums of money provided by the Quaiti government to help in water development for the Sear and the Manahil. The ideas come from

248

AAND and the money from the Naibs; the latter are quite willing to hand it over.

*JAA Kharusi* is in charge of the western area of Northern Deserts, being based at Al Abr with his wife and family. Kharusi is quite invaluable when he is fit and holds the respect of the Bedouin in his area — the Sear, Kurab and the Breiki Musheikh of the Shabwa area. He can be called upon to help in anything, and his local knowledge of most of Northern Deserts, either by experience or by hearsay, is pretty extensive.

### Relations with the Yemen
The actual boundary can be seen from a map in JAA Kharusi's office: we are bounded by the 'Violet Line' which effectively cuts across our tribes' grazing grounds. One has to be tactful over this and while not discussing the existence of the line with the locals, one has to discourage them from taking the law into their own hands and carrying out reprisals on the Dahm tribe of the Yemen, for heavy camel losses in the past. I believe that this is an annual problem: when the rains have been good both our tribes and the Dahm get ideas about raiding and an occasional motor patrol on our side of the line is necessary to discourage those individuals who want to return to the bad old days. We had trouble with the Abdullah bin Aown section of the Sear last year (November 1959) when a party picked 17 camels from the Dahm, and the threat of a reprisal from the Dahm hung over the area for a short time. However, Kharusi has one or two contacts who slip over from the Yemen with more or less reliable information on when a raid is expected.

### Relations with Saudi
We have a contact in Sharora.

### Security Western Area
It is fairly easy to keep the peace in the Al Abr area owing to the terrain being suitable for fast motorized patrols. However, after any rain there always arises trouble in the Maashar area, round the Ramlat Sabatein, where a number of different sections argue over to whom the land belongs. Kharusi sorts them out pretty quickly but the removal of

Annasir Post may give rise to extra disorders. (Likewise the Quaitis are likely to complain about the increasing number of rifles being smuggled into Wadi Irma.) Shabwa, incidentally, is kept out of by us, but many of its inhabitants are seen at Al Abr.

## Pumps, Northern Deserts

PCL in different seasons have drilled for their own use boreholes at Zamarkh, Minwakh, Hazar, Thamud, Dhila, Sanau, Sheher and Shahan. The last two are either capped or u/s. The others are meant to be kept running for the use of the Bedouin when PCL are away, and this task comes to be one of the more arduous of the ND duties, if too many of the wells break down at once. The situation is as follows:

*Zamarkh*. This well was broken by PCL who did not have time to repair it before the end of the 1959 season; they are due to repair it but we need a pump. Owing to Mr Guthrie, the manager of the Madhramaut Pump Scheme, going on leave the matter was quietly shelved by the HPS. It is of some importance that we get this pump going; not because there is not another well, there is, but because although we may close the well later ourselves, to leave it broken and not do anything about it because PCL have left the area gives the Bedouin a chance to point out how their interests do not count, etc.

*Minwakh* is now working well under the charge of a young Seari who did a course in the HPS workshops and who has been surprisingly good. His wages and rations are paid by the Quaitis, but from funds held for water development held by AAND. Whenever this pump does break down there is a terrible scream from the Bedouin, owing to the large number of animals watering there, many of whom have arrived from the Sharora region. One therefore calls on the HPS Saiun to send up a mechanic immediately.

*Hazar* is at present being used and therefore being maintained by PCL. This is also an important pump for the Bedouin in the summer, and one of the best operators is put there.

*Thamud* is being used by PCL at present. Government does not use this much as the old well suits the Bedouin requirements, though it gets very low in summer. However, it is useful, if the key is around, to fill up one's own barrels.

*Sanau* is probably the biggest headache of the lot. When this breaks down not only is there the problem of the locals being left without water but also the garrison. The old well, Bedou built, has little and unpleasant water. Therefore when this pump breaks down, it is essential to get a mechanic from Saiun immediately because of the great distance.

*Dhila* has just been repaired by PCL and being used if necessary by them. This is not an essential pump for the Bedouin but if this pump is kept going at the end of the season it must be kept in a good state of repairs as large numbers of Bedouin will move north and will be left high and dry if it goes u/s.

## General Notes
Firstly, there is a large number of boys from the HBL training in the HPS workshops. They are still young and it is undesirable to put them by themselves in charge of a pump each. However, they may have to be used this summer. Secondly, if a pump does go u/s, it is undesirable to allow any HBL mechanic to try to repair it. Most of them are not diesel trained and it is better to get everyone to wait until a mechanic has arrived from the Wadi. Also, if all the empty barrels are kept filled round each well, it is possible to move the locals on to other drinking points until the well is repaired.

## Relations with PCL
This in its way is far more difficult than getting on with the Bedouin. There are approximately 120 Adenis, etc., some 14 Europeans, and Mr Abdullah Hassan Jaffa. The Europeans play no part in the running of the camp virtually, but get on with their drilling and seismic jobs. The real man behind the scene is Abdullah Hassan, a most powerful figure who is of help with the political set-up and relations with the tribes. He and the Europeans are very generous with PCL bounty as long as they don't think they are being abused or unnecessarily take advantage of.

But Abdullah Hassan is concerned with one thing, the smoothing out of the way for the PCL work for the immediate future only. That is to say, he is prepared to take action, such as give bribes in cases where government policy might be to get round the difficulty by other ways. The HBL usually get wind of these transactions and AAND is informed, but there has been a tendency for A/H to work along his own lines without reference to AAND.

As to the rest, it is necessary to make certain that the local Bedouin have as little chance as possible to mix with either the Adeni Arabs or Europeans. This is because both groups affect to despise the locals as well as being rather scared of them, and unnecessary incidents have occurred in the past when some Adeni or European has been too hurried or cannot be bothered to talk with some locals reasonably — shots have been fired and then that means more work for AAND. So, as a general rule, up to the present, it has been considered wise always to have one HBL *jundi* (soldier) with every PCL vehicle. This has been successful in cutting down the friction. AAND also finds it necessary to be very severe with PCL over bowser drivers and others who go out of their way to visit women, chase gazelle, etc.

Finally, it must be added that one's own existence is improved considerably if one keeps in with PCL. The party chief and the camp boss are the two most important individuals who, if roused, can make life uncomfortable, but who are prepared to be most generous and cooperative if they get on with one.

### Relations with HBL

It would be impossible to work in the area without the active cooperation of the HBL and the company commanders in particular. The latter are on the whole most useful but are rather too eager to drag one into matters military, questions of discipline, etc., which I normally steered around, but until there is (if there ever will be) a European HBL officer to take over all the worries of the HBL in the north, AAND works very closely with the company commanders in everything, including political matters. (One has tended to concentrate on seeing that the company guarding PCL should be as soldier-like as possible to avoid the usual PCL criticisms about the HBL, and the company commander is very willing to support the drive for cleanliness, etc.)

## Supplies of POL to ND

One of the perpetual worries is to ensure that there is sufficient petrol in the north, especially in Al Abr. I think that much of the wastage has now been cut down, but nevertheless areas such as Al Abr use large quantities each month, and the HBL has continuously to be reminded to keep the supplies flowing. It is also normal to keep an emergency dump at Al Abr of ten barrels (to deal with raids, etc.) which can be touched on the personal orders of AAND *only*. It was also the custom to borrow spares and POL from PCL who have been generous in the past. However, where possible, this is only resorted to as a last measure as these debts run up and HQ HBL seem to run out of spares suddenly and leave AAND with a large debt on his hands.

## Resthouses ND

With the completion of Sanau and Thamud AAND will be better equipped for housing than at any time previously. It was intended that Thamud should be the most commodious of the forts and the present room and extension will be more comfortable in the summer than previously. Likewise the provision of outside sanitation will be useful, but it is suggested that a pretty tight control be kept on who uses it, i.e. visiting European officers only, otherwise the place will become filthy. The fort commander is at present i/c the building in the absence of AAND and sees the rooms are kept clean. When the generator is installed at Thamud it will be necessary to see the machine is only used in the presence of a European officer and that the fort mechanic is put in sole charge of stopping and starting it, otherwise there will be a breakdown, with a necessity of getting a mechanic from Saiun, etc.

## 2. Summary of Tribal Set-up at Present
### (Only mentioning the ones of note)

### The Sear

This is divided into two main sections, the Al Ali Ballaith and the Al Mohamed Ballaith (Al Hatim). The former live in the lower end of Reidat Assear, up on the jol (plateau), and are difficult to get at. The paramount chief of the Sear and *muqaddam* of the Al Ali Ballaith is the Hakm Ba Rumeidhan, whose relations with government have been strained for some time. Most of this has arisen from the PCL convoy hold-up at Qaa Fadhul in June 1959, when a few Searis made a nuisance of themselves. The account has never really been settled as Ba Rumeidhan was persuaded by his followers not to meet the Naib and AAND at Merkaz al Hagr when a meeting had been fixed. So there is a state of armed neutrality between government and the Al Ali Ballaith; every truck that passes along the Al Hagr/Sollasil road, i.e. to Thamud, has armed guards, just to discourage any discontented Searis. But the sooner some firmer form of agreement is reached between us and them, the better, as this is not a very satisfactory state of affairs. They have been warned they will receive swift punishment if there are any incidents, but they are doubtless hanging about, waiting among other things to see what the oil prospects are and what will be the behaviour of other tribesmen, such as the Manahil.

## Al Hatim

The Al Hatim, as the other section are more frequently known, although the largest section have been very quiet and considerably more civilized in behaviour. The chief is old Hakm bin Jerboa who has been restrained in his behaviour for some time now. He is to be found at the Merkaz al Hagr end of Reidat as Sear whenever you want him. These people are much more under the influence of JAA Kharusi. Most notable among the Searis around Al Abr are the Abdullah bin Aown who have been well behaved, with the exception of a recent raid into the Yemen to seize 17 Dahmi camels. Although privately sympathizing with them (the Dahm owe them plenty) we had to round up the offenders and caution them that this action was frowned upon. We met with obstruction from the *muqaddam* Surror who had something to do with the raid, but after various threats all the raiders were produced and the incident closed.

Finally, also from the Al Hatim, are the Al Mahroof section. They are mostly rather un-gettable at, living between Minwakh and the Wadi Hazar area and going into Saudi territory, and there are occasional reports of trouble between sections, and so on, which are difficult to act on. I have often sent desert guard Sergeant Salim Baregan, who is one of them, who has been able to sort things out. At the present there is one section, the Bait Thaweet, which is in trouble for breaking an oath made before one *muqaddam* and it is expected that they may ask government to intervene to help the situation.

## Appendix

### The Kurab
For all details on these people please see the *District Book* and consult Kharusi.

### The Musheikhi Breik
Ditto.

### The Manahil
We are rather in the same position with the Manahil as with the Sear: the No. 1 *muqaddam* is Aidha bin Hareez who is also *muqaddam* of the Bait Kazani. He has always made a practice of staying away from the Quaitis and is only to be seen occasionally in Merkaz Thamud or Som. Recently the excitement over petrol and the inter-state agreement for the sharing of the oil profits, if any, has made Aidtha even more difficult to deal with. He is refusing to have anything to do with anyone official, and has plans of uniting the various tribes so that the Bedouin of the north can speak with one strong voice to government. This last idea has not so far been successful. Aidha (as my predecessors agree) is no fool and it is pleasant to meet him, but we are definitely at logger-heads with him at the present.

The progressive outlook from the tribe comes from *muqaddam* Misaed, the No.2 and head of the Bait Maashani. He, supported by Tomatum (the ex-Manhali raider turned PCL foreman who lives at Thamud) is constantly trying to improve matters between government and the Manahil. Misaed is in no doubt as to where his interests lie, and by hanging around PCL has earned himself a sort of PCL stipend of Shs. 400/– per month. He is another clever man and so far has been of help in keeping opinion in the tribe from swinging completely with Aidha. This has culminated in Aidha's plan to contact the premier *muqaddams* of other tribes immediately, being thwarted by a sugges-tion of Misead's being adopted, namely, that Misaed himself should go to Mukalla to talk with the Quaitis. Unfortunately for Misaed, Mukalla has realized that there is no point in this unless there is an assurance (written) that Misaed carries the approval of the whole tribe (including Aidha's) on this action. Such an assurance in the form required would never be given by Aidha, so matters are at a stalemate and we now wait to see if the Manahil manage to resolve their internal differences before making another approach to government.

Lastly, a note on Tomatum. As the *District Book* will tell you, this character can be the greatest help to one. Although not a *muqaddam* he holds a respected position in the tribe by reason of his PCL employment. He will always be ready to help with whatever is going on in the *siyasi* (political) line and will inform one if he feels trouble is brewing.

### The Awamir

Please see the *District Book* for full notes on them. I only wish to add that the Kathiri government has granted Shs. 6000/– to be used on digging a well in the Solassil area; this may prove impossible and I have asked AANA to obtain permission to use the money on water development generally. Secondly, on a different matter, the only trouble you may expect from the Awamir will come in the hot weather when water gets scarce and the Awamir start to draw heavily on Thamud well. There then will arise rows between the Manahil and the Awamir which will have to be smoothed over gently.

### The Ruashid (and others of the Shenafir/Kathiri group)

With the PCL work at present in the Thamud area, certain tribes in he Sanau region to the east have got increasingly interested in oil and possible 'profits' and have been looking around to see who are the most useful people with whom to have contact. Accordingly, in October 1959, a group of *muqaddams* led by Salih bin Ghosfna of the Bait Yamani Ruashid made their way to Saiun and saw the Kathiri Sultan. There, with one notable exception, they swore allegiance to the Sultan, an action which will leave some problems for the future if oil is discovered in the Sanau area (as the Kathiri Sultan will press a claim and the British government will have to support the Sultan of Socotra whose territory we have recognized it is). Bin Gosfna, being one of the poorest but one of the most accomplished scroungers, will doubtless approach AAND on his trips to Sanau with requests for assistance, but I doubt if the above matter will be raised again for the time beginning.

The 'notable exception' mentioned above was Said bin Munnif of the Bait Khawwar who has made it plain (although of the Shenafir/Kathirir Federation) that he is prepared to acknowledge Sultan Issa of Socotra as his boss, if he receives support from the Sultan in his quarrel with a Mahri section, the Bait Zabanat. Much of this confusion might come out into the open if Sultan Issa does pay his promised visit to the mainland, as he asked various groups of *muqaddam*s from different sections to meet him.

*Bait Somada (and other Mahra/Kathiri tribes)*
Apart from individuals my contact with these people has been slight, and you should obtain all details from the notes Ellis has written. The only addition I can make is regarding the Bait Zabanat, who are to be seen from Habarut. The *muqaddam*, Ali bin Hezhaz, has been very friendly, but is slightly under a cloud at the moment as a result of his refusal to let a PCL convoy pass through with two Bait Ali bin Kathir escorts. I gather that the two Bait Ali were offensive and deliberately promoted the incident but bin Hezhaz did not cooperate as was expected of him. In this paragraph, incidentally, should be mentioned the Bait Ali bin Kathir themselves, a group that live on the Muscat side of the border. They have been a nuisance in the past but during my tenure have behaved themselves, though at the time of writing there are reports of disturbances engineered by them. As our position in that area could be delicate, owing to the claims to Habarut of the Bait Ali and Sultan bin Taimur of Muscat, the Bait Ali could be a nuisance.

### 3. Security PCL
I include a separate paragraph to show what the state of affairs is at present. PCL 5H, the main camp, is situated about 40 miles north of Thamud itself. There is one company of HBL responsible for security, and PCL incidentally help us out by supplying water and firewood (one has to battle with Abdullah Hassan over this occasionally). This company carries out its own arrangements regarding guards, etc. In addition to the main camp, PCL put out a 'fly camp' for a base when work is at some distance from the main camp. This means that a considerable amount of equipment with attendant noise, etc. is moved backwards and forwards. Consequently, what with this and dynamite blasts, a certain amount of annoyance is shown by the locals if they consider these bangs, etc. disturb their herds and so on. We have been lucky so far over this, with the exception of a proposed move by PCL (at three-days' notice) into Wadi Armah, in which area are grazing large numbers of goats and camels. It is hoped that eventually these animals and their owners will move away but at this time of year that is the best area for grazing, and I considered it would be inviting an

incident if PCL moved into the area at this time. PCL acquiesced nicely and are doing other work, but I have asked them in future to give AAND a little more warning, in which time the area could be prepared politically.

Otherwise, on this subject as I mentioned before, it has been the policy to see that every PCL vehicle has got at least one HBL *jundi* with it to avoid unnecessary incidents. But there is one further matter, the question of the employment of local labour. It has ben the custom of PCL to take on a certain number of the locals for coolie work, which has acted as a sop to the tribe and kept them interested without resorting to direct bribery. However, these coolies have been such a nuisance in the past and held up work, that I thought it expedient this year to make sure that the reduced number of coolies should be kept in Thamud for any unloading work there; this has been successful in ávoiding delays, cutting out trouble in the main camp between the locals and Adenis, and most important, made it possible to keep *all* Bedouin out of the main camp. Previously, if one Bedouin came who could claim he was a coolie he brought most of his family, his livestock and friends, so there was an unnecessary number of people hanging around, getting in the way.

Finally, I gather that PCL will move their main camp eastwards, probably around Easter, which will be a nuisance for AAND ... no doubt the Mahra and the Kathiris will start wandering around asking for coolie places. There is no reason to give them these unless the camp is east of Wadi Armah, but Abdullah Hassan can be consulted on this.

#### 4. Desert Guards

This is a force that comes directly under AAND for discipline and for any changes, etc. HQ HBL manage the pay side of things, though the payments are actually made by AAND (and a sweat it is). The DGs over to the western area who are managed by Kharusi are considerably better organized and made use of more than their counterparts, Thamud, eastwards. For instance, regular use is made of Al Abr guards as guides, etc. and they are very useful. There are a few sinecures, i.e. positions held by important people in the tribe, but on the whole they are quite a useful bunch of people. The *mulazim* (lieutenant) of the

*Appendix*

west, Ahmed bin Zaid al Kurbi, is, although stupid, helpful in dealing with his men and with any tribal problems.

In the east, on the other hand the people who make up the Desert Guards seldom do much to earn their living, apart from keeping out of trouble. It is very much a political sop for the present, and must remain so for some time. However, there are useful men among them, one of them being Mulazim Mubarak bin Dafnsh al Kathiri, who will do his best to see that order is maintained in his area. (The special DG problems, by the way, are all contained in the DG file and held by AAND.)

Up to now the policy on dealing with the DGs is to make it clear to the fort commander that all DGs are the responsibility of the AAND and JAA only, and without asking AAND or the JAA for permission. However, since the DGs are now no longer being issued rations (they receive extra pay instead) because of the difficulty in getting stores to the north, it is necessary to give numbers of them leave to go off and get their supplies, every so often. This only applies to Thamud, Sanau and Habarut.

Otherwise one spends one's time diplomatically turning down requests for increased numbers of DGs, which come daily. The only big increase lately has been in Thamud, where the Manahil were increased by three, and the Awamir by one. One position was pinched from the Mahra representative (and there will be a scream from them over that, but the place was left vacant by the death of the Mahri DG). It is normally extremely difficult to alter the proportion of places available and the only thing to do seems to keep one's eyes open for good types (preferably who can read and write as they are a help in carrying messages to illiterate *muqaddams*) and gradually ease out the deadwood and the political appointments (which unfortunately abound in Sanau and Habarut).

(M.A. Crouch)
Assistant Adviser

c.c. The Resident Adviser
and British Agent, Mukalla
Assistant Adviser (Intelligence)

259

# Index

and machinations) 155, 166–
7, 172, 180
Balala, Issa Mussallim
(Passport Officer Quaiti
Government) 65
Barahim, Abubakr (wealthy
blind merchant and member
of Mukalla Health
Board) 162
Barashaid, Ahmed Nowah
(company commander
Hadhrami Bedouin Legion in
Northern Deserts area with
author, greeted author and
companions on their 1993
tour) 246
Barnett (see family)
Bazergan, Abdurahman
(member of Mukalla Health
Board) 162
BBC 138, 174, 242
Beavan (see family)
Bedouin Boys School Mukalla
(EAP) 43, 48
Beirut 119, 165
Belhaven, Master of 170
Besse family of Aden 37, 128
Bilharzia 108–9
Bin Faheid, Ali bin Mohamed
(of Amaquin in Wahidi, local
notable) 188–9
Bin Jerboa (one of the titular
heads of his tribe with
reputation for being wise)
(see Sear)
Bin Ndail, Abdullah (Desert
Guard Al Abr who served
with author 1960/1) 83–5,
99, 218, 246
Bin Said (ruler of the Wahidi
state on behalf of the Sultan,

assassinated) 105–6, 108,
114, 116, 191–2
Bir Ali (WAP) 62, 104
Bonnycastle (see family)
Booker, Catherine 49, 65–6
Booker, Pat 44–6, 48–9, 53,
65–6
Boustead, Colonel Hugh 38–9,
46–8, 51–2, 56–61, 63, 73,
79, 88, 113, 163, 214, 219
Bowden, George 151
Bowden, Liz 151
British influence 91, 163, 189,
239, 240
British forces, role and opera-
tions of 47, 99, 114, 118–19,
131, 135, 141–3, 152, 155–6,
169, 178, 189, 211, 217, 224
Bowen, Roderick QC 189, 194
Boyle, Flight Lieutenant
Tony 119
Brown, George (Foreign Secre-
tary) 190, 207, 216, 223, 231
Cambridge 25–8, 30
Carozza, Vincenzo 106–7, 111
Chesney (see family)
Coles, Hon. Bridget 49, 74
Coles, Lieutenant–Colonel
George 49, 53, 77
Commonwealth Services Club
(see Oxford)
Corbett, Captain Hugh RN 191
Crater (the densely populated
living and business area of
Aden) 4, 110, 169, 177, 185,
201, 210–12
Crescent Hotel 35–6, 40, 110,
196, 245
Cribb, Air Commodore
Peter 135
Cribb, Vivienne 135